Managing
and Measuring
Social Enterprises

Managing
and Measuring
Social Enterprises

ROB PATON

SAGE Publications
Los Angeles • London • New Delhi • Singapore

First published 2003
Reprinted 2003, 2006 (twice) 2007, 2008

 SAGE Publications Ltd
1 Oliver's Yard
55 City Road
London EC1Y 1SP

SAGE Publications Inc
2455 Teller Road
Thousand Oaks, California 91320

SAGE Publications India Pvt Ltd.
B1/I1 Mohan Cooperative Industrial Area
Mathura Road, New Delhi 110 044
India

SAGE Publications Asia-Pacific Pte Ltd
33 Pekin Street #02-01
Far East Square
Singapore 048763

British Library Cataloguing in Publication data available

A catalogue record for this book is available from the British Library

ISBN: 978-0-7619-7364-5 (hbk)
ISBN: 978-0-7619-7365-2 (pbk)

Library of Congress Control Number available

Printed and bound in Great Britain by Athenaeum Press Ltd., Gateshead, Tyne & Wear

Contents

Tables and Figures

Key Words

The following are thematic and perhaps unfamiliar concepts. Those reading the book selectively may find the following explanations helpful – along with judicious use of the index, which indicates where else these ideas are developed and applied.

Constructivism. Social constructivism holds that the world as we perceive and experience it is constituted through the lenses of the constructs we use to think about it and make sense of it. It is these constructs that highlight and delineate particular aspects of the 'blooming buzzing confusion' that greets the (unsocialised) newborn infant. So the world is not just 'out there' something that imprints on us as passive perceivers. This active constructing of the world is a social business, undertaken in and through communities of one sort or another, communities that share and evolve their language in responding to the issues they face. Hence, social constructivism is *not* an arbitrary subjectivism (in which every one operates in a self-enclosed world regardless of what is happening 'out there').

Institution, institutional and institutionalised. An institution is a convention, practice or set of organizational arrangements that displays stability and longevity; it is established, widely adopted, taken for granted, normal, and generally seen as having value in itself. No-one bothers to measure the performance of an institution – such as financial auditing – because everyone knows it is worthwhile (until an Enron-style lapse punctures the aura). For a new practice to become *institutionalised*, therefore, it must become widespread, it must last and it must bed down into its context, gaining the co-operation and approval of those directly and indirectly affected. The *institutional environment* is comprised of those established bodies – especially legal, regulatory and statutory agencies – that are particularly important in generating authoritative decisions on potentially divisive issues, and whose pronouncements can therefore convey legitimacy onto other organizations and their practices. The more heavily institutionalised an industry or field of activity – through eg. the presence of multiple professional bodies, statutory funding, legal regulation, etc. – the more difficult it is to bring about changed modes of operation. As regards the study of organizations, *institutional theory* is concerned with the ways in which some management and administrative practices come to possess institutional qualities, and are adopted or maintained independently of their contribution to task performance.

Managerialism. The belief that the sorts of management roles, practices and thinking associated with large national and international companies provide the key to achieving high levels of organizational performance. Hence, even if some changes are needed on account of task and contextual differences, introducing such roles, practices and thinking is fundamental in modernising organizations in, eg, the public and nonprofit sectors, or in transitional and developing economies. Arguably at this political level, managerialism has drawn very selectively on actual management thinking and practice (ignoring developing economies. Arguably at this political level, managerialism has drawn very selectively on actual management thinking and practice (ignoring much that has been written on the human side of getting things done through people). Indeed, paradoxically, managerialism in the public domain has often taken on a certain 'soviet' quality with top-down target setting and monitoring, a reliance on economic incentives, an emphasis on managerial authority and discretion (at the expense of eg. professional self-regulation or citizen involvement), and elaborate documentation of standards and processes for audit. Not surprisingly, the results have often been disappointing – in the UK the introduction of general managers into the National Health Service in the 1980s is now a widely acknowledged case in point. Of course, rejecting the simplistic and exaggerated expectations of managerialism is not the same as belittling or rejecting the contribution either of managers or management ideas.

Social Enterprise. Most simply, an organisation where people have to be business-like, but are not in it for the money. Defined in this way, social enterprise is a generic term, encompassing many very different sorts of organizations (just as private enterprise does). This use is increasingly accepted. For example, Harvard Business Review designates its articles on nonprofit management and social entrepreneurship under this heading. However, it is in competition with a number of more restricted definitions that try to delineate a particular type of organization (usually based more or less exclusively on trading activity for social purposes). A more elaborate explanation and discussion of the term with references to other definitions, is given towards the end of Chapter 2.

Acknowledgements

The text draws on some material previously published in other forms. Grateful acknowledgements are made to the publishers as follows:

Chapter 5 is a revised version of a British Academy of Management Conference referred paper, Edinburgh 2002 'Benchmarking by nonprofits: an examination of the cross-sector diffusion of a management technique' and also incorporates some material from 'Performance comparisons in fundraising: the case of fundratios' from the Journal of Nonprofit and Voluntary Sector Marketing, Vol. 4, No. 4, 1999, published by Henry Stewart, London.

Chapter 6 is a revised version of ' Nonprofit's use of awards to improve and demonstrate performance: valuable discipline or burdensome formalities?' Voluntas: International Journal of Voluntary and Nonprofit Organizations, Vol. 11. No.4, 2000, published by Kluwer Academic, Plenum Publishers, The Netherlands.

Chapter 7 is an extended version 'What happens when nonprofits use quality models for self-assessment?' Nonprofit Management and Leadership, Vol. 11. No. 1, 2000, published by Jossey-Bass, San Francisco.

Figure 7.1 is reproduced with permission of the British Quality Foundation.

Preface

This book originated in work on benchmarking among charities undertaken for the
Charities Aid Foundation. The discussions with Cathy Pharoah and Michael
Brophy that were associated with it first brought home to me how the performance
agenda was set to permeate the world of public and nonprofit agencies. Our
different views on the likely consequences for charities started me thinking about
the gulf between the worlds of policy and management. I thank them both for that
spur and opportunity – and I hope that belatedly they can understand why I felt so
ambivalent about the drive to measurement, standards and benchmarking that they
were endorsing. Those conversations echoed others, concerning the spread of
business practices into public and nonprofit contexts, where I had felt uneasy about
the positions commonly being advocated. Usually, I wasn't sure whether the
enthusiasts for modernisation and management alarmed me more than the critics of
change depressed me (with their relentless negativity and unshakeable conviction
that low performance was only a symptom of underfunding).

Prompted by these concerns the book aims to illuminate practice and policy issues
drawing on (and occasionally developing) theories for that purpose. The worlds of
management practice and of management research are, rightly, very different,
serving different functions and operating to different timescales, with different
perspectives and values. That said, when they drift too far apart (as shown in either
mindless activism or narrow, discipline-focussed agendas) then both suffer. Which
is why I have tried to write in a way that will be accessible to policy and practice.
communities as well as contributing to academic debates. It is for others to judge
how well I have succeeded (the old line about only seeing the full force of human
fury when a friend of the opposing parties tries to intercede, comes to mind).

In the early work on different forms of benchmarking I enjoyed (literally) the
assistance of Geoff Payne and Jane Foot. I learned a great deal from both of them.
Geoff's energy in pursuing enquiries and his willingness to keep challenging me
when we disagreed (which was often) were exemplary. Jane's encouragement helped
me to see that there was a broader story to tell about performance. She kept me up
to date on developments in Local Government her support helped me to focus and
clarify, and she identified many of the key cases. Later John Moss-Jones helped me
with the PHS case, and again the discussions with him forced me to clarify my
thinking. Adrian Sargeant provided the data set for the analysis of ACE ratios,
showing collegial cooperation between institutions is alive and well.

At various times during the book's torturous progress, the encouragement of many
colleagues in the Association of Researchers on Nonprofit Organization and
Voluntary Action and in the Voluntary Sector Studies Network, has been really
important, in particular, but not only, Vic Murray, Dennis Young, Melissa
Middleton Stone, Pam Leland, Bob Herman, Dave Renz, Roland Kushner,
Duncan Scott, Peter Halfpenny, David Mullins and Moyra Riseborough.

Ray Sheath of the Scarman Trust deserves a special mention. It is a delicious irony
that one of the most intellectually stimulating and helpful discussions of all should

have been with a businessman and took place in the Institute of Directors (especially since he argued that I was giving far too much credence to measurement!).

My colleagues in the Open University Business School have also been very supportive, offering constructive comments and encouragement (and showing great patience). Jill Mordaunt, Chris Cornforth, Charles Edwards and Scott Taylor deserve special mentions. The financial support provided by the OUBS research committee was extremely important (as was a grant from the Chartered Institute of Management Accountants Research Trust). It has also been a privilege to have the steady, dedicated and technically highly skilled assistance of Jackie Connell in preparing, without melodramas, a book-length text with full formatting, referencing and bibliography.

Finally, I want to salute all the managers and staff in the social enterprises we studied – and others who came to workshops or discussed the issues with me in other contexts. They all had other, much more pressing things to do, but gave generously of their reflections, ideas and concerns. Without their assistance the whole exercise would have been impossible.

Rob Paton,
Walton Hall

1 The Challenge of Social Performance

How good are we at doing good? This book is about managing organizations that exist in order to make a difference to lives and societies. It is about the challenges of running projects, activities and collaborations in pursuit of high aspirations - and doing so at a time when public trust in those who profess social ideals and motivations has declined. It is about those situations where it may be hard to know how much good the organization is really doing, and how well it is run. In these cases how can those responsible find better ways of doing things and how can they give a meaningful account of their stewardship of resources? In particular, this book considers one solution that has been urged for more than a decade – becoming more business-like, by adopting measurement and other modern management practices. It examines what happens when this is done.

Why social enterprises? There has never been a satisfactory collective term for the independent agencies, campaigns, foundations, self- help federations, semi-detached public bodies and socially-oriented businesses through which individuals, groups and societies have shared their concerns, provided services voiced dissent and pursued vocations. This 'loose and baggy monster' (Kendall and Knapp 1995) has grown rapidly in size, significance and sophistication over the last decade. All the major social changes and challenges of our time – Aids, the environment, an ageing population, urban decay, drugs and crime, the new information technologies, globalisation – have seen the emergence of new initiatives and new forms of social action. And the standing of social enterprises has increased. Often they have what governments and corporations seek - credibility, expertise, public support.

Like an old friend we have not seen for a while, this sprawling terrain is both familiar and changed. The term social enterprise, as used in this book, may not be perfect, but it reflects some of these developments – the innovation and dynamism, the spread of business perspectives, the emergence of hybrid organizations and inter-sectoral partnerships. Moreover, the term is both positive and virtually self-explanatory –more than can be said for the 'nonprofit', 'voluntary', 'charity' and 'third' sector labels. It is also broader, encompassing co-operatives and socially-oriented businesses, even if they do not have a nonprofit or charitable legal form. Chapter 2 considers the scope of the term further, in particular, where social enterprise leaves off and more traditional public administration begins.

In pursuit of performance

Unquestionable successes.... The contribution of social enterprises over the years has been enormous – and enormously diverse. As innovators, as expressions of new social movements and concerns, as society's rapid response expressions of new social movements and concerns, as society's rapid response force for new issues, social enterprises have made a societal difference, again and again. Here are three examples of the very different forms that enterprising socially oriented organisations can take:

1. When the dictator Pol Pot was driven from power in 1979, Cambodia was in ruins and the already near-starving population faced imminent death. Legal and geo-political diplomatic complexities meant any response by the international community would be even more belated than usual. In this situation Guy Stringer, Deputy Director of Oxfam, flew to Singapore and set about taking food, seeds and equipment to Cambodia. He had chosen to work for Oxfam after earlier careers as a soldier and a businessman and he drew heavily on these experiences in the critical weeks that followed. He negotiated large purchases of grain, hired a barge and a tug, and set off across 600 miles of the China Sea. He set up the first relief operations in time to save hundreds of thousands of lives – and shamed an international community made heartless by preposterous cold war *realpolitik*. This may be a particularly striking example of successful social enterprise in the field of international relief, but it is only one of many.

2. In the US in the late 1970s many Christians (and others) became deeply concerned by the dismantling of federal food entitlement and welfare programmes. An important safety net between poverty and outright hunger was being removed. The response was extraordinary – but completely unplanned. Over the following years a complex, sophisticated and extensive system of food gathering and distribution sprang into existence. Many of the initiatives had an accidental quality, started on impulse when individuals were appalled to see large quantities of good food wasted and wanted to make it available to those in need instead. Similar schemes sprang up independently in different places. Networks were formed. Word spread. Business leaders became involved. Governments contributed – through seed corn funding, tax breaks and the removal of legal obstacles. Of course, one can regret the circumstances that gave rise both to this need and the response. But the scale of the achievement was remarkable. By the early 1990s hundreds of millions of pounds of fresh, frozen, cooked and dry foods were being gathered and distributed annually through a two-tier system of warehouses (food rescue programmes, food banks) and food outlets (food pantries, food kitchens, domestic violence refuges, etc). For example, Second Harvest Gleaners Food Bank of West Michigan, is one of 185 regional clearinghouses for donated surpluses from the food industry. By the end of 1997 it was operating through seven warehouses, serving 975 church and charity agencies across an area the size of Scotland, and providing 60,000lbs of food per day.

3. For 50 years the Scott Bader Company and Commonwealth have been a beacon for industrial reformers and those pursuing greater corporate social responsibility. Scott Bader is a UK-based chemical company, specialising in polymer resins, that was founded in 1919, but progressively given away

by its founder, Ernest Bader, to the Scott Bader Commonwealth – a democratic association committed to partnership in industry, community service, peace, international understanding and stewardship of the earth's resources. Only those working for Scott Bader are eligible to apply for membership but unlike worker cooperatives or other forms of employee ownership, the constitution of the Commonwealth tried to prevent members from taking advantage of the company's resources for their own benefit – profit distribution is strictly controlled for example. Hence, the Commonwealth is a framework for collective trusteeship by the workforce of the business for which they work, for boldly progressive purposes. The governance processes that integrate this democratic association with the management structure of the company it 'owns' are distinctive and somewhat arcane, but what was originally a modest family firm, is now a small multinational company employing more than 600 people in Europe, Africa, the Middle-East and America. It has given away millions of pounds to charitable causes, often those in which members of the Commonwealth are personally involved or interested. It has a reputation in its industry for integrity in its business dealings. Clearly, social enterprises can take many very different forms – and whatever performance is, we know it when we see it...

...And demonstrable failures. Unfortunately, social enterprises do not always succeed. Here are three cases to illustrate some of the ways in which they can 'go wrong'.

1. In 1967 Nigeria was plunged into civil war as its Eastern Region of Biafra declared independence. Predictably, the civilian population faced the usual dangers and depredation of war especially in Biafra as Nigerian government forces gradually closed in on the rebel territory. In the hope of preventing what looked increasingly like a humanitarian disaster, aid and church agencies in the UK and Europe began running relief operations in Biafra. Unfortunately, these operations introduced considerable amounts of foreign exchange into the rebel territory, and this was immediately used by the Biafran government to buy weapons, as its leader subsequently admitted. It is now clear that the attempt to save lives prolonged the conflict and helped create what became an appalling famine. Unfortunately this is not an isolated example. In recent years many development professionals have become increasingly concerned that humanitarian efforts in 'complex emergencies' have had the effect of institutionalising conflict. For example, in order to reach refugee civilian populations, relief workers often have no option but to pay a tithe of their supplies to local warlords – thus sustaining military groupings that would not otherwise be viable.

2. In 1993 Second Harvest of West Michigan was being offered high quality food by the food industry at seven times the rate that the agencies and pantries they supplied were giving it out to needy people. On investigation, it turned out that the food pantries had evolved a

shared set of policies and procedures about how much and what sort of food it was considered appropriate to make available to poor people, and in what ways. In consequence, food pantries did not call for many items stocked by the food bank (they were not on the approved list); and they went out and purchased at considerable cost the items that were not stocked by the food bank. Food from these two sources was then bagged up in standard packages, and made available under screening policies designed to protect the system from 'cheaters' and 'abusers'. Even leaving aside the humiliation and resentment such arrangements engendered, they were breathtakingly inefficient: recipients regularly threw away up to half of the contents of the pack provided. The Executive Director of Second Harvest in West Michigan calculated that in Grand Rapids the food pantries were spending $4,000,000 per year on efforts which fell woefully short of meeting the need for food – but that this need could be met for less than $500,000 if practices changed. The key was a different model of food distribution based on client involvement and choice from the full range of supplies available. Though a proven success, the food pantries were highly resistant to this new approach. As the Executive Director put it:

> But over and over again I have been admonished that such a model and approach is much too simplistic, that people *like* giving cans instead of money, and that the food bank's food (a roll of honour of the nation's favourite foods) is the *wrong* food, and that those who are hungry simply cannot be trusted to make reasonable decisions. And so in agency after agency and community after community they keep buying food and giving it out in woefully inadequate amounts, and I continue having to refuse readily available goods at a rate of 3.5 million pounds per month... (Arnold 1998)

3. If one asks 'what is the social return on the (say) £100 million of assets held by the Scott Bader Commonwealth?' no clear answer is available. Of course, it still gives some money to charity every year (recently, about £150,000/annum) – but then the constitution requires that any bonus paid to employees out of profits is matched by charitable giving, a situation in which most people would show some generosity. Over the years any number of initiatives have been launched to 'make the Commonwealth mean something'. But in practice, the vision of a new form of self-management or industrial partnership has been reduced to employee representation on the company's (non-executive) board of directors, a code of conduct, and protection from take-over. Senior managers have no great difficulty in preserving their autonomy (through control of information, the meeting before the meeting, the discreet exercise of patronage) but they have not pursued a social agenda of any consequence, either internally or externally, and nor have the leaders of the Commonwealth. Indeed, the Commonwealth was, until recently, in breach of its own constitution, having for many years

withheld the right to membership from employees of overseas subsidiaries. Attempts to reform the labyrinthine and contradictory constitutional documents have repeatedly failed, bedevilled by distrust between various groupings within the Commonwealth and company. The consensus among outsiders who have been involved either as consultants or 'nominated Trustees', is that the social performance of the Scott Bader Commonwealth has been disappointing. Some Commonwealth members, and presumably those employees who do not bother to join, agree.

Unravelling performance. The contrived presentation of these examples illustrates a number of points about the notion of performance in relation to social enterprises, and about the way the term tends to be used. First, it is easy to project a fine tale on the basis of uplifting purposes and selected information. In a similar manner, it is easy to belittle and denounce on the basis of a particular mistake or period of difficulty. Second, the issues addressed by social enterprises are frequently complex and the consequences of their interventions uncertain. None of the cases introduced – international relief, emergency food aid in the US and the Scott Bader Commonwealth – supports simple, sweeping claims about performance or non-performance. Third, the more ambitious social enterprises are regarding their missions, the more problematic their performance is likely to appear. Our judgements about the food pantries are very different depending on whether we see them as an expression of concern never intended to be more than a stop-gap for those in the most extreme need, or as a means of alleviating poverty and restoring social solidarity. Fourth, our judgements about performance derive in the end from narratives about what is going on and what has been achieved. Rhetoric can only take you so far; in the long run such narratives are usually more convincing when they encompass evidence, analysis and comparisons. Whether or not one agrees with his position, John Arnold's calculations about the inefficiency of the food pantries as a way of providing needy people with food make a very telling point. Which is, of course, where measurement enters the picture. Nevertheless, one should not expect too much of facts: they seldom speak for themselves – or at least, they may say different things to different people. The 'insurmountable opportunities' that social enterprises often take as their missions involve complex and contested issues bound up with different values and ideologies (as John Arnold's experience also shows). If you think that *Médécins sans frontières* is a vehicle for rescue melodramas whose resources would be far more productively used as (say) *Sanitations sans frontières*, then no amount of measurement is likely to change your mind about its performance.

Performance as a social construct. These observations point towards a central issue running through the book. For social enterprises (particularly), performance is not some underlying attribute that exists and can be known independently of the people centrally involved in and concerned about that organisation. Performance is what those people more or less agree, implicitly or explicitly, to be performance, what they have in mind when they use the term. Hence to say an organisation is (or is not) performing is to say that one has (or does not have) confidence in the accounts offered for what it has been achieving. Does this mean performance is not a 'real' issue, that it is all a confidence trick? Hardly. We know that organisations, like individuals, can become 'locked in' to beliefs that others find unconvincing, and become committed to ways of doing things whose effectiveness well-informed observers doubt. First World War generals are the classic example, but arguably each of the three cases discussed above shows some signs of this happening. In such situations, the people concerned will still, in all likelihood, offer positive accounts of their performance, and do so with conviction, screening out information that does not fit the preferred view. And for a time they may carry others with them. Usually, however, sooner or later, some party or another is likely to start questioning the accepted wisdom. Confidence and support may begin to ebb away. An alternative approach may appear offering a new and more convincing account of what can be done. Suddenly, performance is seen as problematic.

So the definition of and evidence for failure and success remain vital issues for those who manage or are interested in social enterprises. This is the case even though what is meant by performance will often be provisional achievements towards a loose-knit and evolving bundle of aspirations more or less shared within a particular network of stakeholders. As the argument and the case material unfold, this constructivist perspective highlights the ways in which performance is a multifaceted, fluid, problematic, ambiguous and contested concept. Performance may sound like some unitary, stable and objectively real attribute – and the management of social enterprises might be easier if it was – but it is far more elusive than that. This is one of the reasons why measuring performance is so attractive – it seems to offer a way of pinning it down, of seeing just what has been achieved.

The performance agenda

Clearly, the management of social enterprise is not made any easier by social performance being hard to define and measure. This does not mean that charities and the like must be badly managed (though this has been claimed by Argenti 1993). But it does raise questions:– how much of a problem is there with the management and achievements of social enterprises? Are there grounds for a general concern over their performance?

Known ways of 'going wrong'. One way of answering such questions is to point to difficulties that social enterprises often experience. Many of these are now well understood, and are associated with the broad array of stakeholders whose often conflicting concerns have to be combined and balanced in governance and in operations. Often, and sometimes unavoidably, one stakeholder is in a dominant position. Stakeholder dominance thus provides one way of distinguishing between different sorts of social enterprise – and of highlighting some of the characteristic pitfalls they face (see table 1.1).

Table 1.1 A stakeholder typology of social enterprises and the challenges they face

Type of social enterprise	Field or example	Potential pitfall
Funder-led	Agencies providing services under contract	Loss of autonomy, local government at one remove; inflexibility; reduced standards; advocacy and innovation gradually circumscribed.
Staff-led	Independently funded agencies providing care to children, people with disabilities, etc. Also membership associations.	Domination by perspectives and concerns of staff at clients' or members' expense. Many well-documented cases down the years in health and social welfare, trade unions, associations, etc.
Donor-led	Fundraising and campaigning charities	Sensationalism, reinforcing public misconceptions about complex issues. Arguably, some animal welfare and mental health charities have illustrated this pitfall at times, in recent years.
Customer-led	Schools, counselling services, arts organisations, etc.	Developing lucrative market segments rather than those originally intended.
Member-led	Self-help and community groups, cooperatives.	Conflict and disarray in decision making; degeneration/loss of social purpose.
Beneficiary-led	Disaster relief agencies	Stress and burn-out; over-commitment; especially among new agencies.

The sorts of difficulties that prompt interventions by regulatory bodies (eg in the UK, the Charity Commission) illustrate some other challenges. These commonly involve breakdowns in governance (eg disputes among the trustees) or stewardship failures (such as the loss or misuse of funds, over-ambitious attempts to expand, maladministration). Both of these are often associated with transitions of one sort or another – such as rapid growth or the departure (or reluctance to depart) of a strong founder or long-serving leader. Such cases may be a–typical but they can receive widespread publicity – which provides another sense in which performance is an issue.

Public confidence. Evidence exists of a decline in public confidence in charities. How far this simply reflects broader social changes and a loss of deference towards established institutions is less certain. But most social enterprises depend directly or indirectly on the public at large for support, and they can hardly ignore signs that the bond of trust on which they rely may be eroding. Moreover, specific issues have repeatedly been a focus for public concern in many industrial countries – high administration costs, inappropriate fundraising methods and excessive fundraising expenditures, poor management, lack of accountability for what they do, not using their resources properly or as they claim, and using tax advantages to compete unfairly with small businesses.

Governmental and policy concerns. Meanwhile, 'managerialism' has been the order of the day in government (Clarke and Newman 1997). Since many social enterprises operate in the orbit of government, this influence has been far-reaching – it is explored further in the next chapter. Suffice to say that performance and accountability have been the watchwords, with a presumption in favour of competitive and private sector approaches. The argument is not that private firms are necessarily better run, but that those that are badly run are likely to be gobbled up by others or forced out of business. These processes are imperfect and erratic, but in general failure is punished, often quite promptly and severely. This does concentrate the minds of business managers. Since no comparable pressures weigh on the managers of social enterprises, the fear has been that chronic underperformance is widespread. An organization may have started out with the creative energy and enthusiasm of youth, but a decade or two (or three) down the line is it not likely to have grown paunchy, staid and myopic? How, indeed, would one know whether or not that had happened? This brings us back to questions of performance and measurement. If these are problematic, as seems to be the case, where can the pressure for renewal come from, sufficient to overcome the normal parochialism and resistance to change that is commonplace in organisations of all sorts? So perhaps the doubters and cynics are right, and the nonprofit sector is a playground for bumbling amateurs, a museum of bygone administrative practice, a sanctuary for those seeking a comfortable, less demanding position than the business world provides...

Inter-sectoral comparisons. Happily, there is now a developing body of work that shows such fears are largely unwarranted. Various studies have compared the performance of private, public and nonprofit providers in fields where they all operate – such as health care (hospitals), nursery provision, schools and residential care for the elderly[1]. These have often involved sophisticated research designs in order to take account of hard-to-measure dimensions of quality, and to allow for differences in client intake. The overall pattern of the results is clear: the differences within a sector are much greater than the differences between sectors. That is to say, although a particular sector may come out on top in a particular comparison, all three sectors always provide a wide range of performance from the very well run to the badly run – with most organisations neither the one nor the other.

One implication is that those seeking instances of sectoral heroism or villainy will usually be able to find them. Risk-taking business leaders creating value for customers and grasping corporate owners putting profit ahead of care *both* exist, as do (some) supremely dedicated and professional public servants *and* (some) time-serving and rule-bound bureaucrats. Likewise, the occasional mould-breaking social entrepreneur coexists with the occasional bumbling incompetent. Another implication is that how such organisations run is not determined to any great extent by sectoral auspices. Management (in a broad sense) does matter.

In summary, performance *is* an issue for social enterprises, but they are not unique in this respect. Moreover, taking the performance agenda seriously does not mean endorsing generalised criticisms of such organisations. It simply acknowledges that managing social enterprises is decidedly challenging, and that it would be reckless to ignore or belittle the concerns about performance held for one reason or another by the public, the media, and in policy circles. Even where they are unfounded they need to be addressed positively and respectfully.

Controversial solutions – and contradictory predictions

The new performance improvement methods. So how are social enterprises to improve their performance, and to show that they are doing so? Over the last decade various consultants, policy analysts, government bodies, and the sector's own leaders have urged a range of performance improvement ideas upon the managers of social enterprises. These have been the main ones:

- more and better performance measurement – especially outcome or impact measurement;

- greater accountability – through improved financial reporting, enhanced public communications, or social audit;

- benchmarking and the identification of best practice – comparing and learning from others;

- ideas and methods from 'the Quality movement' in management, including quality assurance, customer satisfaction, customer care, and the use of the TQM-derived Excellence Model;

- human resource-based approaches, like Management Development, National Vocational Qualifications and the 'Investors in People' standard;

- 'balanced scorecards' giving due weight to financial, operational, client and 'renewal' perspectives on performance.

This is pretty much a roster of the management ideas of the last 20 years, most of which originated in the private sector, though some have been adapted for public and nonprofit contexts. Advocacy of such techniques usually implies a 'genericist' theory of management – as opposed to one that emphasises sectoral distinctiveness (Paton and Cornforth 1991; Osborne 1996) and the danger of adopting practices that may clash with the values and culture of social enterprises. The argument can be reduced to the following three propositions:

i.   the techniques have been shown to be of benefit to significant numbers of companies seeking to improve their performance in various areas;

ii.   the various challenges and circumstances for which they are helpful commonly arise in other sectors;

iii. hence social enterprises will also often gain from using them.

With a few *caveats* and qualifications, this perspective, and the approaches referred to, have been endorsed, sometimes enthusiastically, by many social enterprise managers.

A cure as bad as the disease? Equally, however, it has not been hard to find managers who have accepted these approaches much more doubtfully and reluctantly. Outright opposition is now less common – if that is what government and funders require, then that is what they will be given, albeit through gritted teeth, on occasion. So (nearly) everyone accepts that measurement and business-style management are here to stay and the debate is between enthusiasts and sceptics, about how to measure, and which methods to use in what ways, not whether to introduce them.

The doubters and critics argue that the methods are inappropriate and unworkable, costly and burdensomely bureaucratic to implement, often a cover for cost cutting, irrelevant to the real issues facing social enterprises, and damaging to their values and ways of working. The enthusiasts are quick to reject such claims – they exaggerate the difficulties and are based on instances where the methods have been poorly implemented. Do not the techniques work elsewhere, and is there not a growing practitioner literature attesting to their benefits in social enterprises? Alas, it is not that simple.

Such practitioner writing is open to a number of criticisms: it exaggerates the distinctiveness of the new techniques; the successes tend to be reported in glowing terms, usually by the 'product champions', while failures and difficulties are almost certainly underreported; and important questions are not addressed concerning, for example, the contexts for which the approach is suitable, and whether the techniques pass the test of time. A graphic illustration of these limitations was encountered in the course of the research for this book.

Visiting the Royal National Institute for Deaf People in connection with the use of ISO 9000 (the international standard for quality systems) in its Typetalk division (see chapter 6), it emerged that a recent major 'customer care' initiative had been dismantled as misconceived, ineffective and costly. But this scheme had been reported in glowing terms in the leading journal of nonprofit marketing by its product champion, who had since moved on.[2]

Management fashions? So perhaps these techniques are being adopted by social enterprises but to no very great effect? This might be happening because they are 'management fashions' – transient collective beliefs that particular techniques are quite widely applicable advances in management practice (Abrahamson 1991; 1996). Much has been written on this theme with commentators discussing management gurus and their best-sellers in terms of charisma, panaceas, myths, rituals, cults, witch doctors and the like (see for example Huczysnki 1993; Clark and Salaman 1996; Kieser 1997; Pattison 1998). The general thrust of these theories is to highlight the extent of gullibility and non-rational behaviour in the spread of management practices. The following propositions capture their gist in relation to social enterprises:

  i.   new, identifiable techniques are often widely promoted to managers;

  ii.   those managers of social enterprises who identify with the broader management community will be susceptible to an exaggerated belief regarding their efficacy and relevance to them;

  iii.   use of such techniques in social enterprises is likely to result either in disappointment, or in claims of its effective use that appear unconvincing or exaggerated to third parties.

This is only one possible explanation (and prediction). But it illustrates the point that the policy and practice issues raised by the transfer of new management practices into the sector also have some interesting theoretical dimensions.

The research: scope aims, methods

Research aims. The investigations that grew into this book began as an exploratory study of the issues raised by the spread into social enterprises of the ideas and methods associated with performance measurement and improvement. It grew out of dissatisfaction with the claims of both advocates and critics, and initially the aims were simple: to clarify the issues the methods raised for managers, trustees and sector leaders, and to determine what further, more sustained research was warranted. As an exploratory study it aimed to be descriptive and interpretive: to document how and why the new methods were being used, and to report the sorts of challenges and benefits that the managers and staff of social enterprises associated with them. To this extent the enquiries started relatively 'open', following a grounded theory approach (Glaser and Strauss 1968). At the same time, however, the project aimed to be analytic, in the sense of identifying from potentially relevant literatures (or developing) concepts that would help illuminate the experience and processes reported and also locate them in a broader theoretical perspective. It was assumed that the literature on the use of the methods in commercial and public organisations would be of some, but uncertain, relevance, and thus a subsidiary aim was to explore the significance of sector auspices in relation to these issues.[3]

But how can we tell if they work? The RNID's customer care episode (referred to above) illustrates the difficulties involved in relying on the claims of those whose roles involve responsibility for promoting and maintaining the systems ('product champions'), in judging whether a new management technique has 'worked'. This is a common weakness in the professional and practitioner literature, and some academic writing is methodologically questionable for the same reason (eg Letts, Ryan et al. 1999). Characteristically, staff experience and view the methods and systems involved in different ways, with the costs and benefits often being controversial. In particular, the contrast between accounts of the awards offered by product champions and those who are obliged to enact them, can be striking. But collusion in support of a colleague or boss (to avoid tension, to be a 'team player') is another possibility (Brunsson and Olsen 1993). Hence, as researchers, we soon realised that it was important to disentangle three different sorts of accounts that participants and others might be offering, and to adapt our questioning accordingly:

- Aspirational accounts, as offered typically by consultants, internal product champions and sponsors, are normative, idealised, and rhetorical (employing terms like 'quantum leaps', 'excellence', 'world class', and so on). They may help in attracting attention to new methods, and in building internal support for projects to try them out.

- Cynical accounts contain many distrusting and dismissive elements. They can be a reaction to difficulties encountered, or to inflated claims and overblown rhetoric. Or they may reflect divisions and disenchantment that exists for reasons unconnected to the method.

- Operational accounts tend to be technical and procedural in content, describing the often rather mundane and problematic core of the methods, techniques or systems.

Further difficulties in appraising the methods include the variety of circumstances, and the manner in which the methods are applied. Indeed, did those who claimed success really use the method? Quite possibly not, as it happens (see chapter 5). And perhaps failure is explained by attempts to use a method in an inappropriate situation? Hence, though questionnaire-based surveys of organisations are often interesting reflectors of currents in management thinking, they do not capture what is actually happening 'on the ground', in a way that can reliably inform judgements about the contribution of performance improvement methods. Such considerations meant that, although some other methods were also used[4], the primary method of investigation was the case study.

Research methods. The studies of particular performance improvement methods that make up the heart of the book (chapters 4 to 7) were generally carried out in overlapping phase.

First, familiarisation and focusing. This involved tracing relevant academic and practitioner writing (including articles in professional and nonprofit sector publications, guidance and advice concerning the methods), and through key informant interviews (eg of consultants and others associated with particular methods, staff of lead bodies, managers with relevant experience).

Second, selection and preparation of case studies. In order to avoid the limitations of existing reportage, two principles were central in the choice and execution of the case investigations. In the first place, all were multi-informant studies – based mainly on semi-structured interviews, internal documentation, and occasionally earlier published reports. Informants with varying roles in relation to the method under study were sought, though this was sometimes difficult (and cases sometimes had to be abandoned for this reason). Interviewees were also asked about the range of views towards the method that existed within their organisation. Hence particular attention was given to probing the evidential basis for claims about the benefits of performance improvement efforts, and to checking how far the official accounts given by those responsible were consistent with more local and private impressions formed by others involved or affected. In each case a 'composite account' was prepared and sent back to informants for checking, and this often led to some further discussion.

In addition, the cases were chosen to illuminate long-standing applications of performance improvement methods, often by 'early adopters' of the particular method in question. Sometimes, indeed, the original product champion had moved on, and the system or procedures were now taken for granted. Hence the research generally required follow-up (retrospective) studies, though in several instances a significant longitudinal element was possible.[5] The various cases are listed in tables 1.2 and 1.3 below.

Third, concept formation and testing. Propositions emerging in one location were tested and elaborated in the light of experience in other sites, and they could also, to a degree, be checked against the views of consultants, other researchers and the professional and research literature from public and commercial contexts. This phase also included presentations on the emerging analysis at conferences and workshops (eg under the auspices of relevant professional bodies) and taking notes on the ensuing discussion, circulating draft analyses to interviewees and informants, and publication in professional journals.

Limitations of the approach. Selecting long-lasting examples that would be statistically representative was never a possibility. Potential cases were identified by following leads from key informant interviews and the practitioner literature. Among these we sought, for each method and across different methods, organisational variety – by deliberately including social enterprises of different sizes, working in different fields, and with different legal forms.

Beyond this, such factors as geographical accessibility and willingness to cooperate were probably as important as any more theoretical considerations. The number of cases is still quite modest given the number of methods, and, moreover, it is biased towards successes (because of the longevity criterion) and against failures. Further testing of the findings – either against the reader's own relevant experiences or through more formal studies – is obviously needed.

Overview of the book

The book is in three parts. This chapter and the two that follow set the scene for the research – locating the issues in public policy developments and the literature on measurement. The next four chapters provide the heart of the book by presenting original research on eight different methods of performance measurement and/or performance improvement (see tables 1.2 and 1.3). Some of these are very specific tools (eg ISO 9000, the Excellence Model), others are broader approaches (outcome measurement, benchmarking). The last two chapters draw the discussion together with an emphasis on the implications for managers and policy-makers.

The following chapter summaries indicate how the argument develops, and may help readers locate material of particular relevance.

Performance management as government policy. The basic argument of the next chapter is that governments now aim to manage performance without managing organisations, and that to do so they rely on some mix of a limited number of generic strategies and methods. These strategies are briefly explained with reference to all the main 'industries' in which social enterprises operate (health, education, housing, welfare, international development, local services etc). One effect has been powerful pressures on social enterprises to embrace those measurement and management practices favoured by governments, such as those considered in later chapters – even if their contribution to task performance is unclear. Another effect has been that semi-detached parts of the public sector and contract-entwined voluntary agencies now operate in increasingly similar supervisory and policy environments, to the point that *the regulated social enterprise* is emerging as a distinct form.

Taking measures – lessons from the literature. Chapter 3 offers a review of recent developments in the theory of performance measurement and the extensive research on it in both private and public contexts in the last decade. It plays an important role in the book by introducing several key concepts and recurring themes – such as the tensions that inevitably arise between the different meanings that performance has within institutional, managerial and professional domains. It is argued that a constructivist perspective accounts better for how and why measurement practices unfold over time in organisations, often showing, for example, initial benefits followed by increasing dysfunction, oscillations between different patterns of use, and an ever-increasing turnover of the measures employed ('churn').

Table 1.2 Case studies of organisations

Organisation	Activity or field	Improvement method	Chapter
'Ability'	Large national disability charity	Self-assessment, using the Excellence Model	7
'Disability Homes Network'	National network of care homes	Internal Benchmarking and ISO 9000	5, 6
Groundwork Trust	Environmental, social and economic improvement through community development	Outcome measures, Internal Benchmarking	4,5
'Hillend'	Local night shelter/day centre	Self-assessment, using PQASSO	7
'Health Rights International'	Specialist NGO in the health field	Scorecard review	8
'The House'	Local Authority Day Care Centre	ISO 9000	6
New Economics Foundation	Advocacy, consultancy and policy studies	Social Audit	4
Pioneer Human Services, Seattle	Housing, counselling and employment services for ex-offenders and substance abusers	Outcome measures and Scorecard review	4,8
RNID Typetalk Division	Telephone relay service for deaf people	ISO 9000	6
Royal Society for Protection of Birds	Conservation and advocacy	Benchmarking	5
Shaw Trust	Employment support for disabled people	'Investors in People' standard	6
Standish Community High School	Local comprehensive secondary school	'Investors in People' standard	6
'The TEC'	Quasi-governmental agency, responsible for employment and enterprise-related training	Self-assessment, using the Excellence Model	7

Table 1.3 Multi-organisational case studies

Name	Focus	Improvement method	Chapter
ACE ratios	Variations in administrative costs in four sub-sectors – 'Special groups', 'Christian societies', 'Illness societies' and 'Relief agencies'	Performance measurement and reporting	4
Birmingham Project	Capacity building initiative in a major city	Self-assessment, using PQASSO	7
'Fundratios'	Confidential comparisons of costs and returns in fundraising	Benchmarking	5
Good Practice Unit	'Knowledge sharing' service run by Chartered Institute of Housing	Benchmarking	5
Kids Club Network	National network of after-school clubs	Self-assessment, using a precursor of PQASSO	7
Trade Associations Project	Suite of Benchmarking initiatives promoted to trade associations	Benchmarking	5

The performance of measurement. Chapter 4 asks how measurement is being enacted in social enterprises and whether it is delivering the goods, focusing on three different forms – Administrative Cost Ratios, Outcome Measurement, and the use of Social Audit. The experience of social enterprises generally conforms to the patterns of measurement behaviour noted in chapter 3, and two themes recur through the discussion of the findings. The first concerns the extent to which measurement by social enterprises has itself become a performance undertaken to satisfy or impress others. The second concerns the elusiveness of the central idea of performance and the loose relationship between performance-as-reported and the judgements of 'real' performance made by those who are well informed.

'Best Practice Benchmarking' – why everyone does it now. Chapter 5 examines how the technique of Best Practice Benchmarking has been used in social enterprises. It confirms what has been reported in other contexts – that when attempts are made to compare performance regarding particular processes through detailed measurements, these can be suggestive, but rarely are they anything like conclusive. Moreover, although nonprofit managers do occasionally use Best Practice Benchmarking in its original form, much more commonly, they employ one or more of a family of practices that are far simpler – and arguably, more appropriate. That is, managers seem often to be using the language of best practice and benchmarking for rhetorical effect, even as they (wisely) pursue more realistic 'satisficing' approaches.

Do 'kitemarks' improve and demonstrate performance? Chapter 6 examines the use of awards and kitemarks as a way for social enterprises to show that their management systems meet recognised standards of good practice. Based on five case studies covering two different awards (ISO 9000 and 'Investors in People'), it concludes that organisations can and do use these schemes in very different ways, and hence the outcomes are diverse. These findings run counter both to the 'rational system' assumptions on which such arrangements are based, and to the general thrust of institutional theory with its emphasis on organisations becoming more similar (isomorphism).

Using quality models for self-assessment. Chapter 7 examines the practice of organisational self-assessment, for which an increasingly wide array of rating systems are now available. The two examined both spring from the Quality movement, and hence this is another chance to examine what happens to private sector management ideas when they spread into the nonprofit world. One, the Excellence Model, has been very widely adopted in the UK partly as a result of promotion by the Government. The other, PQASSO, is a derivative of Quality Assurance methods developed to suit smaller social enterprises. The case studies show that self-assessment can indeed enable constructive review processes in a wide range of contexts. However, when the models 'work' it is in rather different ways than is suggested by the terms in which they are promoted.

Towards Practice: Choosing a Suite of Measures. What combination of measures are needed to enable leaders of an organisation to make rounded judgements about the performance and prospects of their organisations? In the private sector this issue gave rise to the enormously influential 'Balanced Scorecard'. Chapter 8 presents (and illustrates) a similar framework devised for social enterprises, within which the various approaches to measurement or reporting previously discussed are easily located. It draws together a number of topics (eg the limits of measurement) from earlier chapters, revisiting some of the case study organisations. In doing so it highlights an issue neglected in most discussions of nonprofit performance: the management of those intangible assets upon which future performance depends. Hence this chapter continues the critical appraisal of the relevance of 'mainstream' management ideas (and their adaptation) to social enterprises. But it also starts to draw together the main ideas of the book, while offering a tool for managers to appraise their information management.

A more measured management? The final chapter revisits the various explanations for the spread of performance improvement methods, and the predictions of their impact, in the light of the various studies reported. While genericist, management fashion, and institutional theorists can all take some comfort from the findings, none offers a very satisfactory account – not least because those who adopt the methods also seem to adapt them quite radically to suit the circumstances. The most striking feature of the experiences reviewed is the variability of the outcomes. Clearly, use of the methods can lead to significant benefits. But equally, the costs and potential pitfalls are very considerable indeed. This means that those funders and policy-makers who pressurise social enterprises to use such methods risk doing more harm than good – promoting a disconnected managerialism, rather than the selective incorporation of useful insights in a grounded manner. In any event, measurement activities, analysis and use are likely to steadily become a more prominent part of managerial work in social enterprises. Managers must come to terms with this development, taking measurement seriously, though not literally, and steering a reflective course between naïve rationalism on the one hand, and a cynical pre-occupation with appearances, on the other.

Sources and resources

The Cambodia and Biafra cases are both discussed in Smillie (1995) though I also drew on an interview with the late Guy Stringer. The contradictory nature of emergency food supply in the USA is well captured in Poppendieck (1998). The discussion also draws on material from John Arnold of Second Harvest Gleaners Food Bank of West Michigan (www.wmgleaners.org). The story of the Scott Bader Commonwealth can be found in Hoe (1995), or in Oakeshott (2001) available through Scott Bader (www.scottbader.com). For an analysis of the Commonwealth's (limited) progress based on many years involvement as an advisor and trustee, see Hadley and Goldsmith (1995). I have also drawn on my own involvement with Scott Bader, over the years, particularly as a Trustee in 1996–2001.

For the UK, the view that social enterprises need to embrace the performance agenda and adopt new measurement methods is more or less explicit in the publications of NCVO (especially the Quality Standards Task Force) and the Charities Aid Foundation (www.ncvo-vol.org.uk and www.cafonline.org respectively). For the US, Light (2000) captures the *zietgeist* admirably, in a way that has wider relevance. Clarke and Newman (1997) offer a strong and sustained critique of the new managerialism in the UK (though it is now somewhat dated) – they take organisational issues seriously even if their interests are more at a policy level.

2 Performance Management As Government Policy

The performance of social enterprises is not just a management challenge, as discussed in the last chapter; it is also a policy issue. Governments have helped make performance an issue and they are actively trying to raise performance. This chapter reviews this institutional and policy environment, locating the adoption of performance improvement methods by social enterprises as one of the ramifications of the new public management.

Managing performance without managing organizations

Over the last 20 years many governments have ceased to provide services directly – the development of what (Milward 1994) calls 'the hollow state'. This trend has been accompanied by the introduction of new arrangements to supervise the variety of more or less independent service providers that have emerged. In other words, 'decentralisation', privatisation and competition in public services (variously in provider markets, consumer markets, and in non-market forms) developed hand-in-hand with the introduction of new supervisory regimes. At the same time, independent voluntary agencies operating ever more commercially have been drawn into this increasingly regulated environment as contractors to government - the 'contract culture' (6 and Kendall 1997) is now a reality. Viewed in these terms, the debate between those who see such changes as an empowering decentralisation, and those who see them as a new and potentially intense form of control, loses its edge. Performance management as government policy involves both centralisation and decentralisation (Hoggett 1996).

The drive to rationalise. It is now a central, underlying, and taken-for-granted assumption of governments in relation to a wide range of social policy, that they can and should *manage performance without managing organisations*. Hence, in a wide range of areas - in health, education, welfare, housing, international development - government policy is now focussed on devising and revising frameworks for performance management. Governments do no to want the burdens of operational management and to be associated with the failings of services they fund. But they cannot wish away deep-seated and widely-shared expectations that where problems are uncovered or new issues emerge in health, education, welfare and the like, it is the job of governments to *sort things out*. Social problems are seen as more or less soluble, by analysing and understanding them, and by designing interventions to deal with them. If there is an outrage and 'something should be done', then it is up to government to see that something is done. Such interventions need to be soundly devised, of course - which is to say rationally constructed from the best available course, which is to say rationally constructed from the best available knowledge and managerial expertise. Indeed, the taken-for-granted aspiration of modern society is that more and more areas of unnecessary distress and disorder can be rationalised in this way – this is what progress means. Governments may feed these diffuse societal expectations, but they are also driven and punished by them.

This chapter offers a brisk tour of the ways in which governments have made performance management a core social policy, and traces through the implications this is having for social enterprises and for those who run them. Most obviously, social enterprises are under increasing pressure, both to deliver improved operational results – to do more for less, often – and to incorporate the latest advances in management thinking and practice. Drawing on concepts from institutional theory (Powell and DiMaggio 1991), the discussion also highlights more of the research issues concerning the possible consequences of these developments. Finally, it also provides the opportunity for a closer look at the idea of a social enterprise. As the tools of performance management are transferred between sectors and industries, the structural similarities and correspondences between different institutional fields are increasing. In the light of this, it is argued that a degree of convergence between organisations in different fields and sectors is now taking place, and that the 'regulated social enterprise' is emerging as a distinct organisational form.

This perspective is developed with reference mainly to arrangements in the UK and necessarily involves passing reference to a wide range of regulatory bodies and policy initiatives. The nature and scope of these may be obscure to non-UK readers (as indeed they often will be to UK readers unfamiliar with a particular field of activity). But the general argument will still be clear – and indeed, various parallels and similarities with developments in other countries will be obvious to anyone familiar with the literatures on both the new public management and third sector organisations in an international perspective (Salamon and Anheier 1997).

The instruments of performance management

So how does a government 'do' performance management? This section distinguishes eight generic instruments used either to form social enterprises or to influence them. Such influence may be direct or, by intervening in the organisational fields in which social enterprises are embedded (DiMaggio and Powell 1983), it may be indirect. The aim is to illustrate the elements out of which performance management frameworks are constructed, and to demonstrate the similarities in different fields. Along the way, some observations are made about what is more or less new in such arrangements, and what is a recycling of familiar policy instruments.

1. Specifying governance arrangements. This has a long history – *vide*, the evolution of the law surrounding charity trusteeship, and the use of Royal Charters in the constitution of universities. The general rationale is to give key stakeholders a voice while safeguarding the integrity and basic purposes of the organisation, and preventing its capture by 'producers' or other interests. Such considerations were very clear in the government's decision to preserve the non-beneficiary status and the independence of directors of housing associations and of trustees of charities, especially in relation to local authorities from which they may have been 'hived off'. Changes to governance arrangements have also been seen as one way to break existing institutional patterns, to check professional dominance, to represent service users and to introduce more commercial thinking at the most senior level (Cornforth 2002). Hence, for example, the introduction of parent governors for schools, and the reconstituting of the governing bodies of colleges of further education with employer representation.

Whether particular governance arrangements achieve their purposes (and with what other consequences) is less clear. Moreover, the dynamics of governing bodies with disparate membership can become very unstable (eg the well-publicised breakdown between parents and teachers in a school in Stratford, London).

2. *Requiring public reports.* This instrument, and the idea of public scrutiny, not just regulatory oversight, is relatively new, or at least one that has been rapidly developed in recent years. For example, in local government the Best Value Performance Plan, to be published annually, is 'intended as the principal means by which an authority is held to account for the efficiency and effectiveness of its services, and its plans for the future' (DETR 1999). Likewise, new reporting requirements have been introduced for charities (the new accounting SORP and the Charity Commission return), for NHS Trusts, housing associations and for schools. The aim has been to ensure that basic information on expenditure, achievements and plans is not just lodged with a supervisory body but placed in the public domain and made accessible to those with a direct interest and to third parties like the local and national press and researchers. As part of this strategy, the Charity Commission is making annual returns available to on-line enquirers – and similar developments have taken place in the US in respect of the IRS 990 form.[6]

Of course, the trustees and managers of social enterprises have often seen such reporting in terms of avoiding anything that might prompt the interest of regulatory bodies or adverse media interest; and more broadly as an occasion for presenting a positive public image. Not surprisingly, complaints have been made, at least regarding charities, about data quality, the self-congratulatory tone of such reporting, and comparability issues (Gamblin and Jones 1996; Stevenson, Sales et al. 1997).

This instrument has been developed most energetically and intrusively through the requirement to provide data for performance comparisons. 'League tables' have become a familiar feature in the landscapes of schooling, universities, housing and local government and most recently hospitals. This goes far beyond annual performance reporting: it involves major initiatives to create new data (eg, in schools, national test scores); and to ensure it is available to the relevant stakeholders (eg, the Housing Corporation providing individual reports to local authorities on the Registered Social Landlords operating in their areas). The argument is usually in terms of consumer choice and competitive pressure. However, where choice is not realistic, the rationale is in terms of 'naming and shaming'. All this is, of course, controversial – not least among professional evaluators (for a recent exchange, see Perrin 1998; Bernstein 1999) and statisticians (Goldstein and Spiegelhalter 1996).

3. Financial leverage. This instrument must be as old as government itself and it is widely used to induce social enterprises to undertake programmes, join collaborations, or make decisions that will help achieve performance as the government construes it. Recent UK examples that illustrate the diverse possibilities include:

- the offering of contracts to run a wide range of services, often out with the customary ambit of voluntary agencies and NGOs;

- 'City challenge' and the operation of the Single Regeneration Budget with their 'partnership' elements;

- financial rewards for General Practitioners achieving, for example, immunisation targets;

- a more generous financial regime for schools that 'opted out' of local authority control;

- grants under the 'Make a Difference' scheme to promote volunteering.

However, the extent to which such schemes produce the results intended is less clear – and probably very variable. As with grant giving and grantsmanship in the nonprofit sector, so government departments may end up paying for what would have happened anyway, or for schemes that, for better or worse, were never what the criteria had been intended to allow, or for projects that are opportunistic and ill thought out. But equally, some schemes do work, show-case projects can be found – indeed, sometimes projects yield greater success than predicted in quite unexpected directions – and at least the government is able to point to *something* it is doing to address what are, it may be said, insoluble issues (Seibel 1990). Moreover, regardless of the content of a programme or scheme, funding arrangements require particular budgetary and reporting practices, which may themselves embody government policy. Such concepts as logical framework analysis (currently *de rigeur* in international development programmes – see Commission of the European Communities, (Communities 1993), and outcome funding (Williams and Webb 1991) have changed the way in which proposals are made and reporting is required.

4. Setting and inspecting standards. The rationale for inspection is in terms of ensuring minimum standards, though this may be supported by claims that the expertise of the inspectors means the visits can also serve a developmental function, identifying weaknesses and transferring good practice. The Social Services Inspectorate (SSI), the Office for Standards in Education (OFSTED), the Quality Assurance Agency (QAA) for higher education, the Best Value Inspectorate (for local government), and the Housing Corporation are examples of statutory bodies with a brief to determine appropriate standards and to check, through inspection visits, that they are being upheld.

Nevertheless, the questionable reliability of such inspections has been repeatedly observed and reported both in the press and academic studies. Thus, long-standing physical abuse has subsequently been uncovered in adult residential care homes that have been commended by the SSI. And OFSTED has provoked many challenges to its reports and suffered numerous embarrassments (eg different teams producing contradictory appraisals of the functioning of the same governing body responsible for two schools on the same site).

The reasons are well understood: determining whether the standards have been achieved involves forming a judgement on a limited set of observations open to a range of interpretations. These observations have to be considered along with the subjects' selective reporting and politically motivated responses, in an unfamiliar context. Inevitably, therefore, given this degree of ambiguity, standards are socially constructed and tacitly negotiated, with existing reputations and developing relationships playing an important role (Ashby 1990). Some failures of supervision are therefore inevitable, especially since not all inspectors are as highly astute, dispassionate, experienced and interpersonally skilful as the role demands.

Such well-documented issues are not inhibiting the use of this instrument. The Charity Commission is now visiting larger charities in a rolling programme, and standards are also being proposed for Hospital Trusts. And a new version has recently emerged – the 'kitemark' or award, like 'Investors in People', the 'Chartermark' and the ISO 9000 quality standards. Promoting such schemes offers a way for governments to stimulate performance while still remaining above the details and avoiding the on-going costs of conventional inspection.

5. Giving rights to service users. This instrument tends to be used whenever it is thought that professional or bureaucratic dominance and a lack of responsiveness jeopardise important dimensions of performance. Depending on the field of activity and the political values of the government, the rationale may be in terms of partnerships between clients and professionals, in terms of consumerism and marketisation, in terms of quality, or even democratic participation and community building. This instrument has a relatively short history, but recent examples of statutory requirements and official departmental guidelines include:

- in the housing field, consultation on specific issues has been a legal requirement for social landlords since 1985;

- in local government, the Best Value regime includes a general duty to consult not just on the experience of current service but about improvement targets and the future shape and quality of services;

- in international development and urban regeneration, community groups have to be represented in partnerships and the public consulted in planning processes;

- in education, the parental right to choose schools; the requirement for parental ballots for particular decisions;

- in community care, involvement in individual care programme planning, appeals procedures, the requirement for consultation with user groups in service planning, the right to choose among residential care homes – and so on.

Of course, in practice, the rights of service users are often heavily circumscribed, not least by resource constraints and by deference to professional expertise. In addition; user representatives are easily typified and their concerns reinterpreted in more familiar professional terms. But the recognition of these difficulties has sometimes led to official funding for and support of advocacy schemes. Overall, such legal and quasi-legal entitlements create some institutional pressure to take account of user perspectives, and provide scope for alliances – either with professionals against the managers, or with managers against the professionals.

6. Promoting new and better methods. This instrument refers to efforts to change professional or management practice in different fields either by setting a general agenda or by funding more specific work to identify and disseminate more effective practices. Much government sponsorship of evaluation research in education, international development and other fields, and its emphasis on dissemination, exemplifies this approach. So does support for education and training initiatives concerning governance and management (eg in Schools, charities, the UK Health Service). 'Evidence-based medicine' in health care is a current example, as is the encouragement of 'Beacon' status (eg in the Health Service, in local government) where particular sites are recognised as exemplars and funded to share their know-how with others. Another instance is the use of the Audit Commission to study and make recommendations on particular issues and activities in local government.

Such initiatives have a powerful common-sense logic in terms of identifying 'what works' and providing professional staff and managers with detailed information on how they can improve their practice. And they have a considerable history. For example, in the late 1960s, the US Office of Education (USOE) published the 'It Works' booklets, each on an apparently successful project for educating disadvantaged children. By the mid-1970s the USOE was so determined to propagate best practice in educating disadvantaged children that it set up an Office of Educational Replication. This was charged with developing and distributing boxed kits for use in school districts to replicate as exactly as possible projects that had been found effective elsewhere. The kits met with very limited success – according to the evaluator involved (Hawkridge 2001).

In fact, the identification, the transferability and the willingness to adopt 'best practice' are all *deeply* problematic and the whole approach can easily become crudely mechanistic. This is well illustrated by recent research on the relationship between R&D and clinical practice in health care (Dawson, Sutherland et al. 1998). This found that, even with clear-cut, well-researched guidelines and scientifically trained practitioners, evidence-based recommendations offered by journals, education and guidelines were rarely seen as authoritative and were filtered and interpreted in relation to the individual's accumulated experiences and that of peers and mentors. Echoing similar findings in other fields, the researchers concluded that tacit knowledge, the particularity of the case, and various aspects of organisational context shape clinical behaviour and learning far more powerfully than exposure to explicit knowledge, the implications of which can always be contested.

7. Adjusting sector boundaries. This usually takes the form of requiring private sector involvement (or its threat in the form of market testing). It has been used as a way of creating incentives for cost reductions, breaking up established institutional patterns, stimulating the development of a more commercial culture less influenced by producer perspectives, enabling greater focus on an agency's 'core tasks', and introducing greater expertise. There may also be financial advantages (in terms, for example, of reduced borrowing). Examples include the requirement on local authorities to seek out private investment, engage in partnerships and collaboration with private and voluntary sector organisations, and to make use of competition exercises within Best Value, the Private Finance Initiative (PFI) now penetrating throughout government and the public sector and the requirement for Registered Social Landlords to seek some commercial finance. Private sector involvement, either as sponsor or commercial partner, has also been required in environmental, arts and education initiatives (eg City Technology Colleges).

8. Intervention. The more common form is to instigate an investigation but, as a last resort, governments usually hold reserve powers to impose changes. Examples of the former include judicial and SSI enquiries into child abuse, and the Charity Commission probing and reporting on political activity by Oxfam. Such investigations can be a way of responding to public concern over the activities of social enterprises. Less formally, a request by a minister for departmental officials to report on a controversial issue may legitimise concern, reinforce media attention, and inhibit repetition of the doubtful behaviour by tacitly threatening some further action.

The more drastic step of imposing change, by 'stepping in' to close down, take over, or replace the leadership in failing social enterprises, is now clearly on the agenda. For example, inspectors have powers to find a service failing and refer it to the Secretary of State for intervention. So far, this instrument has attracted most publicity and attention in relation to certain schools (eg the Ridings School in Yorkshire). It is less well known that in 1998 (for example) 20 receiver-managers were running charities on behalf of the Charity Commission.[7] The government is currently developing the capacity for comparable interventions ('hit squads') in local government (through the Improvement and Development Agency), and the possibility has also been discussed in relation to NHS Trusts.

The rationale, on both pragmatic and theoretical grounds, for such a capacity is strong: even in a market environment where performance signals are much clearer, it is well known that senior managers can screen out unwelcome information and persist for long periods in demonstrably ineffective courses of action (Slatter 1984). Even if the phenomenon of 'permanently failing organizations' (Meyer and Zucker 1989) is unusual, the error-correction process can be ponderously slow – especially when a governing body comprising diverse stakeholder groups cannot sustain a coalition for change. Nevertheless, the difficulties, costs and limitations of such interventions are bound to be considerable – as the press reports concerning some of the schools seem to confirm.

From government policy to management practice

Tension and churn. Performance management frameworks put together from these instruments, can be designed to reflect and give 'bite' to a very wide range of policies and ideological positions. Governments can pick and mix between several different, widely understood, institutional logics. These different logics – of control and accountability in public administration, of relying on professional expertise, of the competitive pressures of the marketplace, of democratic involvement and responsiveness – all command substantial degrees of popular support (though there are important cultural differences between countries in this respect). Each can provide a legitimate basis for performance management initiatives, indeed these different logics actually imply different conceptions of performance and point to different situations as problematic. Since performance management frameworks subscribe in varying degrees to all of the different institutional logics, a degree of tension and inconsistency is built into them. For example, schools are obliged to concentrate on their league table results, but also urged to meet the expectations and preferences of parents (which research shows are much broader and more balanced). Similar dilemmas face health care providers – patients often prefer treatments, especially for mental health problems, other than those deemed most effective by researchers.

More importantly, performance management frameworks tend to be constantly revised. Most obviously, new foci for public concern rise and fall, and policy rhetorics come and go. Moreover, any particular framework will have some unintended consequences, which will need to be addressed – for example, in the UK the priority given to agency results (narrowly defined) accentuated the problems of inter-agency working (James 2000). In response, the need for 'joined-up government' became more of an issue and this gradually began to feature in performance management frameworks. More generally, most frameworks will either be seen as not working well or fast enough in some respect, or as having ceased to work. This is because many of the issues that social enterprises exist to address are not amenable to this sort of rationalised solution. As was noted in chapter 1, cause-effect relations are often poorly understood and in any case the issues are imbued with political and value dimensions that render apparently rational solutions unrealistic. The point is not that the programmes are pointless and unwarranted, but that they only work sometimes, or up to a point, or for a time. All these tendencies contribute to what may be called *policy churn*.

The public and private faces of performance. But what can managers do if their results are equivocal – even if they are the best that current understanding of the issues can achieve? In such situations they cannot rely on performance in terms of self-evident operating results to secure the confidence of government agencies or other key stakeholders. Performance in its other sense – that of acting to convey a particular impression and evoke particular responses – becomes important. In other words, managers have to give increasing time and attention to securing the confidence of key audiences by building relationships with them and projecting favourable accounts of necessarily ambiguous activities and figures.

The problem is that the language of performance takes no prisoners. Through its lenses, the world is straightforward, situations are or should be controlled, the issues are clear, the criteria unambiguous – and results have either been achieved or they have not. Uncertainty, patchiness, ambiguity, riders and qualifications – all these can be read as excuses, signs of weakness. 'Performance' is categorical – that is precisely its attraction. By comparison, evaluations are thought to muddy the waters, raise more questions, and fail to come to the sorts of conclusion a busy decision-maker can act on – as well as being expensive (Davis 1999). Hence performance management seems to be accentuating the familiar discrepancy between an organisation's public and private faces. Whatever the strains, stresses and disorder that are occurring 'backstage', the 'frontstage' impression is still upbeat, a tale of rationality and order, progress and achievement (to use the terms of Goffman 1959). Moreover, there is a lot more to this 'frontstage' impression than annual reports and good stakeholder relations.

Internalising the environment. It is a truism that organisations adapt to their environments. However, in some strands of management and organisational theory this seems to imply no more than some tactical ducking and weaving for economic advantage, while the organisation itself continues as a self-contained entity (though perhaps smaller or larger, depending on its success). In practice, however, meeting environmental expectations often means incorporating new practices.[8] Thus the performance management frameworks described require that the organisations subject to them undertake extensive measurement and reporting (the second, third, fourth instruments, in particular) and do so in particular ways. These requirements come to be reflected in management language and job titles,[9] and (as we shall see) they may also shape the spreadsheets that are the basic mechanism for internal reporting and management. Moreover, even when particular methods and procedures are not specified, frameworks for performance management usually require that issues of governance, benchmarking, service review, quality assurance, service user involvement, etc are being addressed. This requirement may be expressed in terms of standards or of 'best practice' (ie the fourth or the sixth instruments). Again, it means new roles being created, and changes in the way tasks are carried out. External changes require internal reconstruction.

Hence, government policies variously require or encourage the adoption of favoured practices believed to improve performance. As we shall see, the performance improvement methods examined in this book often provide ways for social enterprises to show that they are well run, and doing things properly.

This perspective on how the new public management has unfolded conforms to a considerable body of institutional theory. This has shown organisations can increase their reputations and improve their prospects by incorporating those formal structures and practices believed to be associated with superior or more reliable performance:

> Organizations that do so increase their legitimacy and their survival prospects, independent of the immediate efficacy of the acquired practices and procedures. (Meyer and Rowan 1991, p 41)

Indeed, the more problematic and uncertain the outcome, the more attention is likely to be given to the conspicuous use of the proper formal procedures. Jefferson and Meyer (1991) may well have had the situation of many NGOs in mind when they suggested that the drive to rationalise takes on a 'manic quality':

> ...in the peripheries of the modern system where external pressures make elaborate organization seem crucial in the struggle against failure and entropy. (p 209)

The state of the debate

The preceding analysis may explain the spread of the new performance measurement and improvement methods, but it remains much less clear how far they help or hinder social enterprises. The debates among managers and professionals are mirrored by competing perspectives in the research literature.

Pessimistic perspectives. Critics and pessimists can say the dangers are substantial and have often been reported: performance management by government distorts organisational priorities as attention goes into deflecting, limiting or circumventing the impact of the statutory initiatives that generate ever-changing and incompatible requirements. On this view government activism in the name of performance management is doubly wasteful. It misdirects resources into unproductive audit and reporting that are often largely ceremonial, de-coupled from the real work, and which actually feed the public anxiety they are supposed to assuage. And it corrupts organisational functioning encouraging a concern with impressions rather than substance (Power 1997). So 'managing performance without managing organizations' means governments exercising power without responsibility – creating ever greater strains for the staff of organisations that must do more with less, while disclaiming any direct involvement.

Innovation will continue to happen more often despite than because of performance management. In particular, for many, the break up of established institutional patterns will provoke resistance and defensiveness, while the controlling tendencies of performance management will restrict the scope for experimentation. For example, in social housing many of the most important developments of the last 10 years concerning community-based economic development, training and neighbourhood improvement ('housing plus' is the usual term) had no place in the performance indicators used to assess housing associations during that period. These focused entirely on financial and managerial matters – voids, response times, etc – while ignoring the more important and difficult factors that affected the quality of life of tenants.

The optimists accounts. By contrast, supporters and optimists say that even if performance management is sometimes a blunt weapon, it addresses real issues stimulating more functional than dysfunctional behaviours. It is introducing constructive tensions into the planning and management of social enterprises – tensions that reflect the diversity of stakeholders that need to be satisfied, some of whose concerns have not been given due weight in the past. The succession of different imperatives is no more than the familiar pattern of sequential attention to goals – an intelligent response to complex issues and cognitive limits (Cyert and March 1963). There is evidence that a far better integration of professional and managerial rationalities is beginning to occur (Ferlie, Ashburner et al. 1996; Llewellyn 2001), along with more diverse, if still fitfully effective, ways for service user concerns to be expressed and represented. Moreover, fears that the new methods restrict what can be done are frequently exaggerated. In many cases they are loosely defined leaving ample scope for interpretation – to the point where some have complained that they are largely rhetorical (Hood 1998) Nor is it the case that the adoption of performance improvement methods whose efficacy is uncertain leads to cynicism and demoralisation. The contrary view is that they boost morale:

> Participants not only commit themselves to supporting an organization's ceremonial façade but also commit themselves to making things work backstage. (Meyer and Rowan 1991, p 59)

Conclusions

This chapter has argued that managing performance without managing organisations is now the order of the day. In practice, this means combining and elaborating different versions of the limited number of generic instruments available. These 'frameworks for back-seat driving' can always be adjusted to respond to emerging public concerns or to pursue particular agendas. Activist governments can and will move goalposts.

While chapter 1 introduced 'genericism' and 'management fashion' as rival explanations for the spread of performance improvement methods, this chapter has introduced institutional theory as a further possibility:

1. The techniques are believed in government and policy circles to be

effective means of raising performance; and governments (directly or indirectly) encourage social enterprises to adopt the techniques, through their own frameworks for performance management.

2.   Securing the confidence of external stakeholders will be an important consideration in the adoption of the methods by social enterprises.

3.   Adoption of the methods will be more common and rapid where there is greater dependence on governmental funding, regardless of their advantages or disadvantages for task performance.

The controversies surrounding these developments have provided a preview of themes that will be explored in the chapters and case studies that follow. In particular, they highlight the question of the relationship between the new formal methods and actual task performance (are they being applied in ways that support and contribute to task execution, or are they a burden?). And they introduce as a possibility (one with horrid methodological implications) that the methods may work indirectly, by helping managers secure the confidence and support of stakeholders. So perhaps they are often a necessary evil or a mixed blessing – enabling organisations 'to maintain standardised, legitimating formal structures while their activities vary in response to practical considerations' (Meyer and Rowan 1991, p 58).

One other issue is raised by this discussion. Given the 'churn' in performance management frameworks and the possibility that some methods may be adopted to build a public reputation rather than to assist the primary task, how can and do the managers involved construct their roles and identities? As the interpreters and exponents of performance improvement methods that their staff and colleagues may view with dismay, do they become true believers in the brave new methods, as theorists of cognitive dissonance would predict, and has certainly been reported (Pattison and Paton 1997; Pattison 1998). Or, ever pragmatic, if sometimes a bit jaded and cynical, do they become operators and impresarios, coaxing colleagues into playing the game?

Coda: the 'regulated social enterprise' as an emerging form

Policy transfer and 'isomorphism'. The idea that organisations operating in the same organisational field are likely to become gradually more alike as they accommodate the same environmental expectations is a tenet of institutional theory. The observation that voluntary organisations drawn into the contract culture tend to lose some of their distinctive characteristics is a case in point (Taylor, Langan et al. 1995). For this reason it can no longer be assumed that the sectoral differences, around which much social policy has been debated, continue to reflect substantial organisational differences.[10]

But some convergence may also be taking place between different organisational fields, and not just within them. As was noted, the performance management frameworks employed in different fields use the same basic instruments and so have many common features. Policy transfer would seem to be widespread – presumably it will continue.   As an example, the Charity Commission recently developed its own version of the risk profiling approach used by HM Inspectors of Customs and Excise. The aim is to identify those factors and financial trends that tend to be associated with different sorts of fraud and mismanagement, and to develop statistical filters to search for 'at risk' charities. It allows the Commission to be more proactive, and to make the most cost-effective use of the investigative effort available.

Increasing similarity. But if policy environments are becoming more alike, and if organisational settings and institutional environments are highly interpenetrated, then one would expect a degree of convergence also to be taking place across different institutional fields, not just within them. If so, we should see a somewhat distinctive organisational form emerging, whatever label it is given (Hoggett 1996, refers to SMPEs – small and medium-sized public enterprises). Its main characteristics would seem to be:

1.   The pursuit of social outcomes in relation to either individuals or communities (and hence considerable goal ambiguity is commonplace).

2.   Governance that involves a substantial lay or non-executive element, and often quite diverse stakeholder representation (multiple accountabilities are normal).

3.   Key staff who are human service professionals or bring other strong and distinct value commitments to their roles (the integration of these with managerial rationalities is often problematic).

4.   Funding obtained from a mix of voluntary, public and commercial sources, increasingly through quasi-market or other competitive processes (commonly generating income uncertainty and complex fund accounting arrangements, even in medium-sized organisations).

5.   Close public scrutiny (underpinned by the prospect, ultimately, of intervention) through some combination of supervision regarding professional standards, managerial arrangements, client or citizen involvement, etc, and detailed performance reporting.

6.   Working in or through partnerships, whether for financial reasons, statutory requirement or because of the nature of the task (these partnerships may involve firms, governmental bodies or other social enterprises).

The first three of these characteristics have long been noted as features of public and private nonprofit organisations. What has been gradually changing is the increasing significance and prevalence of the fourth, fifth and sixth characteristics. And it is these in combination – a greater reliance on earned income, closer public oversight, more cross-sector working – that the term *regulated social enterprise* recognises. This does not mean everything public or social is a social enterprise. The characteristics listed are not those of central government departments, large agencies or the armed forces. Nor does the term embrace the vital undergrowth of informal voluntary action, self-help and leisure networks, and neighbourhood groups that constitute the social capital of a functioning society (Putnam 1995).

Other, narrower definitions of social enterprise have been offered for particular purposes or in support of a claim that the designated organisations are a new, distinct and important form. The difficulty with such arguments are that the boundaries are usually hard to discern; and what is supposed to be new and different (trading activity, business practices) is actually quite widespread, often with long historical precedent. Hence, social enterprise is probably more use as a generic term to recognise the combination of changes that have been taking place in public and nonprofit organisations, rather than as the label for a specific sub-category (these can usually be referred to using more familiar terms – credit unions, fee-earning charity, community business, etc).

And continuing differences. This is not to claim that schools, housing associations, care providers, hospitals, development agencies (and so on) are becoming 'all the same', or that the differences between them will no longer be significant. That will never be the case simply because they undertake very different tasks requiring very different organisational settings. In addition, it is also the case that the intensity of direct governmental control varies considerably, with the Health Service notoriously tightly run, notwithstanding the introduction of Trust status. Indeed, the main difference among social enterprises, beyond those directly associated with their primary task, probably lies not in their sectoral auspices but in their degree of institutionalisation – that is, the extent to which they show continuity and stability, and embody rationalised practices recognised in the wider society. The spectrum ranges from those embedded in large, 'mature', highly institutionalised fields (like health and education), to those in fields where institutionalisation is more limited or emergent (eg community-based organisations, advocacy, micro-finance). The cases in this book range across this spectrum.

Sources and resources

The literature on 'the new public management' is extensive but Ferlie, Ashburner et al. (1996) and Hoggett (1996) are both still useful. The journals *Public Management* and *Public Administration* show how the debate is moving on.

Institutional theory in organisational analysis derives from pioneering sociology of Max Weber as reinvigorated by DiMaggio and Powell's celebrated 1983 article. Key ideas from both are summarised in Pugh and Hickson (1995) but Powell and DiMaggio (1991) is well worth the effort.

Social enterprise and related terms (social economy, social entrepreneurship) are now becoming quite widely used. In the UK, the report by Social Enterprise London (www.sel.org.uk) has been influential in providing a working definition and indication of the principal variants. It focuses on trading activities undertaken for social purposes (but is still wider than the definition used by the Social Enterprise Unit of the UK Government's

Department of Trade and Industry). This aspect is also important in the US, though there the idea of social investment (with Foundations acting as social financiers for portfolios of projects) is also influential. Dees (1998) offers a clear and comprehensive overview of US experience and thinking, with a useful 'Social Enterprise Spectrum' showing the main dimensions on which social enterprises vary. In Europe, the term 'social economy' has a longer, more institutional pedigree, based on cooperatives, mutuals, associations and foundations.

3 Taking Measures - Lessons from the Literature

Introduction

As the previous chapter showed, nonprofits now operate in an environment permeated by expectations of measurement. The reasons usually offered for preferring measurement-based performance management are:

- Defining performance explicitly, and specifying the level expected, demands greater focus and clarity - it reduces the scope for obfuscation, ambiguity and misunderstanding.

- Measures can summarise the important aspects of a complex situation making it easier to spot where and when expectations are not being realised

- Measurement expresses and encourages an approach to decision-making (including recognition and reward) based on facts and analysis, rather than anecdotes and opinion, not to mention wishful thinking and self-serving claims.

- Measurement can assist learning by allowing greater comparability - over time and between units - and by helping identify 'what works'.

To the extent that these claims are sound in particular circumstances, measurement offers some or all of the following benefits - enhanced supervisory control, greater day-to-day autonomy of operating units, steady performance improvement, and reduced supervision costs. But how sound are these claims? Although performance measurement is, at least in the popular mind, practically a defining feature of managerial activity, it has for years been highly controversial, both in practice and in management writing:

> Performance measurement has a chequered history even in the traditional manufacturing and bureaucratic settings ostensibly most conducive to measuring outputs and causally attributing outputs to individuals and organizational sub-groups. There are many more instances of dysfunction - instances where performance measures stimulate less than optimal or even counter productive behaviours - than there are instances of demonstrable success (Austin, Larkey et al. 1998).

Nor is it the case that the critics and sceptics are simply behavioural scientists on the sidelines - while practical managers get on with the real if imperfect business of managing and making decisions on the best (quantitative) scientists on the sidelines – while practical managers get on with the real if imperfect business of managing and making decisions on the best (quantitative) information they can obtain. In fact, the critics of measurement include many practising managers as well as major figures in management thought – Deming, Mintzberg and Handy to name but three. This chapter explores these debates, highlighting the main themes in recent writing on performance measurement. The aim is to provide some conceptual focus for the empirical studies in later chapters.

An explosion of research. The last 10 years have seen an explosion of interest in and research on the measurement of organisational performance inspired by three trends:

- the reduction in data handling and processing costs as a result of ICT developments;

- the vastly increased measurement efforts in the private sector, particularly in pursuit of non-financial measures of performance;

- the impact of the new managerialism in government and nonprofits.

So what does this literature suggest is likely to happen as social enterprises give increased attention to performance measurement? Research on or relevant to this question appears in the following disciplines and fields:

- the extensive organisational and management literature on the uses of performance measurement in (mainly) commercial organisations;

- the literatures of political science and public administration, regarding the use of performance measures as instruments of government control;

- the literatures associated with particular areas of nonprofit activity, in particular development studies/NGOs, but also including others like urban regeneration;

- studies of nonprofit effectiveness, and of the evaluation of nonprofits.

In addition, relevant theoretical ideas have been developed in some branches of economics (the theory of the firm, principal-agent relations) and in sociology (institutional theory). Experiences of measurement initiatives are also described and debated in the journals of professional evaluators. All these sources are referred to in the discussion that follows, but to keep the task within bounds, the views of measurement authorities from leading business schools are given particular weight.[11] The discussion aims to highlight some of the common themes from diverse contexts with a view to clarifying:

1. what is known about the different ways performance information can be used and the issues that arise; but also

2. what may be different about measurement in social enterprises (and why).

As Kendall and Knapp (1995) have pointed out, the main divide in discussions of effectiveness and performance is between those with a rationalist/positivist approach and those with a social constructivist perspective. The discussion starts by considering the practical difficulties associated with 'rationalist' measurement projects and then turns to the contribution of constructivist perspectives to understanding measurement practice. Thereafter, the implications for social enterprises and for research are considered.

The limits to rationalisation

Technical desiderata and flawed realities. The attributes of performance measures that are needed if systems of performance measurement are to assist motivation, feedback control and learning are now well understood. The lists vary as authors express the ideas in slightly different ways, but the same issues and requirements recur, whether with reference to commercial or public organisations (Carter, Klein et al. 1992; Meyer 1998; Kennerley and Neeley 2000), namely:

- they should be *valid* and *reliable* (and 'non-manipulible') and hence provide an appropriate motivational focus;

- they should be *parsimonious*, that is, relatively few in number – lest the 'cognitive limits' of those wanting to understand the performance in question are exceeded;

- they should be *comprehensive*, in the sense of covering all significant dimensions of performance, including the strategic;

- they should be *acceptable, meaningful* and *credible* to a wide range of constituencies;

- they should be *pervasive* and *integrative* allowing the aggregation of results and comparisons both externally and internal;

- they should be *relatively stable*, allowing the tracking of performance over time;

- they should be constructed to have *explanatory* power, aiding diagnosis of low performance, assisting learning and giving insight about future prospects not just reporting past results (sometimes referred to in terms of 'attributability' and 'drill down');

- they should be *practicable* – capable of being quite promptly reported and without adding unduly to administrative costs.

Nevertheless, it is now quite clear that in practice, measurement systems never manage to combine all these attributes. As one leading authority puts it regarding companies:

> I wish I could recommend specific measures meeting these requirements. But I cannot. Such a measurement system, to the best of my knowledge, does not exist and probably it never will exist. (Meyer 1998, p xv)

Many of the difficulties are hidden in the concept of performance itself, which sounds like a unitary attribute but is always multi-dimensional and hard to operationalise ('Performance measures for firms are generally uncorrelated – this has been known for years' (Meyer 1998, xvii). Partly this is because of the time dimension of performance – which may refer to past achievements, current functioning, or future prospects. Thus desired outcomes (including profits in the case of companies) which may be very useful as *incentives*, are of limited value as indicators of continuing and future performance (Carter, Klein et al. 1992, p174; Bruns 1998). Hence, the enormous effort devoted to finding other, non-financial measures (such as quality, customer satisfaction and loyalty, intellectual capital) that may be leading indicators of profit. Unfortunately, however, most of these are extremely hard to measure – which is to say, they subsume many dimensions requiring multiple indicators of uncertain reliability – as the continuing business and academic research effort testifies. As a result, it is commonplace for senior managers to be faced with 50, 60 or more 'top level' measures. So even in companies with their (supposedly) narrow and shared financial goals, the attempt to be comprehensive in measurement leads to information overload (Meyer 1998) and is incompatible with parsimony.

These issues are likely to be even more acute in nonprofit contexts where concepts of effectiveness and performance are often broad (Herman and Renz 1997, 1999; Forbes 1998); and where one important dimension is often a degree of social or community impact – for which 'the flows of information involved are often remarkably high' as Bovaird (1998) puts it. When a single programme has 169 separate performance measures (Sawhill and Williamson 2001) it is clear things are getting out of hand.

Such overload can easily lead to a pattern of oscillation as first noted in Blau's classic study of the employment office (Blau 1963). The use of a limited set of indicators encourages staff to neglect unmeasured dimensions of performance, so new measures are added; but in due course the resulting set exceeds cognitive limits, so there are calls for sharper focus and greater selectivity. This leads to a 'cull' of measures and a much more limited set – and so on.

Other reasons why measurement systems always appear technically unsatisfactory will be noted later. Meanwhile, an alternative view of such lists and the normative theory underpinning them is that they reveal the extent to which performance measurement systems stimulate or express inflated expectations of rationalised control. In consequence, systems of performance measurement rarely provide what is expected of them (Meyer 1998). This does not mean that they fail (though they may do); it does mean that clarity over their purposes and what can realistically be expected from them is essential.

The pursuit of control. Measurement-based performance management assumes that measures of performance provide a basis for organisational control. If a system of performance measurement does not provide an appropriate focus for managerial effort and a sound basis for recognition, then there is something wrong with it. Measures, it is said, should have 'bite'. At the same time, however, the dysfunctional consequences of using performance measurement for control are well understood, not least in the private sector. Neely (1998), for example, starts his book in the following terms:

> The main theme of the book is that the traditional view of performance measurement as a means of control is naïve. As soon as performance measures are used as a means of control, the people being measured begin to manage the measures rather than performance. Incidents are reported selectively. Data are manipulated and presented in ways that make them look favourable. Individuals seek to undermine the measurement system. (p 1)

Such difficulties are not, of course, peculiar to the private sector. Gray (1997), for example, writing about local regeneration programmes draws parallels with the problems generated by planning targets in the former Soviet Union. Rather more kindly, writing about the use of performance indicators in the arts, Schuster points out:

> When one implements an indicator for the purpose of affecting behaviour, one has to expect an entrepreneurial response. (1997, p 257)

Nor do these difficulties only arise in areas where outcomes are particularly difficult to measure. Smith's (1993) study found that the use of outcome-related performance indicators in hospital maternity services (where key dimensions of outcomes are easily and promptly established) produced evidence of the usual dysfunctions – which he usefully categorises in terms of tunnel vision, sub-optimisation, myopia, convergence to a norm, ossification, gaming and misrepresentation.

A key issue, therefore, is how serious these known and predictable dysfunctions are likely to be. Measurement optimists blame major difficulties on poor design and/or implementation failures, and accept minor difficulties as a price worth paying for the demonstrable benefits. Moreover, the difficulties do sometimes subside. Carter, Klein et al. (1992) report cases of initial resistance, denigration and perfunctory compliance (including the 'mass baptism' of existing data) being followed by pragmatic engagement with measurement and the discovery of uses, culminating in constructive dialogue. In passing, it is worth noting that those strongly committed to control strategies also have the option of investing further in measurement – in the form of audit – in order to reduce the extent of one of the major dysfunctions.

Partial measurement. The pessimists argue that the *measurability* of performance is critical. Austin (1996) usefully distinguishes between situations in which measurement sets encompassing all the aspects that make a significant contribution to overall performance can be implemented; and those in which, for whatever reasons, only partial measurement is practicable. Where 'full measurement' exists performance indicators *do* provide an effective and economical basis for control – because the only way to improve performance-as-measured is to improve overall performance as intended. By contrast, in situations of 'partial measurement' the use of performance information directly or indirectly for control (eg as part of gauging the performance of sub-unit managers) quickly introduces 'incentive distortion'. Managers and staff have an incentive (indeed, they may come under pressure) to improve performance-as-measured at the expense of intended overall performance.

Hence the importance of a comprehensiveness measurement set. In fact, however, full measurement or even anything approaching it is rarely practicable (even if possible from a social research point of view). Partial measurement is the norm. As Austin puts it, 'In fact, many critical effort dimensions (for example, quality-related dimensions) have been observed to be especially difficult to measure' (1996, p 40). Again, these difficulties are likely to be at least as severe, if not more so, in nonprofit contexts (DiMaggio 2002).

In passing it is worth noting that the prevalence of partial measurement also offers a possible explanation for the popularity of performance measurement – such systems often work to begin with because the control aspects are not emphasised initially. Later, encouraged by the early results, senior managers raise their expectations and these are transmitted down through the organisation, introducing incentive distortion and in due course dysfunctional behaviour (Austin 1996). If this is the case, the problem is, essentially, one of *over-use*.

The problem of incomplete measurement has long been recognised (eg Eccles 1991), but is usually fudged – eg through appeals to 'managerial judgement' in respect of the important unmeasured dimensions. As Austin points out citing research evidence:

> ...people's confidence in their ability to make subjective corrections to measured evaluations far exceeds their actual ability. (p 72)

Hence, even if some dimensions of performance are measurable, judgements of overall performance may still be and appear arbitrary. Again, there are clear parallels with what has been reported in nonprofit contexts. In particular, Tassie Murray et al.'s important study of the evaluation of a nonprofit highlighted the way that decision-makers, even when using an extensive set of formal criteria (and considerable information pertaining to them), still made use of additional informal considerations:

> As a result, the [Voluntary Social Service Organization] developed a somewhat cynical view of the [Federal Funding Organization's] funding decision process. As one said, 'It's all politics.' In this context, the term 'politics' meant for them a process that was not clear, was subject to influences that the VSSO could not counter, and led to an evaluation

process that was different from the formally pronounced one. (Tassie, Murray et al. 1996, p 359)

Performance measurement for learning?   Another solution to the difficulties facing measurement advocates in situations where only partial measurement is possible is to play down the control aspects and emphasise the informational uses of performance measurement – that is, its value for problem identification, process improvement, logistical coordination, mutual understanding and learning. There are two problems with this approach. The first is that it may not be believed – and for good reason. The temptation for managers to use such information, either explicitly or implicitly, in forming judgements of performance is too strong, and sooner or later they (or their successors) will breech earlier undertakings. Hence those subject to such a regime will be wary. Based on his experience in software development in the private sector, Austin's solution is to call for procedural safeguards against measurement misuse, including restrictions on managerial access to the data. In other words, like Neely, Austin argues for the importance of performance information and tries to develop a basis for its collection and use that will serve dialogue, learning and improvement – and avoid the institutionalised dishonesty that comes with its deployment for motivation and recognition.

The second problem in emphasising the informational uses of measurement is that of attribution. If learning and improvement are to take place, performance has to be measured in ways that allow changes or differences in performance to be related to a particular contribution or to differential conditions. But often performance is co-produced through the joint action and interaction of several parties – some of whom may well be external to the organisation.   So even if it can be established that an improvement in performance has occurred, the reasons for this are likely to be contested (though a shortage of claimants for the credit is unlikely). Likewise, if the situation is changing rapidly, learning by controlled repetition becomes very difficult. Both problems arise in the private sector – but they are also familiar in public and nonprofit contexts, eg NGOs (Edwards and Hulme 1995). Hence, although learning and improvement may be given as reasons for performance measurement, the contribution it makes for these purposes may be very limited compared to discussing the processes in detail with those directly involved.

The social construction of performance

Differentiated constructs, integrated systems. Much writing on performance measurement assumes the feasibility and desirability of close integration between different reporting levels. That is, the performance measures set by the top level should also provide the basis for performance analysis at lower levels, and the information used at lower levels can be combined to inform higher level measures. When it is then observed that the information used to measure the performance of sub-units and the information actually used to manage performance within them are rather different, and moreover, that the organisations performance measures do not help managers improve the performance of their sub-units, this is seen as a weakness of the system.

In fact, what performance *means* is different at different levels and in different domains, and its measurement and management changes accordingly. Hence, it is generally appropriate for levels to be loosely coupled, rather than closely integrated. In the case of companies, external reporting to shareholders (financial accounting) has provided such a poor basis for internal performance measurement and management that a whole profession grew up around management accounting, in order to remedy the problem. More recently, popular guidance for corporate managers on performance measurement takes it for granted that measures of performance at different levels and in different spheres will be expressed in quite different terms. See, for example, the 'performance pyramids' in Lynch (1995) and the relationship between 'perspectives' in the Balanced Scorecard of Kaplan and Norton (Kaplan and Norton 1996). The relationship between levels in terms of performance information then becomes an important and difficult issue. Establishing connections between the information given by centrally designed systems and the local operating context as understood much more intuitively by local managers requires much talking through – it does not happen simply by driving abstracted measures down through the organisation (Ahrens and Chapman 1998).

In nonprofit contexts, the three main levels were usefully described by Kanter and Summers (1987) as the *institutional* (concerned with legitimacy in the eyes of major external stakeholders), the *managerial* (concerned with resource use) and the *technical or professional* (concerned with service quality and outcomes). Characteristically, institutional performance measures create a framework for governance – what needs to be achieved in order to maintain legitimacy and a license to operate. These are given by regulatory bodies, major funders and contractors. Within this framework, an organisation's leaders create their own more elaborate system of performance measurement – to feed institutional reporting requirements, but also to inform their own decision making and to set a performance framework for professional ('street level') activities. In their turn, the team leaders or first line managers may have their own performance-related information, partly explicit in records and partly tacit (in memory). Some of this practice knowledge may be context specific but it is also likely to be more detailed and elaborate, combining much current and background information in complex mental models about how to pursue a range of goals and maintain a web of relationships. This formal and informal information is, likewise, drawn on to provide or embellish accounts of their sub-unit's performance, to inform their own performance improvement efforts and as a basis for dialogue with staff.

The point is that although these conceptions of performance are related, they cannot just be aggregated and dis-aggregated. They are rooted in different concerns and experiences; they involve very different constructs, values and levels of abstraction; they reflect the discourses of different policy, managerial and professional communities and evolve accordingly; their alignment is always problematic (Sanderson 1998).

Competing frameworks. The literature contains three responses to the existence of competing conceptions of performance. The first is to promote some version of one's own conception as fundamental and an adequate foundation for other users as well.   This is what is happening when institutional performance frameworks are imposed on nonprofits, as with the promotion of outcome funding, or the definition of nonprofit effectiveness in terms of their programme effectiveness (for a critique, see Herman and Renz 1999). The mirror image – which might be termed 'educate our masters' – is implicit in the views of many leaders in the nonprofit sector.   An excellent example, from the field of international development, is provided by Rondinelli (1994) who sets out a sophisticated managerial framework and argues that it should be the basis for institutional level performance management (and also project level learning). When this approach is seen to succeed it is likely to be described as 'regulatory capture' (Stigler, 1971).   (For a discussion of this in relation to social housing, see Mullins and Riseborough (1997).)

A second approach is to try to incorporate all the competing goals and rationales of nonprofits into one master framework. This is the approach of Kendall and Knapp (2000) whose framework has eight measurement domains and 22 separate indicator sets. As the authors acknowledge, the cost and feasibility of creating worthwhile indicators in relation to some of the 22 concepts are considerable. How this approach might be used outside of lavishly resourced research contexts remains unclear.

The third approach is to abandon the 'realist' position and accept that performance is and will remain an evolving and contested concept, with particular measurement sets being the expression either of the thinking of a dominant group, or of a negotiated compromise among a wider group, at some point in time. Such a position (described as the emergent approach) has been summarised in the following terms in relation to nonprofit effectiveness:

> Accordingly, in the emergent approach to organizational effectiveness, assessments of effectiveness are not regarded as objective facts but neither are they regarded as arbitrary or irrelevant. Rather, the emergent approach holds that definitions and assessments of effectiveness have meaning but that the meaning is (a) created by the individual or organisational actors involved (b) specific to the context in which it was created (c) capable of evolving as the actors continue to interact. (Forbes 1998, p 195)

From this point of view, measures are not the means of estimating some underlying reality; rather, they construct and imbue with authority the notions of performance associated with particular points of view. The performance constructed by particular measures is bound to be partial, contextual and contingent, constituted partly by the social processes of its selection and gathering, but also by the lenses of those who interpret it. On this basis, plurality, contingency and contestation are signs of organisational life, not failure. Stable, coherent, consensual systems of measurement are probably an indication of domination by some one or some group (Greene 1999).

Implementation issues. Performance measurement systems do not spring into existence fully elaborated and the idea that they may involve an on-going process of social negotiation is helpful in understanding the issues that arise. Designing and operating them requires managerial time, expertise and effort, which is always in limited supply. In particular, those introducing performance management face a dilemma over their approach to those who will be subject to the arrangements. Do they spell out detailed definitions and reporting procedures, and perhaps even police them through audit – and risk generating resistance, introducing dysfunctional rigidities (because they lack information about operating circumstances), and generating additional costs for both parties? Or do they set out general principles and invite cooperation in a shared endeavour – thereby risking the dilution and diversion of the original aims? Up to a point, directive and accommodating elements can be tactically intertwined according to the relative power of the parties, but in general, limited resources are best used in ways that engage cooperation rather than provoke resistance.

> Control systems can be seen as an infinite game between controllers and the controlled in which advantage lies with relatively full time players having direct personal interests in the outcomes. (March and Olsen 1989, p 11)

Even in cases where measurement regimes are largely imposed, some scope for interpretation is likely to remain. If the detailed and highly institutionalised rules of accounting standards still leave scope for creative accounting, it is hardly surprising that operational definitions of performance indicators do so as well. Hence, how a performance measurement system operates in practice will depend not just on the intentions of those who commission it, but on the resources, commitment and approach of those that design and operate it. Its enactment will also depend on the responses chosen by the organisations or sub-units who are subject to it. They may have to adjust their operating policies (in ways that may or may not be dysfunctional) in order to achieve satisfactory performance as measured. But this may not be necessary. The other options are to try to influence the design of the scheme; to engage in creative accounting; and to concentrate on promoting favourable interpretations of what will usually be ambiguous results, eg by building relationships with the performance managers, and presenting strong and favourable narratives ('spin') around the performance data. And obviously, in each case these can only be countered by additional managerial effort on the part of the performance manager.

Hence, even if the intention is integrated control, one can confidently predict that this will be diluted in its enactment. Significant weaknesses in implementation are virtually inevitable – and they will often be benign, in the sense of making dysfunction less likely or pronounced. These considerations have three implications.

First, because such difficulties are actually well understood by performance managers – if not publicly acknowledged – they moderate their ambitions for performance measurement, adopting instead what can be called a strategy of *selective control*. The performance measures become in effect a screening device through which (apparent) low performance can be identified. Such cases are then investigated with the measures being used alongside other, nonquantitative information, to make more considered judgements about performance, to understand it, and to seek improvements (for a description of this approach in health care, see Mannion, Goddard et al. 1998).

Second, faced with 'the same' measurement regime, different sub-units or agencies can and do respond in a wide variety of ways. Depending on local circumstances and leadership, a range of accommodations and adaptations are possible – from dutiful compliance to creative improvisation (Jackson 1998). Again, since the enactment of measurement-based performance management is non-deterministic, dysfunction is far from inevitable.

Third, given the difficulties of carrying through measurement-based performance management, those tasked to do so may (not unreasonably) choose the option of *collusive implementation*. A sympathetic approach to design and operation of the measures, limited if any scrutiny, accepting optimistic interpretations of the results, highlighting 'progress' and overlooking failings – all these make supervision easier, and also allow success to be reported to those who originally commissioned the scheme, rather than difficulties.

The symbolic dimension. This last point introduces the possibility that in some circumstances – especially those where measurement is difficult and cause-effect relations obscure – the contribution of performance measurement may be more symbolic than instrumental, which does not mean it is unimportant. The existence of the system may satisfy institutional level requirements for evidence of purposeful and proper management, thereby sustaining legitimacy and ensuring continued access to resources (Meyer and Scott 1983). Scotch, reflecting on many years involvement in programme evaluation, describes such a situation, albeit in relation to evaluations, rather than measurement:

> Over the course of these assignments, I often experienced a substantial inconsistency between what was demanded by the national program sponsors and what local agencies were able to provide, even when the local agencies were doing their best to fulfil expectations... when I interacted with other local evaluators in these programs, I typically learned that my local agencies were doing no worse than most similar agencies in other communities, and that there were few really successful cases of local program evaluation in these multi-tiered programs... And in fact, very little in the public discourse or internal discussion around the programs involved, suggested failure in either program performance or evaluation practice. Rather, there seemed to be a form of collusion taking place ... in which the national staff responsible for evaluation tacitly said ... 'we must articulate high standards in our public discussion, but we understand the problems you face, so just do the best you can and we will accept that.' Apparently (I was not privy to all the communication that took place), agencies that made a good faith effort were excused from negative consequences from their lack of outcomes, as long as their process demonstrated good intentions. (Scotch 1998, pp 1–2)

Moreover, within the organisation, the development and introduction of performance measurement may be useful, by expressing and reinforcing the organisation's commitments, by stimulating dialogue and greater clarity over what the organisation is really trying to do – as is often claimed (and intermittently reported, eg Leland 1998). This could be true even if the measures were of limited value in informational terms. As DiMaggio (2002) puts it, the information may 'improve the quality of discourse ... even if it provides no clear implications for action'.

The dynamics of measurement. One implication of the constructivist perspective is that, despite stability being one of the desirable features of measurement systems, one would not expect measurement systems to be stable. Rather, they would be expected to change and evolve over time – which is, in fact, what is increasingly reported. Some patterns have already been referred to, including 'gradual acceptance' (resistance giving way to creative accommodation), 'oscillation' (between completeness and parsimony), and 'over-use' (initial benefits leading senior managers to expect too much). Another trend is a steady, underlying increase in the number of performance measures in use by organisations – hardly surprising, given falling relative costs of information handling. But more importantly, there is the phenomenon of 'measurement churn', that is, the continuous replacement of old measures with new, and the redesign of measurement systems (Meyer 1998, among others). Several factors probably explain 'measurement churn', including:

- the fact that 'all measures lose variation' (Meyer and Gupta 1994) and hence the need to create new ones;

- Campbell's 'law of corruption of measurement indicators' ('the more any social indicator is used for social decision making, the greater the corruption pressures upon it' (Campbell 1979);

- the steady proliferation of new measures which may be prompted by changes in strategy and goals, problems with old measures, or the emergence of new concerns – since it is generally problems that give rise to new performance indicators rather than performance indicators revealing new problems (Carter, Klein et al. 1992, p 112).

Whatever the reasons, in the private sector, at least, reported dissatisfaction with performance measurement systems is increasing, and the life expectancy of measurement systems is falling (Meyer 1998; Frigo 2000).

Performance measurement in social enterprises.

What is different about social enterprises? The preceding discussion suggests that where conceptions of performance are largely shared, where measurability is high, cause-effect relations well understood, attribution possible, and the scale of operations large enough to spread the costs of designing and operating measurement systems, the situation can be considered favourable for measurement. Likewise, where performance is a contested concept, the measurability of important dimensions impractical, cause-effect relations poorly understood, attribution problematic, and the scale of operations modest, then the situation is unfavourable for measurement. Such situations are certainly not uncommon in private and public organisations. However, it is likely they arise even more often in social enterprises, where as we have seen, performance is often a contested concept, measurability of important dimensions is in question, cause-effect relations obscure, co-production through partnerships and collaboration common, and organisations usually small or medium-sized. Indeed, it can be argued on theoretical grounds that the very reasons why activities are undertaken in the nonprofit sector are also the reasons why performance measurement will be deeply problematic (Krashinsky 1986; Hansmann 1987).

Against all this, it may also be the case that social enterprises also provide a more favourable context for measurement in one respect: to the extent that they are smaller organisations with strong shared missions, they may be less prone to certain measurement dysfunction (eg sub-optimisation, myopia) than others. (It may or may not be a coincidence that the boom in measurement in the private sector has coincided with great emphasis on a 'strong culture' as the primary means of management control.) Nevertheless, overall, high expectations from performance measurement in such contexts – for example, that it can be a substitute for more discursive modes of management – look decidedly unrealistic.

Assessing performance measurement systems. One theme of this discussion has been the need for modest expectations regarding the contribution of performance measurement – more or less wherever it is undertaken. The technocratic fantasies of control that haunt discussions of performance management imply success criteria against which any actual system will be seen to fail. But what is the alternative – how, for example, might one distinguish a crude and imperfect but 'good enough' system of measurement from one that was more trouble than it was worth? And would the difference between such systems lie in its technical features or in the manner of its use? How do we know if performance measurement 'works'?

The obvious answer – through a systematic study of the costs and benefits – is problematic: how are the benefits to be measured? If the increases in performance-as-measured are taken as benefits, then one has already assumed much of what is at issue. But if other independent measures of performance are used, then on what basis are they assumed to be better indicators, rather than merely different (Meyer and Gupta 1994)? The costs of measurement, being diffuse, will also be challenging to measure. Moreover, without some kind of control or comparison, one cannot know the counter-factual. These problems may not be insuperable, but it is ironic that we still await the first rigorous quantitative evaluation of performance measurement.

One success criterion is simply that the system continues to have the confidence of senior managers – it is seen by them as worthwhile. Another test would be that, to an independent observer, the system appears to deliver a number of benefits whose value outweighs the negative effects of any dysfunctional behaviour also triggered or accentuated by the system; and that the administrative burden of measurement is not excessive in relation to the benefits. Clearly, any such judgement would need to be based on the views of a range of participants from the different levels or domains involved and not just 'product champions'. It would need to take into account both specific instances of benefit (eg the use of information in forming a decision) and possible diffuse benefits concerning the communication of priorities, the negotiation of commitments and values, or the increased confidence of external stakeholders. It would have to explore, as far as was practicable, whether the different sorts of dysfunction commonly associated with measurement were significantly present. Clearly, the outcome of such an appraisal might well be equivocal.

Some initial research questions. The preceding discussion suggests some of the concepts and issues that will be relevant in understanding what is happening in social enterprises as they give more attention to measurement in situations highly unfavourable to measurement.

First, we need to understand how managers view these issues and the different approaches to the challenge that are being adopted. Do they 'believe' in measurement? Is more measurement seen as a threat or an opportunity? What strategies are they pursuing?

Secondly, how are measurement changes being implemented? For example, are there efforts to use the new systems as a basis for greater control either of, or within, the organisation – or is implementation much more gentle and exploratory (eg selective control, collusion)? And how are managers dealing with the issues of 'domain alignment' – are institutional reporting requirements driving the development of the information systems of nonprofits at the expense of managerial and operational needs – or are these being loosely and creatively linked?

Thirdly, what sorts of benefits, both direct and indirect, are being claimed, and are the usual dysfunctions becoming apparent (and at what levels)? What about costs (and timescales)?

Fourth, are any longer term patterns becoming apparent? These include aspects of measurement behaviour such as loss of variation, and measurement churn, but also possible impacts on the organisational culture: are the managers of social enterprises now displaying a greater commitment to measurement? How do they combine this with their awareness and experience of behavioural responses to measurement?

Conclusions

Since an important rationale for increased use of performance measurement in social enterprises is the adoption of private sector practices, this chapter has explored that experience as reported in the research literature, along with a wide range of other measurement studies from public and nonprofit organisations. The aim was to highlight more of the practice and research issues that the use of the new performance measurement and improvement methods in social enterprises raise, and to identify from the literature concepts that would help in exploring them. The main questions and associated concepts were summarised above.

In addition, some broader ideas from chapters 1 and 2 have been reinforced. In particular, the constant tension between the drive to rationalise (expressed in a pursuit of coherence, consistency and control) and the constant tendency for the best laid plans to unravel in the face of unexpected or changing circumstances, or methods that cease to work. As politicians try to restore or extend performance management arrangements that sooner or later decay and disappoint, so they create churn for the managers of social enterprises – who in their turn create churn for their staff and colleagues as they revise and replace their own arrangements in order to cope with new demands and address emerging problems.

Another theme has been the contested, controversial nature of performance measurement, which contributes to its limited stability. One consequence is that although most performance measurement is undertaken with a positivist and realist outlook – to get to the bottom of things – most measurement systems clearly fail if appraised in these terms. However, a constructivist perspective seems to accord more comfortably with the churn of measurement practice, and still offers a meaningful basis for undertaking measurement activity, albeit one with more modest ambitions.

Sources and resources

The single most useful examination of performance measurement is *Measuring and Managing Performance in Organizations* (Austin 1996). This combines a comprehensive discussion of the literature with a powerful analytic framework and interesting empirical material. It is also a model of clear exposition. Much interesting and important work on measurement in nonprofit contexts still languishes in conference papers, but the important discussions of Tassie, Murray et al. (1996), Herman and Renz (1997) and Forbes (1998) are all readily accessed. For more up-beat and uncritical guidance on 'doing measurement' in social enterprises, Charities Evaluation Services (www.ces-vol.org.uk) provides useful resources. For North America, Harry Harty's Hatry (1999) *Performance Measurement – Getting Results*, is thorough, clear and well referenced, though mainly concerned with programme evaluation. It also shows how the Government Performance and Results Act has spurred the growth and institutionalisation of the measurement industry.

4 The Performance of Measurement

This chapter begins the reporting of empirical researches into the issues raised in the first part of the book. The studies explore two broad areas. The first is at a policy level and addresses the issues raised in chapter two: is increased effort and attention towards measurement delivering the goods? As a means of institutional oversight, *how well is measurement performing*? Secondly, at the level of management and organizations, and in the light of the issues and concepts set out in the last chapter, what has been the developing experience of social enterprise managers as they learn to operate in this new measurement environment? Or to put it another way, *how are social enterprises are performing their measurements,* The studies examine what is happening as social enterprises try to accommodate the increasing expectations of measurement in the two forms in which they are commonly experienced:

- *Greater attention to established measures*. It examines how UK charities have been responding to the increased interest being shown in one of the few measures of performance that provides a degree of comparability, the Administrative Costs to Expenditure (ACE) ratio.

- *Calls for new and better measures*. The experience of three organisations that have pursued new measurement approaches currently topical within the nonprofit and policy communities are examined. Two of these 'measurement leaders' were pursuing the idea of outcome measurement; the third provides an instance of Social Audit.

So three different measurement methods are examined. ACE ratios provide a broad view across the sector – it is a measure that can and will be applied to many social enterprises whether they like it or not, as most have now realised. Outcome measurement and Social Audit are less well established, but they provide a window not just on the methods themselves (which may well spread widely), but also on what happens when organizations embrace the measurement agenda positively and proactively.

ACE ratios were examined through a mix of statistical and qualitative methods. The 'measurement leaders' were examined through case studies – two of outcome measurement, and one of Social Audit. Hence this chapter condenses and weaves together a considerable body of empirical material. It starts by explaining the three methods, relating them to earlier theoretical concerns. Then the research design for the study of ACE ratios is explained, and the main findings are presented. Next, the research design for the investigation of measurement leaders is described and the experiences of the three case study organisation are summarised. Then the common themes in those experiences are discussed. Finally, these various findings are considered in relation to the broad questions set out above.

in relation to the broad questions set out above.

The measurement methods: ACE ratios, 'Outcomes' and Social Audit

Comparability, focus and comprehensiveness were seen in the last chapter to be highly desirable attributes of measurement systems. The three forms of measurement explored in this chapter are each designed to deliver one of these attributes.

Comparability: the ACE ratio as a measure of efficiency. The ACE ratio presents administrative costs as a percentage of total expenditure. It is a good example of an institutional level performance measure: broad-brush, easily calculated, directed towards significant areas of public concern regarding charities (waste, efficiency), and promising some comparability as well as being of interest in absolute terms. It has often attracted media interest and recently policy and academic researchers have given it increasing attention. Confidence in the measure may have been increased by recent efforts towards greater standardisation in charity accounting. These include the introduction from 1995 onwards of a new and much more prescriptive charity accounting standard (referred to as a Statement of Recommended Practice or SORP), and new accounting regulations issued under the Charities Act of 1993 – themselves both expressive of public and policy concern about the administration of charities (Williams and Palmer 1998).

Essentially, the SORP requires charities to report their expenditure under four headings:– Direct Charitable Expenditure (DCE), Support Costs (ie costs directly associated with DCE), Fundraising costs, and, residually, Administration. Many expenditures fall obviously under these headings but some central or head office activities (eg those of IT and finance staff, the Chief Executive) can and should be divided up as they may contribute variously to the support of charitable activity, to fundraising, and to 'core' administration. The SORP guidelines for such reallocations are very clear on the underlying principles, and in the course of the research examples were given of things that the new SORP had prevented the finance managers from doing (eg reporting a failed fundraising venture as negative income, in order to keep the costs out of the accounts). Nevertheless, and not surprisingly given the diversity of charitable operations, considerable discretion over the application of the principles remains. Hence proper accounting practice can still vary, though this is also where the scope for 'creative' reporting arises. There is also the issue of how many charities have changed their practices to conform to the new SORP (Connolly and Hyndman 2001).

Despite this, the ACE ratio is assumed to be a measure of efficiency, even by researchers aware of possible limitations, and the main research issue has been to understand the reasons for variations in ACE ratios. This work has shown that ACE ratios vary by sub-sector, and by organisational size – large charities seem to be more efficient (Sargeant and Kaehler 1998). But large variations in ACE ratios (and thus apparent efficiency) remain unexplained, prompting expressions of concern. Thus, Sargeant and Kaehler refer to some of the variations in ACE ratios as 'astounding'; and Hyndman and McKillop (1999) hope that 'the publication of standardised ratios and associated research will increasingly provide an incentive to management to eliminate inefficiencies'.

Focus: outcome measurement. The general idea of outcome measurement is simple – a matter of focusing on the lasting benefits produced, not just the activities undertaken and the immediate results or outputs. In its most vigorous form it is tied to a 'social investment' view of funding that derives directly from a business perspective. In this, the often heavily bureaucratised processes of grantmaking and service contracting are replaced by a model of business planning, clear performance targets, and the support of agencies to ensure they yield a high return (the seminal work is Williams and Webb 1991). The obvious question is whether the sorts of goals pursued by many nonprofits, including the quality of their work, and the experiences of participants, can sensibly be reduced to uni-directional service delivery outcomes. In dementia and hospice care, for example, the process is all, and the 'outcome' a foregone conclusion. In practice, therefore, it is hardly surprising that the term has come to be used much more loosely, as a way of referring to broader programme evaluations (of a sort Williams and Webb view with great circumspection). Indeed, in their study of outcome measurement, Morley, Vinson et al. (2001) introduce a distinction between 'intermediate outcomes' (essentially concerned with service quality) and 'end outcomes' (covering the consequences or results achieved). This is the comprehensiveness versus focus issue discussed in the last chapter. While there will always be strong arguments for comprehensiveness, outcome measurement is clearly an appeal for focus, and hence if the concept is too heavily diluted it ceases to offer anything distinctive.

The current vogue for outcome measurement and the legitimacy it affords leads to another definitional problem. Advocates (eg Plantz, Greenaway et al. 1997) write as if outcome measurement systems already exist, but it would appear that for many areas of nonprofit activity much of what they report is research on outcomes undertaken in the hope of developing measures and systems. Even when studies focus on those believed to be 'advanced' in collecting outcome information, this discrepancy between aspirational and operational descriptions of outcome measurement is very apparent (Morley, Vinson et al. 2001). Hence it seems important to distinguish between the journey and the destination, with the latter referring to a measurement system that has the following characteristics:

- it gives most attention to outcomes or impacts, not just activity levels and outputs;

- it employs a (more or less) focused and manageable suite of measures: it doesn't simply reproduce extensive data-sets of the sort that have often underpinned evaluation studies;

- those measures are fairly meaningful and informative to the leaders and/or the funders of the organisation;

- the system shows some signs of being, or at least becoming, stable and 'embedded'; it is not still in an early phase of development.

Comprehensiveness: Social Audit and stakeholder responsiveness. The ideas of social accounting and audit developed in the 1970s as part of efforts to promote greater corporate social responsibility. They were pursued in different ways in different countries (eg in the US they led to systems of corporate rating aimed at influencing consumer and investor behaviour). In the UK in the late 1980s an assortment of alternative business and progressive companies led by Traidcraft and then the Body Shop took up the idea and began to make social accounting a regular part of their public reporting. Comparable developments were soon taking place in other European countries and since then the number of established companies practising some form of social or ethical accounting has increased steadily and now includes some substantial multi-nationals – for example Shell, BP, BT, Diageo and Nike (Gonella, Pilling et al. 1998). The New Economics Foundation (NEF) played a significant role in this development, having helped develop and promote an explicit stakeholder-based methodology, involving the following sequence of activities:

1.   Identifying stakeholders

2.   Designing the consultation process

3.   Choosing performance indicators

4.   The 'year-end' process: collecting and analysing data and preparation of a draft social statement

5.   External verification and use of a Review Panel

6.   Disclosing (publishing) the social statement and acting upon the results

However, although probably the best known, NEFs is not the only approach and so 'Social Audit' is not a precise term. Partly in response to this proliferation of approaches and terminologies, an Institute for Social and Ethical Accounting (ISEA) has now been formed to establish a common language and international standards for Social and Ethical Accounting Auditing and Reporting.

Most of these developments have concentrated on the corporate sector (the main exception is Richmond 1999) aspiring towards social accounts that will complement the established procedures for financial reporting. Recently, however, the idea of social audit has attracted the interest of voluntary agencies in the UK and Canada (Dow and Crowe 1999; Raynard and Murphy 2000). Those adopting it see Social Audit as a flexible but credible framework through which they can test, develop and demonstrate their accountability to multiple stakeholders and the effectiveness of their programmes. It is also of some theoretical interest, given that stakeholder dialogue and assessment is the central, defining feature of Social Audit. In the face of the apparently insuperable difficulties of defining and agreeing on a workable notion of nonprofit effectiveness, it is sometimes suggested that stakeholder responsiveness may provide an alternative approach (Herman and Renz 1999). There are potential problems – in some contexts service users may effectively be in competition for scarce resources and the most demanding may not be the most needy, suggesting that 'a degree of insensitivity' could sometimes be appropriate (Carter, Klein et al. 1992). Nevertheless, the approach is interesting, if only because complex patterns of stakeholder involvement have long been seen as a characteristic of nonprofits (eg Paton and Cornforth 1991; Herman and Renz 1997).

What has been happening to ACE ratios? The research design

Research questions and approach. Since the ACE ratio can be easily calculated from information in the public domain, it provides a convenient way of examining the response of charity mangers – both collectively, and at the level of the individual charity – to the increasing interest in their performance. The research addressed three questions:

1. What has been happening to ACE ratios – have they, as theory would predict, been showing improvements in performance and loosing variation?

2. What are the reasons for variations in ACE ratios? What factors, other than variations in efficiency, might convincingly explain the variations in ACE ratios?

3. How are managers responding to the increased interest? Are they useful as a performance measure for managers and is there any relationship between external reporting of efficiency, and internal efforts to increase efficiency. Alternatively, is it beginning to encourage behaviour that might reasonably be classified as measurement dysfunction? In the terms of the last chapter, this is the issue of domain alignment and integration – whether and how well this institutional performance measure supports a managerial understanding of efficiency.

The first question – also the simplest – was examined by calculating the relevant statistics using a data-set of the summary accounts of the top 500 charities between the years 1992 and 1997, prepared by the Charities Aid Foundation. However, addressing the second and third questions meant getting behind the figures in order to understand the reasons for any ACE variations, and this pointed towards selectivity and the use of qualitative methods. This led to the decision to focus on the extreme cases within sub-sectors that varied in their degree of competitiveness. Limiting the number of charities made the task tractable. Focusing on variations within particular fields controlled for one already identified source of variation. Focussing on those who appeared to be high and low performers (in practice, the top five and the bottom five) provided the greatest scope for understanding the factors affecting the ACE ratio. Finally, choosing sub-sectors where organisations were more and less vulnerable to invidious comparisons, allowed a test of whether differential organisational responses on the lines predicted by theory were occurring.[12]

Procedures. The four sub-sectors are referred to as the special groups societies, the illness charities (all operating in relation to the same major illness type), the Christian organisations, and the relief agencies.[13] The Illness charities and the Relief agencies were selected as operating in highly competitive domains. They appealed to broad cross-sections of the population and differences among the charities in these fields would often not be obvious or salient to potential supporters. By contrast, the special groups and Christian organisations were chosen as relatively non-competitive sub-sectors, since most of the organisations that comprised them had distinct constituencies. The special groups societies were particularly interesting because they were all of a similar size (with expenditures between c. £1,000,000 and c. £4,000,000) undertaking very similar activities, and therefore highly comparable. They also showed one of the widest ranges – the 'best' charity had a ratio of 0.2%, and the 'worst' a ratio of 38%.

Detailed tableaux were created to compare the published accounts of the charities with the five highest and five lowest ACE ratios in each of the chosen sectors. These ratios were presented both 'raw' and 'adjusted' for greater accounting consistency where appropriate, and carried annotations on the accounting issues. Comments on this data were then sought from the senior finance professionals in the charities concerned, by telephone or face-to-face interview, and later in group discussions.[14] A major issue in the discussions was the reasons for particular accounting practices and for changes to them. Given the considerable quantity of data collected, what follows is only a summary of the main points in relation to the theories of performance measurement discussed.

What has been happening to ACE ratios? The findings

Trends in ACE ratios. The CAF data-set covered the years 1992–97 but was missing data for the year 1994. If charities were also missing data for other years they were excluded – reducing the total from 500 to about 350. The mean ACE ratio and the standard deviation of ACE ratios for each year were calculated and are shown in table 4.1.

Table 4.1   The trends in ACE ratios of c 350 major UK charities, 1992–97

	1992	1993	1995	1996	1997
Mean ACE ratio	11.4	10.8	9.8	8.5	7.3
Standard deviation	9.0	7.6	6.8	6.6	5.4

As expected, efficiency-as-reported improved substantially over this six-year period, and the variation in ACE ratios was sharply reduced.

Understanding variations in ACE ratios. Neither 'high' nor 'low' ratio managers thought the differences had anything much to do with efficiency. From the discussions with them, both individually and in groups, the variations could be convincingly explained by two factors. First, the finance managers pointed to the different patterns of activity, which had different implications for administrative costs. For example, although all in the same field, the illness charities approached their work in very different ways. Some pursued research on the illness, others provided care for sufferers, and others supported both care and research. Moreover, they differed on whether they themselves provided the care and undertook the research, or whether they funded others to carry out this work. Each of these combinations had different implications for administrative costs – most obviously, charities which only funded work by others had markedly lower ratios than those that provided a range of services.

Secondly, different approaches to cost allocations often gave rise to large variations in ACE ratios. This was particularly obvious and important among the special groups societies – for example the ACE ratio of one of the charities fell from 15% to 2% once they had apportioned £274,000 of central costs to Support. In this field, those charities with (apparently) very high administrative costs showed the following tendencies:

- To have managers who were less familiar with the SORP and the ability to apportion elements of central costs to Direct Charitable Expenditure (DCE), to Publicity and Fundraising, and especially, to Support costs – the charities with the highest ACE ratios apportioned only modest amounts of central costs to Support.

- To have conservative views as to what does and does not constitute charitable expenditure (eg one charity felt that only amounts paid to beneficiaries should be shown as DCE and hence that *no* central costs, other than beneficiary payments, should be apportioned to DCE or even to Support).

- To employ a lay or private sector definition of administration costs – judging it to mean all central administration costs

- To be locked into that lay view by historical precedent – 'we have always done it this way' – and by trustees who were very reluctant to change.

Common to both low and high ratios were accounting oddities and unusual circumstances. Examples included one with no central costs (they were administered by another organisation); one that had understated their total expenditure (netting off some of its expenditure against income); and one that had overstated their administration costs (by including those relating to a sister charity).

How are nonprofits responding? As expected, ACE interest and awareness was noticeably higher among the more competitively exposed and higher profile illness charities and relief agencies than among the special groups societies and Christian organisations:

> Over the last five years, I reckon every year I have had twice as many enquiries about the figures as the previous year. (Finance Director, relief agency).

> It's very different for [us]... In general we don't get lumbered with those kinds of enquiries. (Financial Services Manager, Christian organization)

In consequence, a greater convergence of accounting practice had already taken place in these 'competitive' fields – and they were much more interested in supporting the research. It seemed they were also more likely to compare their ratios with those they saw as their peers. However, to the extent that finance directors were concerned with the ACE ratio, it was for external purposes. To this end, and without much difficulty, they managed the flow of reported figures:

> We'd be shooting ourselves in the foot if we didn't present the figures in the most favourable way. I have vigorous discussions with my auditors (Finance Director, relief agency)

Commonly, re-allocations were carried out at the year-end, using a rough-and-ready formula, or a set of rules worked out a bit more carefully in a previous year. These were done for external reporting ('they are only carried out for the pie charts in the annual report'); they had not been internalised into the monthly management accounts. In one case, where a finance manager thought it prudent to make major 'improvements' to the reported figure this was done gradually – re-allocating one member of head office staff each year – to avoid attracting the notice of the auditors. But none saw themselves as misusing the SORP, or misrepresenting administrative costs, citing other items they could have re-apportioned if they had so wished, but had not bothered to adjust.

Nevertheless, the finance directors expressed strong concern about administrative costs and efficiency and readily discussed the ways in which they pursued improvements. These varied, of course, but included analysing cost trends over time, tracking the figures of carefully selected external comparators, and studying tables of comparisons in the trade press (eg of charity shop performance). For example, the finance director of a small illness charity with a 'poor' ACE ratio had his own extensive portfolio of performance indicators through which he tracked trends over the last five years. He claimed this was what really drove improvements, describing it as 'my most useful document'. He also used these figures selectively to embellish the annual report or to help deal with questions from the press or supporters. A major theme in the discussions was the crudity of financial ratios as measures of performance and the need to educate the public. Many examples were given of the misleading impressions they could give because they were unrelated to actual service outcomes (eg reliance on volunteers, because it reduced salary costs and thus total expenditure, tended to increase one's ACE ratio). One contributor from a special groups society made a more general point by asking 'Is it a good or a bad thing to spend more on a nursing home this year than last?' He pointed out that the expenditure might be because the roof of one of your nursing homes fell in due to poor maintenance. The discussions also revealed several cases of investment in new accounting systems, new financial management practices (eg rolling three-year budgets) and increasing attention to non-financial measures (including in one case the beginnings of an outcome measurement programme).

When asked if the increased public interest in their administrative costs was actually preventing them doing things, the general answer was 'no', though one participant was less sure:

> It's possible that sometimes the pressure to keep down 'bad' costs has meant we have not made investments in new systems as soon as we should have. (Finance and Administration Director, large relief agency).

Overall, the impression from these results is that nonprofits have been responding to the increased public interest in administrative costs primarily by managing their reported ACE ratios. As one would expect, those charities more exposed to public scrutiny have been doing so more promptly and vigorously. These efforts undoubtedly explain a very great part of the apparent improvements over the last six years. Some charities have also been responding in other ways – such as anticipating scrutiny and preparing a clear explanation of administrative and other costs with appropriate figures and comparisons. Even if this managing of the figures is what is often termed measurement dysfunction, it is doubtful whether the label is appropriate in this case as no great costs have been involved.

It is possible that this generalised public concern has reinforced efforts to contain administrative costs and increase efficiency, and contributed to greater measurement efforts within charities. However, this is entirely speculative and not even particularly plausible. The most striking feature of the data is the lack of alignment between the institutional and the managerial domains in relation to a shared concern with administrative costs and efficiency. The performance measure that expresses this concern at the institutional level was consistently seen to have no value at a managerial level.

Measurement leaders – the research design

The experience of measurement leaders is interesting for several reasons – even if it is by definition, a typical in some important respects. In the first instance, by pro-actively addressing the measurement agenda, they show a particular strategic response to the emerging concerns of funders, contractors and partners. The reasons for adopting this strategy, the issues associated with it, and how far it is a possibility for others are therefore worthwhile questions in their own right.   Secondly, with all such organisational reforms and improvements, there is a problem over premature claims of success (often, of course, by 'product champions', who will also be key informants). Therefore, to the extent that the leaders in measurement have been pursuing their particular approaches for longer periods, their experience offers a better basis for observing the dynamics of implementation.

Case selection and approach. The main criteria for case selection, therefore, was that the organisations should have pursued innovations in the measurement of social performance over a period of time and with strong organisational commitment, preferably in contexts displaying a range of measurement challenges typical of the sector. In the event three organisations were selected, as shown in table 4.2, and as described in more detail in the next section. Though all clearly satisfying the criteria, no exhaustive search was undertaken, and other nonprofits may have be even further ahead in developing measurement innovations.

Table 4.2   The 'measurement leader' case studies

Organisation	Measurement innovation	Data sources
Groundwork ('Social and economic regeneration through environmental action')	Various, including use of indices and ratios; and latterly community impact as a form of outcome measurement	Interviews and discussions with national and local staff over a period of three years; internal documents and published reports
Pioneer Human Services (PHS) ('Improving the lives of ex-offenders and substance abusers through jobs, social services and housing')	(i) Monthly 'mission outcomes' reporting; (ii) Sustained client outcomes project	Interviews/discussion/ correspondence with product champion over two years; visit and discussions with senior managers; internal documents (memos, reports, charts) and published material (press coverage); comment on draft case
New Economics Foundation ('building a just and sustainable economy')	Social Audit	Detailed analysis of five published 'Social statements' going back six years; interviews with staff; comments on draft case study

The innovations at Groundwork and PHS both encompassed several different aspects of performance measurement, but in both cases these included sustained efforts towards outcome measurement. The enquiries were focused on the four broad areas concerning performance measurement systems noted at the end of the last chapter.

The main sources of data are given in table 4.2, and their limitations need to be acknowledged. In particular, there was very little scope for gauging any of the wider and more indirect effects (eg on the organisational and management culture) of the greater emphasis on measurement taking place in the organisations examined. More detailed accounts are available in the full-length case studies (Paton and Payne 2002; Paton, Payne et al. 2002).

Groundwork and its recent history of measurement

Groundwork's mission is 'to bring about sustainable improvements, through partnerships, to the local environment and contribute to economic and social regeneration.' Since its formation in 1981 it has grown into a network of 42 independent Trusts and is now the leading environmental partnership organisation in the UK. The Trusts seek to improve the quality of life for the residents of deprived inner city, urban fringe and countryside areas through projects aimed at making physical improvements and by involving local communities and businesses in regeneration. Groundwork receives some core funding from central government and the private sector but most of the federation's £40m annual income is project related. Brokering and sustaining partnerships between local government, national and local companies, and community organisations is therefore central to Groundwork's approach. For various reasons, in these circumstances the financial management of local trusts is often extremely challenging. Groundwork's national office represents the federation at national level, manages policy and development, builds relationships with sponsors, and is responsible for establishing standards and monitoring performance. The culture of the organisation is one that takes management seriously – for example, it has a long-running and well-resourced management development programme.

The main measures in use during the last five years are summarised in table 4.3. However, several other important evaluations have also took place during this period. The main ones were:

- Value-for-Money Review. This considered the cost-effectiveness of Groundwork activity and its contribution to the Government's regeneration objectives. It was commissioned by Groundwork's principal central government funder and was critical for maintaining its confidence.

- Stewardship Study. This was initiated by Groundwork and concerned local resident involvement in the continuing care or management of improvements/facilities developed through Groundwork projects

- 'What works' evaluation. Likewise initiated by Groundwork, but externally funded. This examined the factors contributing to the long-term durability of benefits developed through Groundwork projects.

The chronology of these various measurement-related initiatives – not including, of course, many purely local efforts – can be summarised as follows:

1995 – Revision of longstanding National Performance Measures (NPMs) by a working group of local and national staff, and involving stakeholder consultation.

1996 – Exploration of performance indices and ratios ('scattergraphs') – an elegant way of condensing much data, but use not sustained following departure of 'champion'.

1997 – More revisions to NPMs; project team searched for new ideas externally, reduced the number of measures and simplified definitions, guidance, etc.

1998 – Consultants recruited to help develop impact measures; constitutional change process initiated to clarify centre-local relationships; 'stewardship' evaluation sought and undertaken.

1999 – 'Impact' pilot projects running, constitutional change process brought to successful conclusion; 'Value for Money' study undertaken; 'What works' study launched. 2000 'Impact' project continues; new posts and committee created to pursue measurement initiatives (following constitutional changes) – new quality-related initiatives being contemplated.

Two developments deserve particular comment. First, the pursuit of coherent and standardised approaches to performance was held back by the lack of clarity over the respective roles and responsibilities of local offices and the National Office. Measurement was far from being the only issue contributing to the decision to embark on the very time-consuming process of a structural-constitutional review – but it was certainly one of them. Now those changes are in place, new more senior roles with performance measurement responsibilities have been created. Secondly, the experimentation with community impact indicators (in the Prove It! scheme – see table 4.3) and their incorporation into the Groundwork approach has been a major undertaking involving Groundwork-wide discussions and pilot schemes in 16 localities. This is likely to lead to a huge increase in the number of outcome-related measures in use. It has much to recommend it, not least the 'fit' with central Groundwork values, but it is early days for the new approach which also has definite limitations (the cost, and the fact that it leads to diverse and incommensurable measures being used).

Overall, the level of resource – both in terms of money and managerial time – devoted to evaluation and measurement has been considerable and it has been increasing. The experience also illustrates why, in Groundwork's case, it will be extremely difficult to develop the sort of stable, focused and meaningful array of indicators urged by the advocates of measurement. The difficulties do not just reflect the usual anxieties about the ways in which the measures will be interpreted. Other factors have included:

- the multifaceted nature of *what* Groundwork is trying to achieve, and also *how* it is trying to achieve it;

Table 4. 3   Principal approaches to performance measurement at Groundwork, 1995–2000

	Focus	Primary stakeholder	Approach	Time period	Perceived limitations
National Performance Measures (NPM)	The results of projects aggregated for the Federation as a whole	Central government funder	30–40 indicators grouped under headings – eg hectares of land improved, no. of people involved ; no. of businesses involved, etc, some of which are clearly outcome – related	Late 1980s onwards in various versions	Data not reliable; Mechanistic, not capturing important dimensions of Groundwork's approach and contribution.
Financial measures	Ratios and benchmarks to track progress in resource acquisition and management	Local Trust managers and Hon Treasurers.	Eg project to total costs: £ turnover p/person employed; % targeted income secured by specific points in year; working capital > 10 weeks turnover, etc	Evolved through early 1990s	Useful as far as they go – but no help on the big issues
'Scattergraphs' based on indices and ratios	The comparative success of Trusts in accessing, and using resources	Groundwork national office	(i) Ratio of funds raised to local opportunities available, using index for latter; (ii) ratio of performance to expenditure, using NPM – derived index for former	1996–97	Scattergraphs of points around a regression line deemed too complex; involve contestable assumptions
Prove it!	The social impact of projects, and clusters of projects, on particular communities	Local communities, and project staff; other local partners	Participatory social research – residents involved as a way of building social capital as well as measuring it.	Piloted from1998, and rolled out in 2000	Useful locally, but costly and very variable

- the fact that performance is understood in different ways by the wide range of interested parties (one interviewee described Groundwork as 'stakeholder hell'); allied to this, the issue of the *unit of analysis* (project, neighbourhood, Trust or Federation);

- the diverse contexts in which the Trusts operate and the extremely wide range of activities they undertake – a function of the fact that their mode of operation is one of flexible and innovative response to local needs and partnership opportunities;

- the continuing evolution of government policy on regeneration and of trends in the discourse of relevant policy communities (post-Rio 'sustainability'; 'social capital', etc), both of which generate new objectives and new measurement requirements

In addition to these conceptual and political difficulties, the technical and administrative challenges involved in agreeing and embedding measurement systems have been formidable, even in an organisation committed to measurement and with extended experience of it.

This does not mean that Groundwork's measurement efforts have been in vain. Rather, their clear commitment to measurement and evaluation seems to have stood them in good stead with their major funders and partners. They have been ahead of, not following, the measurement agenda, and demonstrably 'on the case' in their dealings with funders. This has meant they were generally able to present their own conception of performance lucidly and with evidential backing, in terms of the developing policy agenda and discourse – as evidenced, in particular, by their success in convincing the Value-For-Money consultants that their work was indeed very cost-effective.

PHS and its recent history of measurement

Seattle-based PHS was founded in 1962 by a recovering alcoholic and ex-felon. Its aim was to provide 'chances for change' and for its first 20 years it was not unlike many other nonprofits in the field of rehabilitation. In 1984 a new CEO, Gary Mulhair, embarked on an unusual growth strategy. This involved, among other things, developing partnerships running facilities for major companies and seeking soft loans from foundations to finance the purchase of viable small businesses. In both cases, PHS wanted to run the operations so that it could offer job training and employment to PHS clients.

By 1999, PHS had revenues of over $50,000,000, about half of which were generated in such 'commercial' activities as manufacturing, printing, distribution, and food operations. Its mission ('improving lives through jobs, social services and housing') and target population ('persons living at the margins of society; ex-offenders and substance abusers') have remained basically the same; its range of services has been greatly extended. In 2000 it served more than 6,000 clients in accommodation-based programmes (residential recovery services and low-cost housing) and social and probation services ('community corrections'; counselling and chemical dependency schemes). Perhaps more significantly, it was employing, at any one time, more than 1,000 staff, about 75% of whom were ex-convicts and ex-addicts.

Hence, PHS is able to offer housing, social service and employment support, either singly or in combination. As a consequence it has become a large, highly diverse and complex organisation, containing a range of activities that are usually undertaken in different sectors as well as organisations (eg high technology manufacturing for Boeing, but also addiction counselling).

One consequence of this combination is a senior management team with many of the attributes of a business culture manifest through a strong results orientation and a commitment to measurement. This takes four main forms. First, PHS tracks its financial performance in conventional ways – it claims an average 13% return across its enterprise division. Second, it undertakes a range of quality assurance activities to ensure it is meeting the requirements and expectations of the major customers with whom it aims to work in partnership. Thus, PHS staff prepare for and assist an extensive range of inspections, programme reviews and audits undertaken by external agencies (including the ISO 9002 Certification of some of its enterprises), in relation to such major contractors as the Department of Corrections, the Federal Bureau of Prisons, and Boeing.

However, the third and fourth areas – 'mission outcomes' and 'client outcomes' – are where PHS's most innovative initiatives are being pursued. These initiatives follow a strategic decision in 1997 to develop this area, by the appointment of a senior vice president (Larry Fehr) to lead a small team tackling the work, and by drawing in foundation support. According to Fehr, the aim of the 'mission outcomes' system 'is to report monthly programmatic performance, similar to a monthly budget report's display of financial performance.' And the aim of the TOMS system which tracks client outcomes is to provide the basis for regular client impact reports comparable to the half-yearly reporting of company results.

Mission outcomes. This is a monthly reporting system through which the sub-units of PHS report on their progress based on a variety of indicators of goal achievement. When Fehr was appointed, senior management was already receiving reports on 98 indicators from 24 PHS units. By 1999 this had increased to about 240 indicators from 52 units. At that time the indicators were a varied mix of the sorts of measures that one might expect to see used in managing much larger service and administrative operations. They mainly drew on operational data (activity and throughput levels, completions, etc) and on quality data of a broadly QA nature (error rates, rule violations, incidents etc) but also making extensive use of satisfaction surveys (variously of clients, trainees, internal customers and external customers). Some professional assessment data was also used (eg risk reduction, improvement in functioning, cognitive restructuring, progress towards goal attainment).

A major objective at this stage was to embed a monthly cycle of procedures for data gathering, reporting and target setting. To be useful, this system had to provide units with graphical displays of their performance over time on their key indicators. For this, data analysis, aggregation and presentation were severe challenges. The solution chosen was to use *percentage variances* (using the term in its budget control sense) as a common metric. This means – to take specific instances – that if a course has the target of an overall rating of four from trainees and achieves five, then it is 25% ahead of target on that measure; and that if a particular programme aims for 65% successful community releases and achieves 89%, then 24 points ahead of a 65% target means it has a 38.9% positive variance. The resulting tables of data were very extensive, but were automatically summarised each month in two ways. First, the arithmetic average of the variances was calculated for each of the 50 units. These were then subjected to a Pareto analysis with the results presented graphically on a single page. In effect, this highlighted those units that had contributed most to the totals of negative and positive variance. Secondly, the average variances were calculated for each of the four main divisions of PHS (based on all the unit indicators for which data were available in each case). These results could then be presented as bar charts, showing month-by-month and year-to-date performance against the target of a 12% positive variance.

In 2000 the system was revised to focus more clearly on client-related outcomes. The effect was to reduce the number of indicators by about half, with the more operational items relocated in a new system focusing on operational results.

Sustained Client Outcomes. In 1998 PHS attracted foundation funding to support a programme with the acronym 'TOMS' ('Tracking Outcomes and Managing Services'). As the name implies, its purpose has been precisely that promoted by the 'outcomes' movement – to identify the lasting impact of their various programmes and to do so in ways that can lead to improvements in programme design. The TOMS programme has been pursued through a series of sub-projects. Some of the work has been undertaken in-house, by staff of the Outcomes Group, some undertaken by the University of Washington, and some carried out jointly. An important aim has been to lay the foundations for an enduring system of data gathering and analysis (rather than to carry out a once-off follow-up evaluation of recent clients). Hence, for example, one of the projects is aiming to develop and test a standard instrument for clients to self-report various aspects of personal growth, on departure or discharge from a PHS programme. Likewise, a data architecture for the system has had to be developed to align and collate records from the following sources:

• PHS Central client ID data-base and central operational systems;

• PHS Units' records of admission/discharge, client assessment, and so on;

• official records from the Department of Corrections (for criminal history, and relapse/reconviction);

• official records from the Washington State Employment Agency (*re* pre- and post-PHS involvement);

- TOMS periodic follow-up surveys, concerning current employment, housing and life-style.

The development of data-handling capacities is only one of the challenges that TOMS has faced. Other issues include:

- the fact that ex-clients of PHS are a transient and mobile population, making them extremely hard to trace and contact;

- the range of outcome indicators – concerning economic well-being, housing, life-style, drug use and criminal activity – that are relevant to judgements of success;

- the need to gather pre-PHS baseline data from clients or other sources, regarding these indicators;

- the scarcity of external benchmarks regarding what constitutes success for PHS's particularly challenging client group;

- the number of different sub-groups within the population of ex-PHS clients (generated by the range of services and scope for combining two or even three); this will make it difficult to draw inferences with confidence about 'what works' until a much larger data-set has been accumulated.

The Outcomes Group includes professionally qualified researchers and the reports that they, and collaborating researchers, produce are dispassionate, intermittently noting negative aspects or making references to the relevant literature or external comparators. They are written within the discourse of social research rather than management or public relations. As such, they present a rich and convincing, though necessarily incomplete and uneven, picture of client outcomes. There are clear indications of success – and also some disappointing figures. Some of the data reported are seen as puzzling – and understandably a consistent message is the need to further develop the tracking methodology. The reports are said often to be controversial within PHS, and some information has already informed service planning. The major example of this is the decision to expand the Employee Assistance Scheme in Pioneer Industries rather than reduce it as had been intended. This was heavily influenced by the focus group findings concerning its importance to former clients when they looked back on their time with PHS.

Appraising progress. The sheer complexity and challenge of the undertaking, especially regarding sustained client outcomes, is striking – clearly, it is a long-term project. It has also been costly. By 1999 the planned run-down of one major contract had put some financial pressure on PHS and the Outcomes Group lost one of its two professional researchers. The major achievement is that the information infrastructure at PHS, both technical and administrative, has been substantially enhanced. And the information from the new system is being used in ways comparable to that delivered by more familiar systems in other organisations. That is to say, it provides a basis for recognising particular unit progress and achievement.   It helps in spreading understanding of developments across the organisation ('conversations happen because of the availability of the performance measurement system', as one interviewee put it). And it is used (along with other sorts of information) to inform decisions. Perhaps too, it contributes in a more general way. In a measurement-oriented management culture where financial outcomes are (and have to be) taken very seriously, it may give additional weight and legitimacy to client outcomes and social performance.

The New Economics Foundation (NEF)

NEF is a London-based independent research and policy institute committed to 'building a just and sustainable economy with ideas and actions that put people and the environment first'. It was set up in 1986 to provide the intellectual input to The Other Economic Summit (now the People's Summit), an event that shadows the G8 Economic Summits. NEF has since grown and evolved into a centre for innovative approaches to economics that are responsive to social, ethical and environmental issues. It provides consultancy and training services to the private, public and nonprofit sectors and collaborates with partners such as NGOs and research institutes – carrying out research, writing reports, exchanging information and organising events. It is however also developing an increasingly active campaigning arm around corporate accountability and global economic issues

NEF is one of the leading organisations in the field of social auditing having been involved in social auditing in the corporate and nonprofit communities, both in the UK and internationally. In this role, NEF has acted as external social verifier for a number of organisations, including The Body Shop and Ben & Jerry's, and acts as adviser to companies in the development of their social audit practice. It has contributed both to the development of a methodology and its use, through its combination of research and publications, training and direct social auditing activities.

Both staff and income have increased substantially in recent years – since 1993 staff numbers have grown from 4 to 22 while income has increased from £50,000 pa to its current level of over £800,000 pa. Social auditing is not just politically important to NEF. It is also important in financial and public relations terms – it accounted for some 30% of NEF's total income in 1998 (down from a 1996 peak of 50%) and it is probably the area of work for which it is best known. NEF itself was the first registered charity in the UK to carry out a social audit, issuing its first Social Statement in 1994.

How the method has been described and implemented at NEF since 1994 is summarised in table 4.4, along with a summary of the auditors' comments and recommendations on each occasion. A key issue for any such method concerns how many of the underlying data to report or summarise. On the one hand, it is clearly out of the question to present all the information gathered – that could run to volumes. But equally, it would not be satisfactory for an organisation just to make general claims about their overall social performance, and to report an auditor's endorsement of those claims. Readers of such reports will rightly expect some indication of the sorts of information on which claims of performance are based, and how that information was gathered. But how much is enough? NEF has addressed this dilemma in different ways over the years, as the varying length of the reports indicates.

NEF emphasised the general benefits that arose from making the relationships with stakeholders explicit – *'once relationships are explicit one can deal with them.'* Interviewees also stressed that many issues thrown up by a social audit, especially those involving external relationships, cannot be 'solved' so much as worked on and improved. An important function of the audit is to *'make nagging problems visible and to help resolve them'*. They offered three examples of specific issues that were illuminated by the social audits and had to be addressed in consequence – though they did not claim to have 'solved' them: governance, equal opportunities, and workloads and stress.

Social Audit as a method. A striking feature of NEF's use of social audit is its variability – both as regards the stakeholder approach, and at the level of measurement. As table 4.4 shows, the way the method is described has varied considerably, as have the parties awarded stakeholder status and involved in the process. This has concerned the verifiers in 1995,1997 and 1999 – for example:

> More consideration could be given to weighting the importance of different stakeholder groups – a desirable outcome would be to re-balance the focus of consultation towards external bodies...(NEF 1999, p 39)

The issues here concern the weight to be given to various stakeholder's views vis-à-vis each other and in relation to objective-style indicators of project outcomes and impact, especially given repeated references in the Social Statements to low survey response rates and 'questionnaire fatigue'. It is worth noting that 'indicators and benchmarks' only enter the description of the method from 1995–96 onwards. Arguably, the latter remain underdeveloped: some external referents are given in relation to environmental matters, but not in other areas where this might have been straightforward (eg administrative cost ratios). Interestingly enough, and to NEF's considerable credit, stakeholders' opinions on the effectiveness of the consultation have been canvassed within the Social Audit process. While the responses were generally positive, they were certainly not uncritical:

> ... There were suggestions (from staff, trustees and networks) that NEF needs to try and assess the real impact of its work and of the New Economy in general.... There were repeated stakeholder requests for future audits to contain summaries of NEF's work for the audit period; a basic but overlooked necessity. (NEF 1999)

Such comments echo those of the auditor in the first social statement:

Table 4.4   Social audit method at NEF

	1993–94	1994–95	1995–96	1996–97	1997–98
Description of social audit	Draws on participative research and organisational development to assess 'the social impact and behaviour of an organisation in relation to its stakeholders'	'… a way to assess the impact of an organisation on people's lives…can be thought of as reporting on a conversation between an organisation and its stakeholders… guided and validated by an outsider…'	'… four key building blocks… are stakeholder consultation, indicators and benchmarks, external verification and disclosure'	'Social auditing is an approach which aims to redefine and measure progress, so as to understand and improve the social impact of organisations as well as promote accountability…'	'Social and ethical accounting and auditing are methods of measuring and reporting on an organisation's social and ethical performance'
Stakeholders consulted (1)	A,B,C,D,E,F	A,B,C,E,F,G,H,I,J	A,C,E,F,G,H,I,J	A,B,C,G	A,B,C,F,I,J,K
Length, format and scope	10-page summary published; full accounts available for £5	24-page summary published, including a one-page account of action in response to the auditor's comments in the previous year; full accounts available for £5. Focus on the Indicators Programme	46 pages including much more data from surveys. Also includes 'NEF response and next steps,' section by section. Focus on the Community Economics Programme	20 pages, mainly presenting data that often shows comparisons with previous two years. An interim report only, reflecting decision 'to move to a two-year cycle of fully verified reports'	42 pages, starting with a one- page executive summary. Report addresses three key themes (Getting our message across, Learning from others, and Practising accountability), then reviews environmental impact and views of most stakeholders

Auditors observations and recommendations

'...social impact... receives insufficient attention...' and urges more emphasis on views of organisations representing disadvantaged groups. Stakeholders need to know NEF's mission/strategy and values if they are to appraise performance. Various suggestions for more and better monitoring of equal opportunities environmental practices, health and safety, role of volunteers, relationships with partner organisations, etc

Various improvements in reporting endorsed – 'a quantum improvement in the quality and presentation of the accounts.' Reiteration of call for various improvements made in previous year. Recommends some new areas for attention, eg suppliers. Highlights data collection issues, eg low response rates. Urges data collection and presentation to show changes over time

General endorsement and welcomes use of focus groups and social capital analysis. Calls for more impact assessment ('to complement stakeholder analysis... need to include intended beneficiaries not yet among the stakeholder groups so identified'). Repeats various suggestions from previous years, and suggests some new areas for attention or improvement, including whether audit findings 'are translated into strategic plans and actions'.

Not externally verified.

Endorsed as 'useful analysis and representative disclosure of the views of its stakeholders... the scope of the audit in terms of the themes pursued was appropriate... a comprehensive account of its performance'. Calls to 'further formalise the social audit process to ensure continuity and consistency' and to 're–balance the focus' of consultation towards external bodies' and for some improvements in consultation methods

Note:

(1) **Stakeholder key:** A – Staff; B – Trustees; C – Supporters; D – Patrons; E – Volunteers; F – Network groups and partners; G – Suppliers; H – Funders; I – Subscribers/Publications buyers; J – Staff families/partners; K – Clients.

> ... the social impact of NEF's work receives insufficient attention. There
> was a lack of clarity in stakeholders' responses about what criteria to use
> to do this.... I recommend ... all stakeholder groups are provided with
> mission, strategy and value statements...(NEF 1999, p 1)

Some continuity among the measures used is now emerging – for example
regarding media coverage, energy usage, hidden and visible hours work – and
the latest report contains far more comparisons with previous years. But in most
of the regularly reported domains a stable set of measures seems not to have
emerged. Such apparent methodological looseness and variability may have
been exaggerated by the fact that the method was still being developed, and by
NEF's particular circumstances. During this period NEF grew rapidly and one
would expect its measurement system to evolve along with its aims and
activities. Moreover, advocacy and campaigning for social change are by far,
and notoriously, the most difficult areas of work in which to track impact (6 and
Forder 1996). Indeed, one could just as well argue that the observations about
the variability of the method and the data presented demonstrate one of Social
Audit's great strengths – its wide applicability and flexibility.

Common themes among the measurement leaders

Measurement as a strategic opportunity. Most obviously, none of the cases
involved the top-down imposition of measures designed to support a conception
of performance passed down from an institutional level. All three organisations
undertook their measurement initiatives with a clear strategy, rationale and
approach. All were closely involved with the private sector and had a 'business
case' for embarking on what was bound to be a challenging undertaking. Both
Groundwork and PHS had long claimed a businesslike approach to the
management of their activities and so they were honour-bound to respond to the
new measurement challenge. But in both cases the challenge was seen as an
opportunity – to build stakeholder confidence, to enhance reputations, to attract
additional resources – and not just a threat to be minimised and contained. NEF,
too, were honour-bound to practice what they preached – but as well as the
benefits they believed inherent in Social Audit, using it was also an opportunity
to learn more about the procedure they were promoting, and to explore its
applicability to a smaller, nonprofit organisation. Later on, this would open up
a new market opportunity. In all three cases, too, the benefits of measurement
were articulated in similar terms. Measurement was a way of underpinning
organisational commitments (do we really do what we claim to do?) and of
demonstrating performance externally. It was a means of learning and process
improvement ('what works' was an expression used in both Groundwork and
PHS). And it was a basis for 'selective control' (identifying issues that were
hurting, or sub-units that were struggling, as a focus for management attention).
However, the control element was downplayed and no one advocated the use of
measurement data in the performance appraisal of individual managers.

Finally, the measurement initiatives were all pursued in a participatory mode (painstaking consultation at Groundwork; a 'let a thousand flowers bloom' phase at PHS; staff having stakeholder status at NEF) since 'buy-in' was seen as essential.

Implementation and the problem of domain integration. All three organisations were hoping their measurement initiatives would provide internal and external benefits. That is, they hoped the information they generated would simultaneously support requirements for performance information at institutional, managerial and professional/sub-unit levels. As expected, this was proving very difficult, though all the organisations did attempt to do two things at once, wherever possible. Some of the ways they attempted this are familiar – for example, PHS's research reports, which presented a rich, qualified and complex account of client experiences or outcomes relevant to senior professionals, were prefaced by executive summaries. These presented a simple, more categorical picture of the findings, appropriate for managerial and institutional use. NEF addressed the problem by selecting particular areas of work to examine in more depth in each accounting round. The idea was that such occasional reviews would be of value to those working in the area, as well as providing greater insight to the management team and other stakeholders – and without making the whole process too cumbersome and intrusive.

The concept of performance was particularly differentiated at Groundwork – between project, community, Trust and national levels. The NPM were an attempt to define a common currency for results and they always contained some outcome elements, even if no one was really satisfied with them. Several different forms of measurement or evaluation were being (or had been) explored for different aspects of performance, mainly to serve particular needs. Latterly, the most integrated approach was the development and testing of a form of impact assessment that would serve the needs of project staff and Trusts as well as contributing information to address stakeholder concerns at an institutional level.

The costs of measurement. In all cases the costs of the measurement initiatives were considerable. In part these showed up in the staff and other costs directly associated with measurement work: the posts created at PHS and the research funded at the University of Washington; the post created at Groundwork, the consultants appointed, and the significant additional funds provided to local Trusts participating in the pilot schemes; the consultants hired to assist with stakeholder consultation at NEF. But the managerial time spent discussing measurement issues was also very considerable. Another cost was the time and effort of staff who recorded or contributed information – all the organisations admitted to considerable on-going difficulties in 'embedding' procedures for routine data capture.

Proliferation and churn. Several of the patterns of measurement behaviour noted in the private sector seemed to be appearing in these cases – in particular 'oscillation' in the number of measures in use (PHS, Groundwork, NEF), a gradual increase in the number of measures in use (PHS, Groundwork), and a turnover in the measures in use (NEF, Groundwork). Overall, the prospect of a stable, coherent and focused measurement set seems as far off as ever. These measurement leaders were travelling in hope – and none thought they were going to arrive in the foreseeable future. That said, NEF's case is slightly different – in so far as the Social Audit approach is neatly stable and complete (producing an externally verified social account) even if the measures within it show little continuity.

Conclusions

This chapter set out to address two questions: how are social enterprises performing their measurements? And is measurement performing – does it look like delivering the goods? These are of course far bigger and broader issues than the limited investigations reported here can resolve. In particular, one has to be very restrained in trying to draw generalisable conclusions from a study based on a small number of cases. Nevertheless, to the extent that clear patterns of behaviour that make sense in relation to existing theory have emerged, they, and their possible implications for practice, are worth noting. The discussion starts with some general points and then considers the three specific methods of measurement in turn.

How nonprofits are performing their measurements. Considering together the data from the investigation of ACE ratios and the study of measurement leaders, it appears that many nonprofits are:

- devoting more managerial attention and resource to measurement;

- introducing new or improved measurement systems offering more detailed analyses;

- giving increased status to the finance function and to others associated with measurement;

- making more frequent changes in measurement practices designed either to improve reported scores (eg cost re-allocations) or to provide better information.

But their responses also vary widely (and predictably) depending on their circumstances:

- Those in sheltered niches tend to give less attention to possible public perceptions of their performance – their stance is essentially reactive.

- Many, probably most, are pursuing strategies that might be described as 'active management', through such tactics as

  - managing the flow of publicly reported figures to ensure acceptable appearances
  - developing strong stories about their performance with selected internal or comparative performance data to support it

-    staying abreast of developments through sectoral and professional
     networks, and seeking incremental improvements in their own
     measurement practices.

An important feature of these strategies is that internal efforts towards
performance improvement appear to be pursued quite independently of
concerns about external reporting. Internally and externally oriented
measurements are largely de-coupled.

•   A smaller number are seeing the measurement agenda as offering strategic
     opportunities to develop their relationships with stakeholders, and to
     develop their internal capacities. Such initiatives may also be a way of
     staying in control of the measurement process. In these cases, the
     aspiration is to create measurement systems that serve both internal and
     external constituencies. Since, in practice, this is extremely difficult and at
     best likely to take many years, 'leadership' strategies may involve such
     elements as:

     -    re-organisations or the creation of new roles or departments
     -    participative design and development efforts to encourage 'buy-in'
     -    seeking social research expertise externally, to assist them;
     -    seeking external resources to fund the work
     -    adopting the discourse of outcomes and measurement in relation to more
          or less familiar evaluation studies
     -    using the *existence* of measurement initiatives, rather than information
          provided by them, to address (or pre-empt) institutional concerns about
          performance, outcomes, impact, etc

Is measurement performing? What light do the various studies reported here
throw on the broader policy issue of whether the increased emphasis on
measurement is actually 'delivering the goods'? In general, there was no
evidence of the increased attention to measurement 'driving' performance
improvements in a direct way. Performance improvement efforts were
generally pursued independently of concerns about one's publicly reported
performance. When these were linked it was because particular organisations
saw a strategic opportunity. Likewise, there was no real evidence of pressures
for measurement leading to measurement dysfunctions (though that may well
reflect the decision to focus attention on measurement leaders). On the other
hand, the direct and indirect costs of measurement can be considerable – and
have to be borne by someone, even if not the social enterprise itself.[15] In
addition, the technical/administrative practicalities of routine performance
measurement are consistently found to be challenging. And those anticipating
the emergence of stable and coherent measurement sets also look doomed to
disappointment. An era of measurement churn and continuous search, seems
much more likely.

ACE ratios. The revisions to the charity accounting SORP are gradually
bringing about greater consistency in financial reporting by charities. In
addition, the greater public attention being paid to this measure means charities
are considering, or considering more closely, the possible public reception of

what have hitherto been seen as arcane cost allocation decisions. Together, these trends have led to a marked overall improvement in reported performance: there is a clear trend for ACE ratios to fall, and for their variation to reduce. In consequence, charity accounts are probably becoming less obscure, and ACE ratios are offering less scope as a focus for public and media concern. In the longer run it may be that in fields like the Special Groups Societies, where activities are very similar, ACE ratios will come to converge closely. In other fields, where size and activity mixes vary much more widely, a wider range of variations will remain. But instead charities will become proficient at explaining the reasons for their distinctiveness, and in using trend data or other comparisons with 'more similar' charities in other fields to back up their claims to administrative efficiency. Either way, ACE ratios will gradually cease to discriminate.

Outcome measurement. Four criteria have been given for deciding whether a system of outcome measurement had actually been realised. Groundwork and PHS, each in their own way, have made some progress towards that target but neither is near to realising it, nor would claim to be, despite sustained and well-resourced effort in a supportive context over several years. Indeed, it is unclear whether a focused system serving a range of external and internal purposes will ever be realised in organisations like Groundwork and PHS. This is not to criticise the value of their outcome-related work – simply to question whether it will ever take the form of a stable and integrated system, as has been envisaged by the proponents of measurement. The two key challenges are first the problem of 'churn', and second that of domain alignment and integration. It seems that in these cases, as others reported in the literature, outcomes reporting has been captured by the professional domain and construed in terms of research on programmatic outcomes. This can, of course, be useful in its own terms, and at the same time be used to satisfy institutional concerns about effectiveness. But it is seldom managerially useful[16] – and it is very explicitly *not* what the early proponents of outcome measurement intended (Williams and Webb 1991). So where does this leave the case for outcome measurement – what, in other words, are the policy implications?

Two responses seem possible. The more pessimistic one is to say that the whole idea is deeply flawed – because it confuses what is possible in terms of social research with what is feasible in terms of routine management information. There may well be benefits in social enterprises (or better, their funders) commissioning and undertaking social research if they have the skills and resources to do so. But it will be exceptional, in the circumstances of most social enterprises, if such studies lead to the creation of systems of routine data capture and analysis that yield managerially useful information and that are affordable by medium-sized organisations (let alone smaller ones).

The division of labour within the UK National Health Service may be instructive in this respect. All hospitals are expected to keep basic records on the outcomes of surgical interventions. But the purpose of these management and professional records is that the hospitals can monitor their own performance in the conduct of what are taken to be sound medical procedures. They do not themselves attempt to demonstrate the clinical or cost effectiveness of those procedures – that is undertaken as a research exercise by other individuals and bodies (Medical Research Council, National Institute for Clinical Excellence, etc). It would be far less effective and far more expensive to expect every hospital to undertake its own outcome and cost effectiveness studies of all, or even a few, of its treatment areas. But when, for example, funders ask small agencies for outcomes data the collection costs (and duration) of which would far exceed the value (and timescale) of their grant, this is in effect what they are doing.[17] In practice, of course, things are not usually so bad – 'outcomes' information is, wisely, given a generous (collusive) interpretation. Nevertheless, there are worrying trends. Even small social enterprises undertaking challenging enough work in pursuing their missions now risk being criticised for being poor social researchers – for not using control groups and carrying out enough long-term follow ups (Hoefer 2000). The costs hardly bear contemplating.

A more optimistic response is to suggest that outcome measurement is better understood as a potentially worthwhile journey rather than an actual destination, useful, like evaluation, for the dialogues that surround it and the shared purpose and understanding to which it can give rise. Arguably, this makes better sense of much of what is reported about 'successful' outcomes initiatives in the professional and practitioner literature.

Whether one is an optimist or a pessimist, the message for policy-makers and funders is more or less the same: go easy on outcome measurement, lest you discredit a useful aspiration, waste resources, and start to stimulate dysfunctions.

Social Audit. The examination of NEF's experience of using the still developing method of Social Audit over five years in particularly challenging circumstances may be an unreliable guide to its use in other contexts. That said, as a procedure for reporting and accountability, NEF's social audits have obvious attractions: the procedure is under their own control, but still involves independent scrutiny and an unusual degree of organisational self-disclosure (for example, they regularly quote critical views from clients and supporters, and report staff concerns). The statements are also pragmatic about blending narrative and measurement, and are presented as expressing and contributing to a dialogue among stakeholders. They thus display a wider range of perspectives and concerns (and the tensions among them) than is afforded by approaches that rely heavily on objectified performance measures.

However, since there are as yet no established standards for Social Auditing, the discipline can, in the end, be as tough or relaxed as the organisation's leadership chooses. NEF are clearly committed to it, and show every sign of using it in good faith – as is probably the case with most early adopters. But from their experiences as verifiers to other organisations, NEF staff are well aware that organisational reports can conceal even as they reveal. Indeed, one interviewee said a rule of thumb had emerged from NEF's audit work at clients: *'In a 30 page social audit report the token bit of bad news will usually be found around page 26'*. Verifiers may provide something of a safeguard. However, their contribution, too, will depend crucially on the emergence of agreed standards; and their contribution should not be overstated (Power 1997).

Until such standards are more widely recognised, and given the considerable variability shown in NEFs own practice, it may be misleading to think of Social Audit as a distinct product – a specific tool to address particular reporting and accountability issues. The reality is that those who chose it are effectively joining a loose-knit community of practice engaged in what is bound to remain, for the foreseeable future, a problematic undertaking.

Sources and resources

Anyone wishing to understand the issues surrounding the definition of administrative costs in charities in the UK should start from the latest Statement of Recommended Practice – it is generally well presented and comprehensible to non-accountants. The relevant SORP can be obtained via the Charity Commission website .

The best presentation of the case for an outcome-focused approach to performance remains Williams and Webb (1991), though this may be hard to obtain. It is lucid and succinct, offering a powerful (if optimistic) critique of much grantmaking and contracting. Indeed, it can also be read as a critique of the way outcome measurement has developed, as it has been absorbed into the procedural morass the authors had hoped to by-pass. For a 'state of the art' account of outcome measurement with lots of practical advice see 'A Look at Outcome Measurement in Nonprofit Agencies' (Morley, Vinson et al. 2001). But do not look to this for a critique.

For Social Audit, the Canadian and UK reports on Social Auditing (Dow and Crowe 1999; Raynard and Murphy 2000) are the places to start, and contain references to the evolving practitioner literature. Or visit the New Economics Foundation website (www.neweconomics.org.uk).

The sites for Groundwork and PHS are (www.groundwork.org.uk) and (www.pioneerhumanserv.com). The latter is the subject of an interesting piece in the on-line magazine fastcompany
(www.fastcompany.com/online/33/pioneer.html).

5 'Best Practice' Benchmarking – Why Everyone Does it Now

Introduction

On the evidence of the last chapter, the prospects of a breakthrough in the measurement of social enterprise performance are not good. A synoptic indicator of 'Return on Social Investment' - to match ROCE (return on capital employed) or other established and comparable measures of company performance - is hardly a realistic aspiration. Among the reasons for this conclusion are the many different dimensions of social performance, the difficulties in aggregating non-financial measures in a meaningful way, and the diverse activities undertaken by social enterprises which render comparisons problematic. But perhaps these difficulties can be reduced and rendered tractable by focussing on particular functions or processes, instead of *overall* performance? Perhaps it is possible to define, say, particular administrative processes or fundraising practices, and then to measure the costs and results achieved in ways that are much more strictly comparable? If so, this really would allow one to discover 'what works', and one would know what sort of changes to introduce to raise performance in the same activity elsewhere. This is the essential idea behind the technique of process benchmarking, or, as it is more commonly known, Best Practice Benchmarking (BPB).

The origins and spread of process benchmarking. BPB emerged in large US corporations in the mid-80s, as part of the response to the challenge of Japanese manufacturing success (Camp 1989). The general concept is one of seeking improvement through discovery of the methods used to achieve superior performance elsewhere. This is elaborated in different ways by different authors but the commonly recurring features are:

- careful study of a *defined set of activities*, often an economically important, cross-functional, *operational process*; but it may also be a function or policy

- a concern with the definition and *measurement of performance*, often using non-financial measures, cost-activity ratios, and the like, in order to compare and track performance levels

- *identification of others from whom one might learn* ('industry leaders', 'exemplars', etc), *ie*, those carrying out the same or a similar activities either in the same organization, in a competitor, or in a different industry, but who may be doing so more efficiently or effectively

- setting targets in relation to external standards, rather than past internal performance;

- *a collaborative orientation* to the sharing of performance data and/or process methods, expressed in the idea of benchmarking partners, benchmarking clubs, visits to study successful operations, etc;

- *adopting and adapting ideas* used elsewhere to one's own situation, in order to achieve steady, or sharp, increases in performance

- *formation of a project team*, usually including some of the staff directly involved, to carry out the study and champion the introduction of changes.

The terms 'benchmarking' and 'best practice' have since become widely used. However, the defining characteristics of BPB as a technique are that it involves careful search for, and then detailed learning about the methods of, those who achieve superior performance in a selected activity important to one's organisation. Projects tend to be carried out either by one organisation selecting a particular process or activity to improve, and identifying others to visit and learn from; or by a group of organisations forming a club to share data and experience concerning a particular process (Spendolini 1992).

BPB spread rapidly in the international business community, as evidenced by a burgeoning professional literature, widespread coverage in the business press, the emergence of benchmarking clubs attracting subscriptions from large numbers of well-known companies, and by specialist consultancies inviting selected companies to join particular benchmarking projects (Cox and Thompson 1998). By the mid 1990s, the UK government had made the promotion and subsidy of benchmarking an important element in its strategy to improve the competitiveness of small and medium-sized businesses (DTI 1996). Interest had also spread to public organisations where it was seen as offering a constructive alternative to the imposed comparisons of 'league tables' (Associates 1998; Foot 1998; Samuels 1998). Finally, our own earlier survey research showed high levels of interest among the managers of charities: many claimed to practice BPB while others saw it as potentially important and something they should know about (Paton and Payne 1997).

So how well does BPB work in social enterprises? What happens when managers have tried to use this method of performance improvement? The chapter starts by briefly reviewing the literature on the use of BPB. The main case studies of BPB are then summarised before presenting the findings in terms of a series of propositions about the use (and, much more often, the non-use) of BPB in social enterprises.

The BPB literatures

The practice literature. Many hundreds of articles, books, brochures and web sites have been prepared by consultants or managers with experience of BPB in order to explain, promote or advise on 'how to do it' (the following are fairly typical: Sheridan 1993; Zairi and Leonard 1994; Cook 1995; Lincoln and Price 1996; Unnamed 1997; Wood, Jones et al. 1997). Overwhelmingly, these are based on corporate or public sector experience (the most notable exception is chapter 5 of Letts, Ryan et al. 1999). Among the themes that recur, many writers warn against becoming preoccupied with comparisons of performance. The consensus of experienced practitioners seems to be that these will always be a bit rough and ready. Rather than trying to make measures more strictly comparable, effort is better spent in discovering *how* those who seem to perform rather well carry out their operations, with a view to improving one's own operations. Likewise, many experienced practitioners emphasise that the choice of benchmarking partners is crucial to the success of a project. There may be little point studying the practices of a company whose processes are completely different (because of size, or because they are *so* far ahead in performance) and therefore offer few adaptable lessons.

Survey reports. A second strand in the literature reports surveys of BPB activity. Thus, BPB activities are reported much more frequently (and seem to be carried out more systematically, on more processes, more successfully) from larger organisations; there are marked differences between sectors regarding the extent of BPB activities reported; and BPB continues to be seen as an important tool, with more respondents planning to increase activity than reduce it (see for example Coopers and Lybrand 1994; Partnership Sourcing 1997). The common reasons for launching BPB projects are to find out how well one is doing, and as a source of ideas – it is *in*frequently undertaken in the hope of becoming 'excellent' (Holloway, Hinton et al. 1997). The problems most often reported concern the time and resources that BPB requires, the difficulties involved in finding suitable partners and in making reliable comparisons, and the internal resistance to change encountered (though overcoming such resistance is also cited as one of the advantages of BPB).

Unfortunately, the methodological limitations of these surveys make the findings hard to interpret. Self-reporting of BPB activity is meaningful if respondents are referring to the same sorts of thing, and this requires either that they share a fairly stable concept or that they are prepared to learn and adopt the researchers definition. However, neither seems to occur. Respondents' own definitions of benchmarking are frequently much wider than, and/or the activities they describe do not match, the definitions offered by the researchers (see especially Partnership Sourcing 1997). For example, many of Holloway, Hinton et al's (1997) respondents worked in government, health and education and seem to have been referring to the 'compulsory benchmarking' within the UK public sector – performance comparisons which have been criticised precisely because they have not in any way enabled those involved to identify the transferable practices that would raise performance (Stephens and Bowerman 1997). Likewise, much of the activity reported by Partnership Sourcing's (1997) respondents appears to be either internal benchmarking, or unsystematic (only 25% report involvement in a Benchmarking network or association). One is left with the definite impression that, in the context of a survey on Benchmarking, a wide variety of different activities – quantitative and qualitative performance comparisons, the opportunistic copying of ideas from others, aspects of traditional competitor analysis – may all be reported as BPB.

Theoretical analyses. The third, and noticeably the most limited, strand in the literature comprises academic studies that attempt to theorise BPB. The main issue to emerge concerns whether and when it will be appropriate for managers to spend time on BPB activities. Cox and Thompson (1998) have lambasted the concept of best practice (it is 'contingent on [a company's] individual commercial circumstances' and, echoing arguments from Porter (1996), have claimed that BPB is strategically misconceived – at best it offers a means of catching up, not leading, and the capabilities gained will be imitable by others. While they raise important issues, their claims are almost certainly overstated. A more rigorous and measured economic appraisal is offered by Elnathan and Kim's (1995) analysis of BPB collaboration. They argue that when the rate of change surrounding key processes generates high levels of uncertainty it is worth expending managerial time and effort, and even assisting competitors, in order to ensure one is keeping abreast of critical developments affecting competitiveness. They suggest that the costs of benchmarking depend on the number of partners, falling initially (as data-handling costs are spread) and then rising, due to increased complexity, and a loss of trust and data quality. They observe that benchmarking collaborations offer participants three potential benefits:

i.   they may learn about the innovations of others;

ii.   they may learn about the 'nuts and bolts' know-how needed to deliver such innovations;

iii. they may generate their own new ideas through cross-fertilisation (eg observation of comparable processes in different industries).

Because any process being examined in a benchmarking project will have many aspects, everyone, including the best performer overall, has an opportunity to learn from other participants. However, organisations need to choose suitable partners – those from whom they can be most confident of gaining significant insights and information. The authors suggest companies try to find such partners through a preliminary process of information gathering from trade sources, specialised business analysts, and so on. In practice, though, reputation seems often to be an important consideration. The result is the self-selection of clusters of organisations, whose participants expect to share similar levels of technological information, as benchmarking partners. This account of BPB suggests circumstances under which it is likely to be useful, and both builds on and makes sense of a wide range of observations from the practitioner and survey literature (eg the problems of comparability and contingency, partner selection, the considerable time required).

Taken together, the three strands of literature suggest that this is a practice that has an original or core content capable in certain circumstances of generating valuable learning about ways of improving performance. However, in this strict sense its application is often problematic, and very little rigorous research on its costs and benefits has been undertaken. Moreover, it seems that as it has become fashionable the terms associated with it have been used more widely and loosely. Hence what people mean when they talk of 'best practice' and 'benchmarking' is now far from clear.

The scope of the research and the main cases of BPB

Case selection was essentially a search process – through key informants and sector networks – for social enterprises where BPB (as described above) or some recognisable approximation to it, was being used. Three clear examples were identified, and several others were explored in a more limited way, either because practical issues made access difficult, or because the BPB project had been abandoned. The aim was simply to establish how the ideas had been used, what benefits had been achieved, and the costs and difficulties encountered. In all four of the main cases particular efforts were made to gather independent assessments of the value of BPB project – mainly through the use of sample telephone surveys of those involved in or affected by the changes. In addition, as the research progressed, a support service for a derivative of BPB was identified as having a number of interesting features, and this also became the subject of a case study. The research was undertaken as part of a project on benchmarking in charities (Paton and Payne 1997; Paton 1998) and the initial findings were tested out with professional and sector leaders in workshops and conference presentations. The experiences and views shared in these sessions were a further source of information. Summaries of the four main cases follow – further details are available elsewhere (Paton 1999; Paton and Payne 1999a, 1999b, 1999c).

Improving the purchasing process at the Royal Society for the Protection of Birds (RSPB). This was nearest thing to a textbook case, using detailed metrics, process mapping and employing three recognised variants of benchmarking (Camp 1995). The exercise, which began in 1994, had the objective of achieving 5% savings on a £20-million purchasing bill while maintaining quality. Consultants (whose fees were recovered from the first area tackled – janitorial supplies) provided initial advice, and the Board approved a cross-functional project team. Research and extensive interviewing was undertaken to establish the range of actual current practices and what was already being done well ('internal' benchmarking). The profile of activity was then compared with the consultants' model of best practice to identify areas and parts of the process where more time and attention was required and those where less was required (typically low value orders). Four benchmarking partners were found from among other large charities, and their processes were compared with the evolving proposals for the RSPB, using process-mapping software. Not all were comparable since, for example, the RSPB did not intend to adapt a fully centralised model of purchasing like one of the partners. But the discussions clarified issues and led to later collaboration. As well as this 'competitive' benchmarking, project staff visited Ford and Royal Mail as 'generic' benchmarking partners.   This led to further important changes in the new proposed new arrangements. The proposals involved:

- the designation and training of 'key purchasers' whose involvement in major purchases was mandatory, across the Society;

- the creation of Sourcing Teams in five areas requiring coordination;

- the introduction of a Purchasing Card for low value items, eliminating some 11,000 invoices at a stroke;

- introduction of comprehensive new procedures for buyers and training for them – but promoted to all staff through a two-page Guidelines document;

- introduction of a Suppliers Guide to Prompt Payment – an idea from Ford – which has cut sharply the number of calls from suppliers; and new expediting procedures;

- collaborative purchasing arrangements with other charities in areas of limited strength;

- contract splitting to avoid expensive sub-contract arrangements by chosen agencies – learned from Royal Mail;

- introduction of more appropriate targets for the purchasing process.

Four years on, the direct costs of the activity were estimated at 200 person days, plus consultant costs and some incidentals. At this stage, £560,000 p.a. savings had been realised, and a further £100,000–£200,000 p.a., had been targeted and were in the process of being realised.   Further areas with considerable potential had been identified and the project leader forecast that the original target would be reached within six years of starting the project. Within the RSPB, the new arrangements faced considerable difficulties and critics – not least because they challenged important elements in the organisation's culture and sought to circumscribe operating unit autonomy. In some parts of the organization the new arrangements seemed to be largely ignored. Implementation was a far bigger challenge than design.[18]

The Trade Associations project. This turned into a family of benchmarking activities undertaken with and for various groupings of trade associations. The first exercise was initiated at the end of 1995 by the then Director General of the Association of British Insurers.   He convened a meeting of 25 large associations and a steering group was appointed.   Respected non-profit consultants were chosen to manage the exercise and the UK governments Department of Trade and Industry (DTI) agreed to meet half the costs, enabling 27 large associations to participate at a cost of £600 each. The exercise started with structured interviews with the chief executives of each participating association. This enabled common issues to be identified and informed the drawing up of a detailed questionnaire covering, for example, the number of members, committee structure, period of office of the chairman, salaries of senior executives and so on. The consultants also interviewed senior civil servants, Members of the European Parliament, and others who were in a position to comment on Trade Association performance – which proved particularly useful. A report on good practice in trade associations was issued, and a summary version much more widely distributed.

The 27 participating associations then agreed to establish 12 benchmarking clubs. Areas covered included finances, governance, relations with members, influencing government, promoting exports and information technology issues. Other large associations were invited to join in at this stage and, in all, 37 associations participated – the DTI again provided some funding, reducing the costs of participation to £200 each. The same consultants were retained to convene and facilitate the initial meeting of each club, and later to review their progress. The most successful ones were those associated with finance, governance, personnel and management, information technology, member relations and Europe, and the most valued aspects were simply meeting colleagues, sharing information and exchanging views and experience.

Meanwhile the DTI wished to extend the work done with larger organisations to embrace others and expressed a willingness to finance a wider benchmarking exercise using the original questionnaire, adapted to take account of the involvement of smaller associations. All associations were invited to participate, and ultimately 135 did so. This resulted in a further report, with similar conclusions to the first report, though with more detailed analysis and greater recognition of size differences. Another exercise analysed trade association communication with their members. This involved 41 associations, mainly smaller ones, completing a questionnaire covering corporate brochures and guides to services, annual reports, regular publications etc. Again, this produced a detailed and well-received analysis of current practice with clear recommendations and examples for excellence.

Overall, participants in these activities considered the major benefits to be gaining a mix of detailed hard and soft information about how other associations operated, and how their activities were viewed by those they lobbied. They used this information to pick off areas for attention and to justify proposals for change within their own organisations. It has led to continuing collaboration and the prospect of some rationalisation within the sector. A survey of a sample of participants confirmed the value of the various exercises, with most able to give specific examples of how the information had been used and concerning changes made.

'Fundratios'. This scheme compares costs and returns in all aspects of fundraising. It has been running annually since 1991 as a collaboration between the Institute of Charity Fundraising Managers (ICFM) and the Centre for Inter-Firm Comparisons (CIFC). While Fundratios itself only aims to provide comparative data on a confidential basis, a subset of 22 participants from the largest fundraising charities (who meet informally as the Appeal Directors Group) discuss the results in detail, in the manner of a benchmarking club. And

other informal discussions around the exercise also facilitate the transfer of ideas and practices.

An invitation to participate is sent out to larger charities early in the year and survey forms then follow in April to those who sign up. For many, completion of the form is a significant undertaking, involving desk research, calculation and estimation covering both financial and non-financial data. A preliminary report based on the charity's individual return is then sent to it for checking. In September the main report is distributed to participants. A summary analysis displays and comments on trends in the different sources of revenue, compared with previous years, and allows participants to compare their performance with others on the key ratios of '% Growth' and 'Income per £1 spent' for the main areas of fundraising. This is supported by a detailed breakdown of costs and returns for each of the major areas of activity, in which each participating charity can, once again, compare its performance with 'high', 'low' and average results. However, participants know only their own results and who has participated in the exercise; the particular results of other charities are presented anonymously, to preserve confidentiality. Finally, later in the autumn, a meeting is held in which participants review the exercise and agree changes in the survey for the following year.

Within this annual cycle, the scheme has expanded and grown more complex over the years. In 1991 there were14 participating charities, and each year some have left while others join, or re-join. In the mid-1990s recruitment and retention both improved and a slow upward trend accelerated to the 1998 total of 40. Since 1993, 16 of the charities have been involved continuously, providing a core membership to the 'club'. These are all among the very largest UK charities. In more recent years efforts have been made to make the scheme more attractive to smaller and medium-sized charities.

The annual changes have been driven by efforts to improve the scope, ease of completion, accuracy and usefulness of the survey. Thus at various times revisions have been made to accommodate new fundraising methods (such as telemarketing) and changes in the significance of other methods (eg corporate fundraising), to exclude information no longer seen as essential, to reduce double counting, and to clarify the requirements and improve the layout.[19] The problem, of course, is that while everyone would like simpler forms *as well as* more useful and reliable comparisons, in practice these criticisms tend to pull in opposite directions.

Everyone accepts that the comparability and reliability of the data is suspect, but those that stay with the scheme consider it is good enough for their purposes – and by far the best available. This is also the view of the CIFC project manager who accepted that there were some particular difficulties in the Fundratios scheme – mainly because charities might be pursuing campaigning and public education, as well as fundraising goals, through their activities, which complicates cost allocation – but such concerns are normal and inevitable. Essentially four different benefits were claimed by participants:

1. 'The reassurance factor'. Often the information confirmed what was already believed to be the case or was otherwise 'nice to know' without prompting new courses of action.

2. Strategic review. Sometimes the information provided by Fundratios played an important part in strategic decision making. More generally, the data was seen as useful market intelligence – 'an incredibly valuable tool that gives weight to the whole function within the organisation', as one of the core members put it.

3. A political resource. Overwhelmingly, the Fundratios data were seen, used and valued by fundraisers as a resource in their discussions with colleagues and staff over resource allocation or performance expectations – 'to bash others over the head', in a respondent's blunt terms. Another said he used Fundratios data with his Trustees 'to get them off my back'.

4. Supporting inter-organisational learning and collaboration. For example, discussions among the larger charities led to plans for a collaboration in a generic legacy campaign – a constructive alternative to 'grinding each other down in competition', as one participant put it.

The CIH Good Practice Unit.   The Chartered Institute of Housing established its Good Practice Unit (GPU) in 1994 to produce 'Good Practice Briefings' and to run what was meant to be a back-up enquiry service. Good Practice Briefings remain part of the GPU's service to subscribers. Three briefings are issued each year. They address the issues raised with the GPU and combine 'how to do it' checklists with examples of leading practice, plus contacts and references. However, GPU staff found that while subscribers appreciated the briefings, they liked to talk to someone. Moreover, the key to their satisfaction *was the provision of actual documents* showing how a local authority or housing association in similar circumstances had tackled the issue. Hence GPU staff started to build up a library of such internal working documents. The growth of this service was subscriber-led. From one member of staff in 1994 the GPU grew to a complement of six in mid-1998 when the service was handling about 4,000 enquiries per year. Document provision accounted for some 80% of staff time and was judged crucial in justifying the GPU's fees. The subscription renewal rate was 98% – only a few small organisations had cancelled.

The key to subscribers obtaining the documents they want was the GPU database – in early 1998, 400 topics were covered with some 5800 records of which about half are supported by documents. It is not unusual for the more popular topics to be supported by 50 documented examples – helping to ensure that subscribers obtained a good match. In this context 'a good match' was a document from an organisation comparable to the enquirers own – a small rural housing association, say, or a special needs housing association in an inner city. All such real examples were included – the GPU did not grade or filter the material it received. Examination of the supporting documents and production of the 10–15 line summary for inclusion on the database were time consuming, and obtaining the documents was always a challenge. Subscribers often failed to send any documents when they joined, as they were supposed to – and needed to be chased. The documents most readily obtainable (Annual Reports, Housing Strategy Statements, media articles etc) were not the ones of most interest to subscribers. The GPU experimented with different ways of obtaining documents and in 1998 had a development officer visiting local authorities and housing associations in order to market the service and obtain documents.

Findings

1. BPB is very rarely used by social enterprises; those that do, or that intend to, are almost always the larger ones.

One of the aims of the survey reported in Paton and Payne (1997) was to identify managers who had used BPB. The intention was to follow these up in order to establish the nature and extent of any benefits that had been realised. In the event, although many respondents were willing to receive a follow-up phone call, only a small number also claimed to have had 'substantial' experience of a systematic BPB project. When these were interviewed it soon became apparent that none of them were carrying out all (or even nearly all) of the steps recommended by BPB experts. They had not, for example, visited their benchmarking partner(s) to understand how superior performance was achieved, nor worked out how to adopt and adapt the practices of others. A similar picture emerged from enquiries through consultants, networks and professional bodies: widespread interest, but very few clear-cut examples. And just as the best examples involved larger organisations, so the most convincing and well-informed *aspirations* concerning BPB were expressed by larger organisations. For example, one chief executive wanted to carry out a project on the processes associated with member services and hoped to persuade a number of even larger 'household name' membership organisations to join a 'club'.

Even in federal and branch-based organisations, which might be thought to offer considerable scope for 'internal benchmarking', BPB seems to be unusual, though efforts are made – such as in the Disability Homes Network[20] (see chapter 6) and the Groundwork Federation.[21] Federal nonprofits generally expect some standard reporting to the centre, and facilitate peer sharing and learning between the managers of the separate units through 'handbooks', procedures, working groups and annual conferences, but it would be misleading to call this BPB. These activities are seldom marked by the systematic search for and attempt to transfer 'best practice'. And even when they are, performance measures may not be owned by local units, and performance improvement agendas are easily caught up in sensitive centre-unit relations. This seems to have been an issue at Groundwork and is frankly discussed in the CARE case described by Letts, Ryan et al. (1999). So although at any one time various formal and informal performance comparison and performance improvement efforts may be underway, these different efforts are rarely carried through in the rationalistic manner advocated by proponents of BPB.

2. Nonprofit managers use the terms 'best practice' and 'benchmarking' to encompass a range of related activities most of which are used more frequently than BPB itself. The activities which may be cited by managers as an example of benchmarking or the pursuit of best practice can be grouped in the following seven categories:

1. *'Broad brush' comparisons* – using data-sets largely based on public domain information created by umbrella, regulatory or professional bodies.

2. *'Fine grain' comparisons* – using purpose-built, confidential data- sets created by consultants, trade or professional bodies ('Fundratios' is the exemplar).

3. *Ad-hoc visits* – informally arranged through professional and industrial networks, to find out more about what appears to be a well-run process.

4. *'Recipe copying'* – seeking policy statements, pro-forma, process maps, good practice checklists, written procedures etc that may assist the introduction or improvement of similar practices in one's own organisation (as per the CIH 'Good Practice Unit').

5. *Purchase cost comparisons* – either through networks, specialist consultants or consortia; used to track and reduce the cost of major purchases (eg vehicles, professional services, banking).

6. *Standard ratings* – using a diagnostic model (usually the Excellence Model – see chapter 7) to identify strengths and weaknesses compared to the scores of other organisations held on a database.[22]

7. *Conformity to a recognised standard* – by gaining third-party accreditation eg for ISO 9000 or IIP, or subscribing to a Code of Practice.

Most of these practices pre-date BPB by many years (the Centre for Inter-Firm comparison, which administers the Fundratios scheme, has been in existence providing essentially the same service for nearly 40 years). But this does not mean that nothing has changed, or that the interest in BPB has made no difference. Most of these practices, especially those involving measurement or involving searching and matching to find an appropriate organisation, have been considerably facilitated by the new information and communication technologies, creating new opportunities for the provision of information services. It seems that the currency of BPB has stimulated more managers to use these methods, or to use them more often.

3.   For most nonprofit managers, benchmarking means performance comparisons, and this element of BPB is of great interest to them. Such comparisons are often undertaken, either as planned exercises or opportunistically – though, as elsewhere, they are often problematic and inconclusive.

Survey respondents and workshop participants reported a range of different ways of comparing performance, and showed strong interest in new possibilities – especially use of the Excellence Model (BQF 1997). These comparisons are carried out in a variety of ways. First, managers cooperate with and are interested in statistical surveys and reports on a wide range of topics (eg voluntary income, shop performance, remuneration) that appear regularly in the 'trade press'. Second, informally conducted comparisons seem to be common, and are often carried out through industry and professional networks. For example, the HR manager of one large national childcare charity approached her counterparts elsewhere to try to determine whether her figures for staff turnover were unusually high (they cooperated, although technically competitors). Third, some charities join together to commission their own more detailed performance comparisons – again, usually through industry or professional networks, or in response to an initiative by respected consultants.

Lots of examples were provided by interviewees and workshop participants of the practical difficulties involved in making comparisons between organisations. These difficulties arose even when dealing with a generic function like HR (as in the example referred to above). In general, the problems lay not in agreeing what to measure, but in agreeing the terms involved. For example, people might quickly determine that they needed to measure staff turnover and training. But agreeing operational definitions of these terms would be another matter. Each organisation already had its own way of deciding what counted as 'staff' 'turnover' 'training', etc. In due course, therefore, the issue might be one of deciding how important the differences in the structuring of existing accounting and measurement systems were, and whether it was worth trying to overcome the differences or compensate for them in some not too onerous way. Such difficulties are familiar, not just in the broader BPB literature, but concerning nonprofits (Rooney 1997; Foot 1998) and may be accentuated by measurement systems being relatively underdeveloped in many nonprofits. Whatever the reasons, some efforts at performance comparison fail in consequence while others (including Fundratios) face a constant undercurrent of criticism about the time and effort they require, and whether they are really worth it.

4. The concepts of best and good practice have enormous appeal for nonprofit managers but their usage of these terms is not that which is implied by BPB .

In the survey results, interviews and discussions, great interest was expressed in being able to access 'best' and 'good' practice (eg as a possible facility of a benchmarking club). It was also noticeable that these terms were used often (and interchangeably) in discussions, and frequently appear in popular discussion of organisation and management issues in sector and professional publications. The attraction of these concepts for managers (in all sorts of organisations) has been noticed by consultants, professional bodies and support agencies – as evidenced by the names chosen (eg 'The Best Practice Club') and the services offered (eg, the 'Managing best practice' series of cases and good practice guidance published by the Industrial Society). Clearly, however, the use of the term 'best practice' in these contexts is not restricted to particular arrangements that have been shown to be the best (or even rather good) as a result of search, measurement and comparison – as the methodology of BPB implies. Rather, the terms are used much more loosely and pragmatically – as illustrated by the CIH Good Practice Unit, described above.

5. BPB can be used to good effect by nonprofits but it requires a very substantial investment of time and effort.

Although the research discovered very few 'proper' BPB projects, it appeared that where projects did not just adopt some of the language of BPB but followed its prescriptions relatively closely, they did result in significant change and improvement. These achievements were neither as great nor as easily realised as had been hoped – hardly unusual in organisational change. But they were acknowledged and instanced by a range of participants, including, in the cases of the Royal Society for the Protection of Birds and the Disability Homes Network, internal sceptics. Of course, one can still ask how much these improvements had to do with the actual content of BPB, as opposed to the fact that the processes received sharply increased managerial attention over a prolonged period. But if, as seemed to be the case, the operational elements of BPB contributed ideas and helped build legitimacy, while the aspirational elements help sustain managerial attention during the necessarily slow and painstaking work of carrying through changes, then BPB is adding value.

That said, all the cases of BPB also indicate the scale and duration of the investment that BPB requires, how other changes may be needed in order to realise potential gains, how the chosen 'best practices' are then unevenly implemented, and how different players in a BPB project may, for all kinds of reasons, pursue the opportunities it presents more or less vigorously.

6. The contexts and purposes associated with the use of BPB in nonprofits tend to be different from those originally associated with the technique.

BPB emerged as a way of improving key processes that were subject to major changes and uncertainty, in the context of intense competition. Although officially limited to performance comparison, the Fundratios scheme matches these characteristics well. But in all the other cases identified, BPB was used by nonprofit managers for rather different reasons, usually in much less competitive contexts where the *need* for improved methods as well as the nature of any changes were likely to be contentious. A common theme seems to have been a concern to review taken-for-granted arrangements, and to open up and challenge closed organisational cultures. BPB was a way of bringing external perspectives and views into the organisation, with the elements of empowerment and delegation making it an acceptable way of challenging staff in semi-autonomous units, and of limiting the amount of senior management attention required. Though not, of course, without difficulties, this use of BPB seems to have achieved some success in the cases reported – as it has done in parts of the public sector when pursued for similar reasons (Foot 1998).

Discussion: making sense of BPB

What is striking about nonprofit managers' use of BPB is that many of them readily embrace the terminology and undertake particular elements – but only exceptionally do they embark on BPB in the systematic way recommended by its proponents. So why do managers chose one or more of the related activities (see proposition 2), rather than BPB itself? Concepts from behavioural theory (Cyert and March 1963) suggest an explanation. Managers concerned to improve the performance have to do two things:

1. They have to decide where to focus *scarce attention*. This involves choosing how much of available management and staff time to invest in particular processes so as to have the best chance of securing (and/or generating support for) improvements sufficient to impact organisational performance.

2. They need to acquire and/or develop ideas for *how* different activities can be improved. Given the cognitive, political and organisational limits to rationality, and the scarcity of attention, this often means 'satisficing', aiming simply for 'good enough' solutions to apparent problems.

BPB assists with both of these – through careful comparisons it aims to pinpoint where there is scope for improvement, while at the same time identifying and accessing know-how about how to achieve the improvement. However, it is clear (from both the literature and the case studies) that the information-handling (transaction) costs can be very high indeed. The leader of a BPB project must have the time and/or the staff to undertake most or all of the following:

1. Identify suitable partners – both crucial and problematic.

2. Secure their cooperation, agree the scope of the study and engage a third party.

3. Negotiate the metrics to be used, gather, share and analyse the information – again problematic, as the cases illustrate.

4. Visit and be visited as appropriate.

5. Discuss internally how best to adapt and introduce the ideas gained – which may raise change management issues on a grand scale.

This much commitment of time and effort may not seem worthwhile, or it may be judged too uncertain[23] – or it may not even be a realistic option, if managers are suffering the role overload that is common in smaller organisations. This presumably explains why many surveys have found BPB to be practised mainly by large organisations – they possess the managerial 'slack' to invest, and they operate on a scale to make such investment worthwhile. Interestingly, even in UK local authorities (much larger organisations than most social enterprises) the cost-effectiveness of BPB is being questioned (Bovaird 1999). By contrast, each one of the family of BPB-related activities requires far less attention, and thus they better match the manager's concern to operate briskly in a boundedly rational manner (indeed, 'shortage of time' was repeatedly chosen in Paton and Payne's survey (1997) or offered in discussions as a reason for not pursuing BPB).

Thus performance comparisons may help managers allocate their scarce attention even if they do not lead directly to performance improvement – perhaps because they reassure that performance appears to be good enough, or by alerting them to environmental trends with strategic significance. Alternatively, performance comparisons may help build a case for expecting improvement in a particular area, even if the improvements are sought other than by BPB. Or they may be used to identify possible sources of expertise to help develop, say, a new and struggling line of activity – through an *ad hoc* visit. Such visits are low cost and flexible even if they are dismissed as 'industrial tourism' by those committed to 'proper' BPB (Unnamed 1997). 'Recipe copying' is another way of accessing improvement ideas quickly. Both can be seen as examples of 'problemistic search' (Cyert and March 1963) – but since they take the search beyond what is 'locally available' they offer the possibility of advancing faster than through incremental improvement of existing practice.

Hence the use of limited elements of BPB that make the best use of scarce attention can be seen as displaying bounded rationality, and such action is generally intelligent and adaptive, as behavioural theory demonstrated years ago. Such an interpretation would of course also apply in other sectors, especially small businesses, and is consistent with the findings reported in the surveys cited above.

Conclusions

Three points seem to stand out from this exploration of BPB and BPB-related activity among social enterprises. The first is that, once again, efforts to pin down performance and to identify the sources of success through measurement achieve only limited success. Of course there are differences in aspects of performance and these show up in the measurements – but the issue is comparability, and that is always in question. One ex-participant in Fundratios said 'It was disillusioning; it made us look inefficient. But it is much harder to raise money for mental health, compared to children and animals'. The general pattern in BPB seems to be that the more comparable two processes are in terms of scale and context, the smaller the performance differences between them – *or* the more obviously problematic the differences in measurement procedure between the two contexts. Indeed, the BPB practitioner literature consistently warns against trying to achieve consistent measurement schemes in order to establish which process *really* works best. Such certainty is a chimera and a distraction from understanding other ways of doing things and gathering ideas for process improvement. For example, Lincoln and Price (1996) include as one of their five tips for success 'Don't fall for the best-in-class fallacy'. They argue that the 'class' in question has to be pragmatically defined in relation to the aims and needs of the team doing the BM study – a robust and self-confident relativism with far-reaching implications for the notion of 'best practice'. The contrast between the official recipes for BPB and the practice as it is usually reported, is striking.

This leads to the second general point, concerning the ways in which BPB is enacted. This seems to be happening in three different ways:

First, the technique has occasionally been implemented in its more or less original or 'proper' form, albeit mostly in different situations and for rather different purposes – though still to good effect.

Second, its prestige has encouraged use of a set of simpler practices that can borrow some of its legitimacy while being appropriate in a much wider range of situations.

Third, its prestige has given rhetorical currency to the terms 'best practice' and 'benchmarking' which are now used refer to a wide range of activities that would have been undertaken anyway.

The final point concerns the interest in performance improvement displayed by the managers in the case study of organisations, and the different ways in which this interest can be expressed and described. Of course, the research does not provide a formal basis for judging how widespread such interest is. But to the extent that a comparable concern with performance improvement is expressed through the extensive networking activity that takes place among social enterprises, it would seem to be fairly widespread. Such networking is epitomised by the professional bodies – such as (but by no means only), the Chartered Institute of Housing, and the Institute of Charity Fundraising Managers who were involved with two of the cases. These groupings represent 'communities of practice' within which experience and ideas are exchanged. Interestingly, the good practice document library at the CIH closely parallels the knowledge sharing and knowledge management activity that goes on within large distributed corporations tackling similar tasks in different contexts.[24] In any event, such networking activity is not new, and when the more rhetorical elements of BPB are stripped away, there is much that is familiar in this practice. Some, at least, among social enterprises have been 'talking prose all their lives' – even if, for others, the currency of BPB has provided a powerful stimulant and justification for starting to seek external comparisons and ideas.

Sources and resources

A lively introduction to Best Practice Benchmarking for social enterprises is Letts, Ryan et al.'s (1999) *High Performance Nonprofit Organisations: Managing Upstream for Greater Impact*. This presents the case for, and illustrates, a range of performance improvement methods. It has one chapter specifically on Best Practice Benchmarking, with a useful account of practice. Beyond this, many 'how to do it' guides exist, and more or less appropriate ones can usually be identified quite easily through the relevant professional associations or by visiting a few websites.

An extended version of the Fundratios case can be found in a journal article (Paton 1999). Much more detail on the other cases is available in published working papers (Paton and Payne 1999 a, 1999b, 1999c).

6 Do 'Kitemarks' Improve and Demonstrate Performance?

Introduction: the audit explosion

When achievements are hard to measure managers have always had another way to build and maintain the confidence of their sponsors and paymasters. This fallback is to show that the organization is well run, embodying the most appropriate modern methods and systems ('rationalised practices', in the terminology of institutional theory). One way of demonstrating this is through the use of *audit* and *certification* – that is, the independent verification that an organisation's procedures for an area of activity conform to a recognised standard of good practice. In some respects this is very familiar. The financial audit is an institution in the fullest sense of the term – widespread, taken-for-granted, and continually reproduced even as the accounting systems on which it is practised change. Likewise, in many countries various professional activities undertaken by nonprofits – teaching, residential care, social housing - operate under supervisory regimes that involve inspection visits. Then there are the appraisals of nonprofit governance and reporting carried out by consumer watchdogs, such as the National Charities Information Bureau in the US.

A new form of audit. Nevertheless, over the last decade or so, an 'audit explosion' has been taking place (Power 1997) and, with concerns about probity and transparency now an international issue, this trend seems likely to continue. Audit is now an important means by which societal expectations of rationality, control and effectiveness are given expression (Powell and DiMaggio 1991). As part of this general trend, a new variant of audit has become increasingly prominent. It differs from the various examples just mentioned by having the following combination of characteristics:

- *Voluntarily undertaken,* more or less, as an indication of high, not just basic, standards – and usually displayed on letterheads and publicity material.

- *Independent certification by a 'third party,'* for a fee – these are not inspections carried out by a statutory supervisory agency, *eg* as a licensing condition.

- Application to broader *governance and management systems,* - and not just to professional activities or financial controls.

- *Regular visiting with scope for interviews and observation,* - rather than relying on documentary reports and declarations.

relying on documentary reports and declarations.

The phenomenon of 'badges' and 'kitemarks' – colloquial terms in the UK for such externally accredited standards – is becoming widespread among all sorts of organisations. The best known example is probably the ISO 9000 standards for quality assurance. This has been widely adopted in parts of the private sector, and has also been adopted by some social enterprises (meanwhile a simpler form of quality assurance has been developed for small nonprofits – see Farley 1997). The UK government has sponsored 'Investors in People' (IIP), a generic standard for human resource management and staff development, and this has been adopted by all sorts of public and private organisations, including some social enterprises. It has also created a 'Chartermark' award for public services that meet a set of standards for quality and responsiveness. Other standards-based initiatives are underway. For example, in the UK the embryonic Audit Bureau of Fundraising Organisations (ABFO), building on ideas already well established in Scandinavia and Holland, is trying to establish a set of standards and a recognised brand that will address issues of public confidence over the solicitation and use of funds from the public. And the NGO community looks set to become involved in two ways: the British Government is working with UK NGOs to develop a code of practice 'People in Aid' for the management of staff in overseas agencies. At the same time, the SA 8000 standard for corporate social responsibility builds in a role for NGOs in appraising the social performance of companies in third world countries supplying goods to Western retailers.

Policy and management controversies. The reasons for this upsurge of interest are not hard to discern. For the leaders of organisations, such voluntary audits and awards promise a way of raising, reinforcing, and publicising their standards of performance, and also of differentiating themselves in the marketplace for contracts, grants and donations. For interested external parties the awards promise reliable information about internal processes (reducing the information asymmetries). And to the governmental and other bodies who promote them, the awards promise a means of stimulating higher standards without incurring the costs and responsibilities of direct supervision. It is a form of regulation that is market-friendly, self-financing and based on choice (Power 1997). So everyone gains – an ideal solution, surely?

In fact, such externally certified standards are highly controversial. In the UK, the ABFO standard has been discreetly opposed by the professional bodies representing Chief Executives and Fundraisers, and so far very few organisations have sought accreditation from ABFO. The ISO 9000 standard in particular has attracted considerable criticism (famously, by the popular cartoon character Dilbert). A lesser degree of cynicism towards other awards has been common, especially when organisations possessing them are seen as behaving inappropriately (eg companies with IIP making large numbers of employees redundant). Opposition to the introduction of kitemarks has been voiced within the NGO community on the grounds that they further extend the power of northern donor organisations at the expense of the autonomy and vitality of southern NGOs (Thom 1999).

Equally, however, other sector leaders and managers of voluntary agencies welcome the development of recognised standards and believe they are essential in order to maintain the confidence of the public (Kingman 1999). Indeed, the Red Cross played a key role in setting in motion what became the 'People in Aid' Code Of Best Practice. As a later section makes clear, these opposing practitioner views are mirrored by the limited, though contradictory, research on this form of audit.

This chapter explores the issues the awards raise for sector leaders, trustees and managers. As usual, it proceeds by reviewing the relevant literature, and goes on to describe the focus of the research and the case study organisations. The main findings are then presented and discussed. First, however, the two awards on which the research came to focus need to be described.

The two awards

ISO 9000. The International Standards Organisation (ISO) 9000 series is a set of procedural standards for quality management systems (also referred to as 'quality assurance'). Such systems are based on a comprehensive set of documented procedures to which staff are expected to conform. This approach was developed originally in armaments manufacture, but attracted increasing attention in the 1980s as quality became a major management preoccupation, spreading into contractor/supplier relations in other manufacturing industries, and then also services, including the public sector. Reflecting their origin in manufacturing, the ISO 9000 standards embody a conception of product and service quality in terms of *consistent conformity with an explicit specification*. It is up to organisations and/or their customers to set those specifications, which may be high or low. Implementation of ISO 9000 involves making procedures, including those for review and improvement, explicit ('say what you do'), documenting them in a quality manual, ensuring those procedures are followed ('do what you say'), and checking that they are effective. Accreditation involves an external assessment, followed by twice-yearly audits to ensure the procedures are being maintained.

Investors In People (IIP). This award was launched in 1991 following several years of development and trials with leading private and public organisations (Alberga, Tyson et al. 1997). It was promoted by the British Government in order to improve economic performance – by reducing the skills shortages that quickly triggered inflationary pressures whenever expansionary economic policies were pursued. IIP is based on four principles:

1. Commitment to staff development and recognition of its increasing significance.

2. Systematic review of development needs of all staff in relation to current and future business priorities.

3. Focused and sustained efforts to train and develop staff both on and off

the job from recruitment onwards.

4.   Careful review of training and development activities to ensure the highest possible return.

Organisations are assessed on their application of these principles. An award is generally for three years, after which a full re-assessment is required, but recently annual re-assessment has become an option.

Hence, although the two awards address very different issues, they both concern the existence and effective functioning of particular management systems, and they share a similar audit methodology based on documentary evidence, interview and inspection.   It is these common elements, and their organisational ramifications as an increasingly common means of establishing one's managerial credentials, which were the focus of the research.

Do you get the award, or does the award get you?

A major limitation of existing research on third-party certification is that it almost always concerns a particular award and appears in the literatures of the fields covered by those awards – HRM, quality, fundraising, and so on (the important exception is Power 1997). However, whatever their field, the main difference among the various reports and studies is between those that are favourable and those that are critical, and so the literature is reviewed on that basis.

Favourable accounts. Most research and reporting comes under this heading, variously claiming that the award in question leads to desirable outcomes, achieving more or less what it is supposed to, both internally and externally. Although sometimes undertaken independently – van Veen's (1995) discussion of the Central Bureau of Fundraising in the Netherlands is an example – such studies are often sponsored by bodies that promote the awards, or undertaken by professionals active in the fields. For IIP in particular a considerable body of work, much of it of a promotional or 'how to do it' nature, has been produced and is referenced in the IIP research directory (1996). Regarding ISO 9000, the studies commissioned by Lloyds Register Quality Assurance (1996, undated) are fairly typical of the genre. They report that registration was associated with markedly superior financial performance on a range of measures; that the perceived internal benefits of ISO 9000 (increased efficiency, productivity and management control) were greater than expected and exceed the external (marketing) benefits, which usually prompted seeking the award; that these benefits are also enjoyed by small firms; and that the level of disappointment with the award is very low.

Unfortunately, the difficulties in making such claims are considerable. The evaluation of IIP commissioned by the UK Department of Employment, who sponsored IIP, illustrates these important methodological issues.   This evaluation tracked the experience of 1,800 organisations (some involved in Investors, some not) over a three-year period, through a series of surveys. It produced a series of publications (Spilsbury, Atkinson et al. 1994; Spilsbury,

Moralee et al. 1995b) culminating in 'The return on Investors' (Hillage and Moralee 1996) in which the authors reported on:

- Employers reasons for pursuing the award – which were mainly to do with better training systems, higher skill levels and improved workforce motivation, but which often also included considerations to do with external image, quality, customer satisfaction, and improving management systems generally.

- What was involved in achieving the award – which was generally seen as harder to achieve than expected, though very few dropped out along the way.

- The impact on practice, which was widely seen to be significant and positive – three-quarters of those who anticipated training benefits said they had achieved them.

- The impact on business performance – where key findings included 60% reporting improved workforce outcomes (understanding, skills, commitment, etc) and a large majority reporting some direct or indirect improvements in such key areas as quality and productivity or anticipating that these would feed through in due course.

Although the author's overall assessment ends up extremely positive – 'Investors is a successful initiative…Investors delivers better training and skills… Investors tackles the parts other initiatives don't reach…' (Hillage and Moralee 1996, pp 71–72) – they readily acknowledge a series of limitations, anomalies and missing outcomes. These include:

- Companies obtaining the award for existing good practice, with IIP as such adding little or nothing – the authors refer to this as 'badging'.

- 'Emulation' – companies copying some or all of the practices required by Investors, but without bothering to obtain accreditation (this can be seen either as a hidden benefit of IIP, or as raising a question about the additional costs and benefits associated with third party-assessment).

- The failure to find associations between IIP and objective indicators of business performance – comparisons between early Investors, newly recognised Investors and non-participants in IIP as regards labour costs, financial turnover and two measures of profitability were all inconclusive, as was a multivariate analysis.

- Achievement of IIP being associated with *higher* (though falling) sickness rates and *higher* labour turnover rates, compared to non-participants; and *not* being associated with higher, or differentially increasing, levels of training activity when compared to non-participants.

- The issue of relative cost-effectiveness – for example, between 60 and 70 per cent of IIP employers reported that the benefits they had achieved regarding skills, motivations and staff relations could have been achieved by other means.

These points do not justify a claim that IIP does not 'work'. They do mean that, not for the first time, the attempt to prove and quantify the impact of a large-scale, 'broad aim' programme was unsuccessful – despite substantial and competent research effort. Moreover, the study is far less conclusive than its authors imply for other reasons. It is essentially a survey of employers' *beliefs* about the benefits of IIP, and reports of their experiences of adopting the IIP standard in very varied contexts. As such, it suffers from a serious (but common) methodological weakness – a reliance on a telephone interview with single informants, who were in many cases at least, in the role of 'product champion'. As one of the authors acknowledged, it is very likely this introduced a positive bias into the results (Hillage 1998). Finally, since it only tracked involvement over three years, the important issue of the longer-term effects and whether benefits are *sustained*, could not be addressed. Hence, although a rich source of information on the thinking of managers closely involved with IIP, what the study actually demonstrates are the difficulties in making judgements about the overall effectiveness of the award as a means of raising and demonstrating standards of good practice in HRM.

By comparison, other 'favourable' studies of both IIP and ISO 9000 are methodologically much weaker (variously: no consideration of 'badging' and 'emulation'; an absence of longitudinal data and controls to address causality issues; no exploration of different industrial contexts; reliance on single informants, etc). Since those who lead organisational reforms often develop accounts of what was achieved that others in a position to make judgements would seriously dispute (Brunsson and Olsen 1993), this body of work cannot really be relied on.

Critical and sceptical studies. Aside from the charge that the awards are vehicles for professional interests (Bell, Taylor et al. 2001), the critics of these awards have made two main claims.

First, the awards are *systematically ambiguous and misleading*, in that they promise far more than they deliver. The argument is presented most generally and powerfully by Power 'The ambiguity of auditing is not a methodological problem but a substantive fact' Power (1997, p 6). He argues that audit failure is almost impossible to define, as those who have taken auditors to court almost always discover to their cost. Auditing and accounting 'facts' are tacitly negotiated, subject to economic pressures, collusion, and even the desire to *avoid* finding mistakes. Thus inconsistencies, deceptions and even absurdities have been reported in both IIP and ISO 9000 assessment procedures (Seddon 1997; Bell, Taylor et al. 2001). Moreover, as has often been pointed out in relation to ISO 9000, the audit simply confirms that standards at whatever level are being maintained. Thus 'Audit can provide assurance that the system works well even when substantive performance is poor... As systems become the primary focus for inspectors and auditors, technical difficulties of performance measurement become invisible' (Power 1997, p 60). This becomes doubly misleading because, as (Bell, Taylor et al. 2001) comment concerning IIP, and Power argues more generally, audit practices commonly draw on emancipatory rhetorics of accountability, transparency, self-correction and the learning organisation, even while the procedural realities are essentially bureaucratic.

Second, the awards are *wasteful and distracting*. Once an award is being sought, organisational activities within the scope of the award have to be carried out in ways that are *auditable*. This gives rise to the phenomena of *colonisation* (the implanting of new practices and procedures to serve the information demands of audit); and *decoupling* (the creation of compartmentalised systems unconnected to the real work which goes on as usual) – to use Power's terms. Even if these are merely common rather than inevitable results, the awards embody an unhelpfully mechanistic philosophy which points organisations in the wrong direction – separating planning and doing, focusing on control rather than improvement, and failing to address issues of culture and values (Seddon 1997; Bell, Taylor et al. 2001).

The critics highlight issues that need to be examined and they open up alternative perspectives. But as with the reports favourable to the awards, one has to take account of the methodological limitations – much of the reportage on ISO 9000 and IIP is either unsystematic or not intended to offer an overall appraisal. Power, by contrast, presents a general social theory of the growth of audit, which is broadly based in a range of theorising and research. However, at a more mundane, organisational level, its implications are far less clear. His main criticisms – concerning the exaggerated claims made on behalf of audit, and the dysfunctions to which it can give rise – are compatible with a much more limited justification of audit practices either in general or in particular instances. For example, one could accept Power's arguments and still view audit as one useful technique among others, not very reliable or well founded, but on balance stimulating more beneficial behaviours than bad, a useful contribution to the 'muddling through' that often characterises political and organisational life (Lindblom 1959).

The contrast between the accounts of the awards based on the views of those whose roles involve responsibility for promoting and maintaining the systems and those who are obliged to enact them without particular conviction are striking. It is unclear how far these reflect different experiences, or the public and private faces of the same experience (frontstage and backstage, in the terms of Goffman 1959). So far only one study has begun to show how the very different findings of supporters and critics may be reconciled. This is the work by North, Blackburn et al. (1998) on the use and non-use of ISO 9000 in small firms, which utilised both a telephone survey and detailed case studies. They found that:

- ISO registration varies enormously between industrial sectors, depending partly on the appropriateness of reliance on explicit specifications, but also on industry *norms*. In some areas this amounted to market coercion unrelated to real system requirements.

- Many owner-managers offered convincing explanations for why they were unimpressed by the 'quality panic' in general and ISO 9000 in particular. Quality was important to them, but explicit quality specifications were not practicable. What the researchers called 'complex informal approaches' were therefore a rational way of handling quality issues. Externally monitored, paper-based quality systems were therefore seen as 'over-engineered', generating significant start-up and running costs, consuming management and staff time, and introducing rigidities.

• Managers who had adopted ISO 9000 held a wide range of views regarding it, and their views often developed over time as they went through the registration process (with cognitive dissonance a possible explanation).

• In general, the arguments of both enthusiasts and sceptics concerning ISO 9000 received support – since much depended on how it was used, and the sectoral context of that use. The award did not guarantee any particular outcome, and was rarely an easy option.

These findings with their emphasis on the context and manner of use of ISO 9000 are in line with reflections and recommendations on the use of Quality Assurance and standards-based approaches in social services offered by James (1992).

The approach of the research and the main cases

As usual, the research proceeded through key informant interviews and a search for 'early adopter' organisations in a range of different settings. The case enquiries focused on the following themes from the literature – which were also issues often referred to by key informants. First and most importantly, North, Blackburn et al.'s (1998) conclusions encouraged a shift of emphasis, away from the awards' *effects on* social enterprises, and towards an interest in the different ways in which subscribing to an award was *used* by managers. From this perspective key questions concerned the reasons managers had for pursuing the award, how the award was seen as serving particular internal or external purposes, and how subscribing to the award fitted with or was shaped by the organisational context. Some possible patterns of use were provided by concepts from both sides of the argument (eg emulation, 'badging', colonisation and decoupling). In addition, the controversies in the literature highlighted the fact that the awards were often controversial, and so it would be particularly important to explore as far as possible the range of views towards an award within an organisation. Finally, the observations of Power and others concerning the problematic nature of the audit process, and the discretion that auditors had in enacting their roles, meant these became another focus of enquiry (and the auditors themselves were interviewed).

Originally, it was intended to carry out two case studies of each award, all drawn from different fields. In addition, however, as dissimilar patterns of use emerged more clearly as an issue in the research, the experience of a federal organisation (the Disability Homes Network – referred to in the last chapter) in respect of ISO 9000 was seen as significant. This therefore became the subject of a fifth case. Descriptions of these five organisations follow – more information on the research methods is available elsewhere (Foot and Paton 1999a; 1999b).

Standish Community High School (SCHS) is a secondary school in Wigan in Lancashire. In 1999 it was teaching 1,050 pupils and employed 65 teachers and 30 support staff. In the late 1980s, the school had an intake of only 90 pupils per year and such poor exam results that it was under threat of closure. Through his involvement with a group of six businesses working with the local Training and Enterprise Council on work-related training, Geoff Ashton, the recently appointed Headteacher, heard about IIP before it was launched. He decided to use it as the vehicle for improving school performance. SCHS achieved IIP status in January 1993, and was the first secondary school in the country to do so featuring as one of a number of case studies in the information about the award published by Investors in People UK (Associates 1995). It has since been re-accredited on two occasions. A wide array of people-related initiatives have been pursued at SCHS and these have made a point of including all staff, not just teachers (eg a lunchtime supervisor had recently completed a certificate in counselling, funded by the school). Training is well resourced (2.2% of the staff budget) and 'demand led' in the context of a training needs analysis undertaken within the line management relationship. Residential weekend meetings of all staff and governors are a regular event, and much of the decision making is through open discussion in cross-curricular teams and staff meetings. In 1999 their examination results and attendance records were excellent placing them in the top 5% of those schools with a pupil intake marked by the same level of deprivation. Their annual intake had increased to 200 pupils each year and was oversubscribed by 60 names. They had achieved Language College status and the Chief Inspector of Schools had declared they were in the 'outstanding' category.

The Shaw Trust aims to help people with disabilities and mental health problems to make the most of their employment potential. It supports 2,500+ people in supported placements and open employment schemes, and provides work preparation and skills training. The Trust works closely with over 2,000 'host' companies (including major employers) as well as Social Services departments, health authorities, TECs and central government. The Trust was started in 1981 and now has a £20-million turnover with more than 200 staff covering England, Scotland and Wales. The majority of the staff work from home, organised into area and regional teams. They support a caseload of employees in a geographical patch. They also negotiate with and advise employers and referral agencies. It claims to have been the first national charity to achieve IIP status in 1995. IIP covers all the staff of the Shaw Trust (those who work within the organisation) but it does not cover the clients of the organisation. The Shaw Trust is often their legal employer, but the clients work on the terms and conditions of the host employer and it is part of The Shaw Trust's job to ensure that their client receives the same training and development opportunities as their workplace colleagues.

'The House' is a multi-purpose resource centre for the elderly run by the social services department of a large city. It has about 30 places for day care, five community rehabilitation beds, seven respite beds and four emergency beds – and seven residents left over from its days as a residential home. The Centre employs 23 people, not including the catering staff who are employed by the council's works department. In 1992, when it was a residential home, The House become known as the first care organisation in Europe to become registered under the precursor of ISO 9000 (George and Casson 1992; Humphrey and Hildrew 1992). This registration had been continued since then.

Typetalk is a telephone relay service for people with hearing impairment or loss. The hearing person speaks to the operator who types verbatim what is said; this comes up simultaneously as text on a screen for the deaf person to read and respond to. The role of the operator is purely as a conduit – they are not required to interpret or translate, unless requested. Typetalk is part of the Royal National Institute for the Deaf (RNID), but run as a discrete operation. Managers think of themselves as part of the telecommunications industry and as a call centre; the majority of senior staff come from a business background, with several from BT. It obtained ISO accreditation in 1993. At that time the rest of the RNID, or at least major parts of it, were expected to follow. Due to changes of policy and senior personnel, this did not happen. But Typetalk has retained its ISO 9000 status.

Disability Homes Network (DHN) is a federal organisation with a head office and 160+ residential homes or other service units across the country. In 1992 the organisation decided to promote ISO 9000 registration within the network and 12 homes volunteered to pilot it at service unit level. After some three years work, eight units were accredited. However developing reservations about the appropriateness of the standard, the costs involved, and some difficulties concerning how it was being implemented across a decentralised network, led to a reconsideration. By 1996 ISO 9000 accreditation was no longer being promoted by the centre (though three units chose to maintain their accreditation). Instead, DHN's own quality standards and review process are used to address quality issues.

Findings

The principal findings are presented in terms of three propositions along with a summary of the more significant data that underpins them.

1. The interpretation, use and meaning of an award or standard can vary considerably between organisations and even organisational units.

In two of the case organisations (and in others that were described to the researchers), the standards were used as vehicles for formalising important processes during or after a period of rapid growth. Thus at Typetalk, ISO was used from very early days to manage expansion in a context where 'consistency and predictability is key to quality'. The HR Director at the Shaw Trust – who as HR Manager had led on implementation – said 'IIP was used to put in place the foundations of HR that were not put in place at the beginning' but that the rapid growth had made a necessity. By contrast, as a local authority school, Standish Community High School, was no stranger to formal procedures and here IIP was used as the vehicle for a *cultural* transformation associated with the quite dramatic turnaround of what had been a failing organisation.

However, the differences between uses of ISO 9000 that arose at DHN were particularly marked. In 'Home A' the ISO documentation did not include any care procedures or standards, beyond the induction training for minimum staff skills. In the view of the manager, it was an inappropriate system for such matters and the procedure manuals referred to other documents that contained professional good practice and the required standards. Instead, he had used ISO to achieve systematic management of the support services – such as admissions, finance, personnel, supplies, visitors, security, maintenance etc. It was seen as time consuming to keep up to date and difficult to make relevant for the 90+ staff, but they used some of their volunteers to come in one day a month to observe and do audit trails and pick up any non-conforming practices. In his view, being ISO accredited shows to the external world – suppliers, purchasers, the service industry that they are part of, and their competitors – that they have attained a certain standard. Nevertheless, not long after the home had achieved accreditation, a DHN Care & Operational Review was carried out and was very critical of care practice in the home.

In 'Home B' a new manager, formerly a nurse with no background in quality systems, wanted to improve standards and used ISO as the framework for this. All the staff and residents met for one day to work up 'The Pledge' – their local vision statement – which over 12 months they developed into a care standards document. When DHN decided not to pursue ISO, the manager decided to put all the work they had done on care standards into one manual, and use it and maintain it as if it was an ISO manual. They have not sought accreditation, but continue to have the internal audit carried out by her husband and a volunteer. She was enthusiastic about the benefits of their manual, including its use for inducting new staff, and the fact that the staff and residents 'own' it. In addition, the highly developed documentation of care procedures has helped the manager delegate tasks to non-nursing staff to an unusual extent, with the back-up of the procedure manuals. She reported that institutional purchasers of the homes services considered the service standards and the documentation were exemplary. The DHN national officer commented that this home had used the ISO process 'more imaginatively than ISO was ever intended to be used' to improve care practice and as a means of team building.

However, in this home, the manual *only* covered care procedures, and associated tasks such as laundry, catering, complaints etc. It did not include support functions such as finance, purchasing and property. Hence, while the interviewees at both homes said similar things about the benefits (systematic, maintain standards) and the disadvantages (time consuming, cumbersome), they were talking about entirely different standards and documents. One only documented the care side and believed it had brought great benefits, while the other only documented the non-care side and did not believe it is sensible to use the ISO approach in relation to care.

A corollary of proposition 1 is that, once a particular construction of the standard has become established in an organisation, a wide range of rules and norms may then be seen as aspects or consequences of the standard itself – rather than as the choices and achievements of the members of the organisation in appropriating the standard for their purposes. Thus in interviewing it was a common experience to hear various features of the way the organisation worked described as the results or requirements of IIP or ISO 9000, even when these features had little if any foundation in the standards themselves.

This occurred in relation to most of the case organisations and was noted in other interviews as well. It was most striking at Standish where there was a clear tendency to attribute a wide range of positive, people-related features of the school to IIP's benign influence. In fact, it cannot be said of many of the successful HR, management and educational initiatives at Standish that they were *required* by IIP – only, perhaps, that they were in the *spirit* of IIP, and in some cases even that is unclear. Arguably, this point would apply to the whole team approach and breaking down barriers among different categories of staff; the flattening of the hierarchy and participative decision making; the on-going use of residential meetings for team building; aspects of planning and evaluation at the school; using the Training Needs Analysis as a means of empowerment, democracy and feedback; and the support of training not directly related to corporate needs.

2. The standing and value of an award within an organisation may change over time; sustained and productive use is more likely where it is adopted in ways that serve significant organisational purposes, and 'fit' with important features of the organisation's internal and external context.

When ISO 9000 was first achieved at The House it was through a highly participative process rather similar to 'Home B' at the DHN (George and Casson 1992; Humphrey and Hildrew 1992), and not surprisingly given the publicity and visits that the award attracted, it was a source of great pride for the staff involved. Over time, however, attitudes changed, so that at the time of the research the staff – including those who had originally created the system – did not wish registration to continue. There seem to have been several reasons for this. Partly, it was because maintaining the documentation and the mutual internal checking to ensure conformance were both time consuming. In addition, relations with the auditors were uneven, as the manager and staff sought, successfully, to reduce and simplify the original, very elaborate documentation. But more importantly, the city's social services department had not pursued ISO 9000 in other units. Instead it had developed its own standards-based inspection which was actually more searching than the continuation audits for ISO 9000. Hence, for The House, certification was no longer contributing to the improvement of care standards as it had originally; its costs were charged to their budget; and yet they could not use it externally as they did not have an identity separate from that of the social services department.

By contrast, the ISO 9000 approach was readily and closely aligned to the essentially industrial requirements of Typetalk. There, individual responsiveness was inappropriate; the strongly embedded message was that there was a right way of relaying calls – so staff should not intervene or offer help, but see the call as 'the deaf person's call'. This need for behavioural conformance underpinned the emphasis on set procedures. But interviewees also stressed that the structure and control of the ISO 9000 approach had been valuable for them in managing change. They believed it had allowed them to maintain consistency while employment was rising rapidly until there were 400 staff on shifts covering 24 hours a day, 365 days a year, and while they were operating from two sites and undergoing major technological changes. It had become so integral a part of their operation that some respondents had difficulty with questions about the benefits of ISO registration: 'We don't distinguish between accreditation and our internal systems.' Finally, ISO 9000 also fitted their external context. 'Charities have the same needs to satisfy their masters, even though they are not making profits', as one person put it. Interviewees believed it was important for their external standing with suppliers and regulatory bodies in the telecommunications industry where ISO 9000 was well understood and widely used. In particular, Typetalk was funded by BT who themselves carry ISO 9000 certification for many activities.

A similar fit between the way the standard was interpreted and important aspects of the organisation's work activities, values and external context is found in the two IIP cases. At the Shaw Trust, for example, IIP did not just provide a spur and a framework in introducing much needed HR procedures; it became an accepted and integral part of their arrangements because it was developed to fit in other ways as well. It matched their own values – which emphasised both personal development and a business-like approach. It was interpreted in ways that addressed other continuing challenges – for example, communications, in a very dispersed organisation. And it was seen as helping with fundraising and winning contracts particularly from government and public sector purchasers – including TECs, the bodies charged with promoting IIP – with whom the Trust's activities were expanding. IIP or similar accreditation was believed to carry weight with increasing numbers of such bodies. In addition, interviewees believed that IIP helped project a professional image to major employers and the public 'rather than the traditional image of ladies in hats'.

3. Assessors can and do approach their role and task in different ways, and this may be a significant influence on the pattern of use that an organisation develops, and how that pattern evolves over time.

Assessment is supposed to be a dispassionate scrutiny and judgement about the existence and normal operation of a particular set of procedures in relation to a clear standard. In fact, because award standards have to be expressed in ways that fit a wide range of circumstances, they must be non-specific and hence are open to interpretation in any particular circumstance. In addition, the fact that scrutiny and evaluation are taking place (and the consequences that may follow) makes the situation abnormal, as all involved are aware. Hence any such assessment process is bound to rely on the judgement of assessors and to allow them some discretion in the way they pursue their enquiry.

It was clear from interviews that the assessors approached the ambiguities of their task and constructed role-relationships in different ways. For example, an

ISO 9000 verifier contrasted two different approaches to auditing. On the one hand there was compliance auditing, based on 'A limited process control conception' and implemented through 'an objective approach' – which was how the standard had originally developed. On the other, there was the 'value added auditing' which he and colleagues tried to pursue, and which he described as a more strategic approach, using the re-assessment visits to focus on continuous improvement in relation to emergent business issues, in collaboration with senior managers. But he acknowledged: 'Some would say it is only process control. We try to take it much further... but it is difficult. Our role is not consultancy, so we offer advice without going that far. Like giving them contacts, based on our observation of good practice elsewhere.'

In a similar vein, the IIP assessor who had assisted Standish and who was also involved with ISO 9000, described her organisation's approach as aiming 'to take people past the standard... We put it in as a culture programme'. She believed this was unusual, though the idea was spreading. She was proud of the fact that in their area all the organisations – private, public and nonprofit – that had gained the standard were seeking re-assessment three years later, something that she thought had not happened anywhere else in the country. The underlying issue of role-relationship was also discussed by the consultant who helped develop the quality system for ISO registration at Typetalk. He talked of the importance of 'soft policing' if ownership of the system was to remain broadly based within an organisation.

These assessors claims about the effects of different ways of enacting their roles were consistent with the views of other interviewees, eg at The House, about how the assessor's approach and interpretation of the standard affected their own commitment to it. Since this issue has been noted before in relation to regulatory inspection (eg Ashby 1990), it is hardly surprising that it also appears in the context of awards.

Discussion

IIP and ISO 9000 are presented as impersonal and unvarying standards – they are intended as a signal that functionally identical systems of control operate in whichever situations the awards have been made. The implication is that they introduce significant similarities (isomorphism) among the organisations that adopt them. And for some this is precisely the attraction: several interviewees reported that their organisations had adopted one or other standard in order to be, and be seen as, more like private sector. Such considerations call out for an interpretation in terms of institutional theory and 'mimetic isomorphism' (DiMaggio and Powell 1983). Nevertheless, the findings of this study extend the claims of North, Blackburn et al. (1998) concerning ISO 9000 in small firms: what matters is not the systems in themselves so much as the ways in which they come to be used. Overall, the formal similarities seem superficial compared to the heterogeneity of meaning and practice associated with the 'same' systems in different organisations. Of course, such an impression may arise in whole or in part from the methodological limitations of this exploratory study – the DHN case in particular was chosen precisely for the differences of use that it illustrated. But equally, the cases fail to cover other important differences by not including any cases where empty formalities and cynicism were widespread, as reported elsewhere in the literature and by some interviewees in this study (eg the recently recruited teacher at Standish; the award assessors).

Arguably, therefore, the priority for future research is to understand the different ways that organisations can relate to and use an award, how such patterns of use arise, how they may develop over time, and the factors that affect them. Four such patterns of use are suggested by this study and the existing literature.

'Integration' is where the award is more or less lived by the organisation; it is taken seriously and most people identify with its underlying purpose and rationale. The processes thus required are taken for granted, part of the normal way of doing things, and broadly appropriate to the task and context. This is the state of affairs that award schemes are intended to achieve, except that the standard on which the award is based may be interpreted idiosyncratically, incorporating unexpected features. Originally, considerable effort may have been required to achieve the award, either because appropriate systems did not exist, or because they were largely informal. Typetalk and Standish most clearly illustrate this pattern of use.

'Bearing' refers to cases where the award requires people to do things they do not see the point of, and is widely experienced as burdensome and treated with little respect, even if those directly responsible continue to believe in it. It may be seen as necessary and continued mainly for external reasons (eg a requirement of many purchasers within the industry). The later experience of ISO 9000 at The House is a case in point. Presumably this pattern can arise for various reasons: because of the way the system has been implemented, because of a pre-existing culture of cynicism in which many managers and staff do the minimum, or because the standard in question is inappropriate to the tasks and context (North, Blackburn et al. 1998). It would include the sorts of situations that Power refers to as de-coupling and colonisation (Power 1997).

'Emulation' occurs where an organisation considers and in considerable measure implements or maintains a standard – but without seeking, or continuing, to have their systems externally certified. In other words, the leaders of the organisation wish to adopt or maintain the general approach or spirit of the standard but see it as in some respects inappropriate, and the external accreditation unnecessary. Home B at DHN is a very clear example. But DHN nationally and the social services department responsible for 'The House' could also be seen as examples of emulation, in so far as they were both either using or developing their own standards-based systems for raising and maintaining quality in their service units

Finally, *'Badging'* refers to situations in which organisations that already have well-developed systems apply for the award mainly for external reasons, rather than to improve their processes. Where 'emulation' is about internal change without external recognition, 'badging' is the mirror image – external recognition without internal change. Though not encountered in this study,

Thorpe and Bell (1996) and Hillage and Moralee (1996) cite instances of badging in relation to IIP – with some organisations seeing themselves as helping IIP by joining the scheme. It seems likely that in the early days of an award the certifying bodies are keen to involve some high-status organisations. Thereafter, standards may, discreetly, be raised and some organisations that expected the award to be straightforward find they need to develop their systems and make sure they work more consistently. Hence badging is more likely to occur among relatively successful organisations whose senior management see themselves as leaders in an industry or geographical area.

Movement between different patterns of use. As ideal types these four patterns are of course simplifications. Real organisations are messier containing divergent views and inconsistent behaviours. Even the relatively coherent stories that emerged from interviewees in these cases showed their awareness of the different views that existed. They talked of the ways they addressed cynicism, of the need to avoid raising expectations too high, of the fact that 'some things like paperwork and communication will always need working on'. Nevertheless, together, integration, bearing, emulation and badging may provide a 'map of the territory' within which the relationship an organisational unit has to an award evolves over time. Figure 6.1 represents this territory in spatial terms and may help in envisioning the various shifts that are possible over time.

An organisation's relationship to an award is likely to shift around over time, especially on the central axis. For example, the commitment associated with integration may erode, as happened at The House (which looked likely to result sooner or later in a further movement from merely bearing the award towards abandoning it, and thereby leaving the field of the award). Likewise, because embedding new practices and building up commitment takes time, some elements of bearing are probably inevitable when an organisation first commits to obtaining an award. The Shaw Trust, for example, at first labelled and justified many activities in terms of IIP, in order to give them profile and priority. Later, they consciously stopped referring to IIP and re-labelled things as 'Shaw processes' in order to mainstream the ways of working. This way of integrating the award seems to have been successful because as they approached re-appraisal in May 1998, they were concerned lest staff fail to recognise the IIP content of what they were doing – and this might undermine their ability to demonstrate conformity to the IIP assessors.

Some vertical movement – that is, a shift in the importance of internal and external reasons for being interested in the award – may also occur. For example, as has been reported more than once in the literature, an organisation that pursues the award expecting to be able to badge itself may find that its existing practices do not meet the standard. It then has to choose whether to change its procedures (be they the de-coupled formalities of bearing or changes that also have operational significance), or to abandon the attempt and leave the field.

Figure 6.1 How organisations may relate to an award

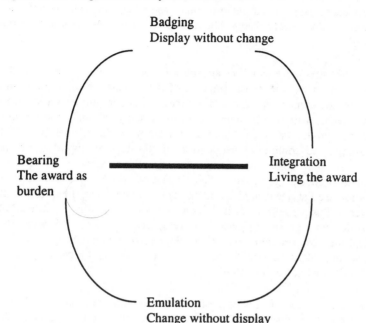

Badging
Display without change

Bearing
The award as
burden

Integration
Living the award

Emulation
Change without display

The bearing-integration axis was recognised by assessors but viewed rather differently. One said: 'It's a Catch-22: either ISO is a sack of bricks or its part of the normal business; so in either case "why bother?" In the past, the standard response from certification bodies to such a challenge would be to say that in the former case the system had been inadequately implemented; and in the latter, external accreditation was still worthwhile because without it standards were much less likely to be maintained. The more developmental approaches to auditing (see the discussion of proposition 3 above) were an attempt to respond more constructively to this challenge.

Patterns of use in context. Other factors may also affect an organisation's pattern of use and relationship to an award. The literature already suggests a number, and these found echoes in the cases:

- The awards become an element in the inter-departmental politics of the organisation (Bell, Taylor et al. 2001). Inevitably, one department or section has to take lead responsibility, and it may thus become a project through which it boosts its visibility, status and resources (at Workplaces the HR department grew very substantially in the years following the decision to seek IIP status). Ideally, other departments will still identify with the standard and it will continue to provide an arena where tensions between competing professional and managerial priorities are negotiated and contained. But one can imagine that strong departmental ownership of an award could easily bring about a shift from integration towards 'bearing'.

- The awards also seem to affect and be affected by the value base of the organisation, as was clearest in the case of IIP. This award combines an affirmation of humanistic values (for example, its commitments extend to *all* employees) with a refinement of instrumentally rational relationships (since the alignment with business priorities is fundamental). Not surprisingly, the continuing negotiation of this tension appeared in the cases, with staff sometimes using the aspirational accounts of IIP to legitimate particular concerns. 'That's not very IIP' was the sort of expression used at one organisation, and at the Shaw Trust, the question of staff versus business priorities had been addressed by putting aside £2,000 to provide some support for personal development activities. Likewise, IIP may legitimate expenditure on staff development which intensely client-led organisations often find difficult – the 'spending money on ourselves' problem (Paton and Hooker 1990).

- The perceived value of obtaining or continuing with the awards is clearly affected by wider institutional trends. At the time of the research the emerging 'Best Value' regime in UK local government had stimulated renewed interest in the possible use of ISO 9000 as a means of demonstrating standards.

- Organisations that achieve one award seem more likely to pursue another, or to be making use of NVQs, which employ a similar assessment methodology (Spilsbury, Moralee et al. 1995a). Thus, the perceived success of IIP at the Shaw Trust (as at a charity addressing homelessness among young people, also an early adopter) contributed to a re-evaluation of ISO 9000 registration which it was expected they would soon seek. Likewise, the choice of ISO by the manager of Home B at DHN followed her use of NVQs as a first means of raising care standards. The cumulative impact of such developments, especially in the context of other regulatory and funding developments that encourage greater formality, may be considerable.

Conclusions

Crests and awards testifying to the soundness of organisational arrangements are now a fact of organisational life. Policy-makers and purchasers considering nonprofit organisations need to understand these schemes and if they choose to promote them, learn to do so skilfully. Managers have to consider why, when and how to adopt the standards involved. But the research base is limited and contradictory, and almost non-existent in relation to social enterprises.

The findings of an exploratory study can only be tentative. But in this case, they challenge important assumptions behind the awards and raise some broader and more theoretical questions. Those assumptions reflect a 'rational system' view of organisations (Thompson 1967) as incorporating well-developed control processes that normally function, in a stable and impersonal way to achieve their intended purposes. On this basis an external party should be able, objectively, to verify the existence and proper functioning of such systems. Nevertheless, as has been noted, the verifiers themselves are acknowledging that this is often an unhelpful basis on which to approach performance issues in an organisational setting. In practice, both the systems themselves and the notion of conformance to standards for them are social constructions, involving considerable uncertainty and ambiguity. Hence issues of meaning, purposes, politics and culture become important in understanding how systems are enacted in different contexts and how those enactments evolve over time. This is not to say that 'anything goes' but that the standards and the audit process are much looser, more limited and variable than either aspirational or cynical accounts of the awards claim.

Finally, allowing that this was an exploratory study, some general implications for practice can be outlined. The findings suggest that policy-makers would do well to moderate their expectations from an award, and accept that they may be used and misused in surprising ways. Such awards may still be worthwhile, but how they are promoted (avoiding *de facto* coercion of social enterprises seeking contracts), and how the audit process is conducted, will be crucial. For managers, the implications seem to be that these awards can unquestionably be used to good effect – but equally, they can easily become a burden and a distraction. Hence it is probably a mistake to think in terms of what meeting the given requirements of the award will 'do to' your organisation. Instead, one needs to think in terms of how to ensure those requirements are construed and implemented in ways that fit one's purposes and context, and reinforce important commitments, in an unobtrusive manner. In doing so the understanding and involvement of the staff involved is crucial. As always, the single most important feature determining the success of a management practice is whether it is accepted by the managed.

Sources and resources

For information on IiP – including lists of guides, case studies and research reports – visit the IiP website (http://www.iiP.uk.co.uk). IiP is now being promoted internationally. For information on the ISO 9000 series of standards for quality systems, visit http://praxiom.com. Note that ISO 9000 is currently being revised. Many professional and sector bodies also offer publications giving advice on when, why and how to use these methods (eg the QSTG, 1998; Darvill, 1998).

The Audit Society by Michael Power (1997), an auditor turned sociologist, is essential reading for anyone interested in this area. It may be rather sweeping in its claims but it provides a superb antidote to the inflated expectations regarding audit that are so widespread.   For a closer examination of organisational practice, North, Blackburn et al.'s *The Quality Business (1998)* is thorough in its approach and measured in its conclusions.   It focuses on ISO 9000 in small firms, but much of the analysis would be relevant to social enterprises.

7 Using Quality Models for Self-assessment

Introduction

The last chapter's discussion of awards alluded to the possibility of their being used in a more developmental way - not as a yes/no indicator of the existence of a particular management system, but as a means of appraising strengths and weaknesses and of promoting gradual improvement. When an organization is appraised in this way - by considering how well the various elements of a model system are being carried out in day-to-day practice - it is a short step to developing a scoring system. Such ratings are another form of measurement, one that provides a rough and ready metric of administrative well being, allowing different organizations to be compared and progress to be tracked over time. Although these appraisals may be carried out by an external assessor (in a similar way to the assessment for an award) this need not be the case. *Self*-assessment - whether by an individual, by the senior management team or by a specially constituted group - is also a possibility. The use of such self-assessment models and rating schemes for diagnosis and improvement provide the focus for this chapter.

Recently, two self-assessment models have attracted considerable interest among social enterprises in the UK – PQASSO (the *Practical Quality Assurance System for Small Organisation)* and EM (*the Excellence Model).* Both have their origins in the 'Quality movement' which has had mixed reviews both in general, and from those who write about public and nonprofit management and policy. Advocates (Martin 1993; Kearns, Krasman et al. 1994; Morgan and Murgatroyd 1994), usually writing from practitioner perspectives, claim that it focuses attention on important issues, especially in so far as it places the concerns of service users (as customers) centre stage. Sceptics (Wilkinson and Wilmott 1995; Clarke and Newman 1997) have seen the quality concept as loose, confused and rhetorical and have viewed the advent of quality ideas as another expression of the new managerialism, promising far more than it can deliver, and best understood as a means for managers to try to control professionals.

However, neither advocates nor sceptics were quick to produce rigorous research. As (Powell 1995) put it writing of Total Quality Management (TQM):

> The researchers know of no other management concept or practice that has ever received so much practitioner attention, with so little academic study, as TQM' (p33).

Interestingly, this is also true of the use of self-assessment models more generally, even though tools to assist organisational self-assessment have long been a feature of the management literature[1]. Such tools may be intended generally, even though tools to assist organisational self-assessment have long been a feature of the management literature.[25] Such tools may be intended simply for the individual manager to consider, or they may be designed for much more systematic use and to surface and reconcile different views by encouraging a shared response by team members. They may focus on a specific issue – Hassell (1998) provides a good example in relation to risk management in social enterprises. Or they may address a broader area of organisational functioning (the schemes of Harris 1993a, 1993b, Herman and Renz 1997) are of this sort.

Perhaps it is because they are so common and taken-for-granted that the research questions these diagnostic models raise have been overlooked. For example, what actually happens when managers try to make serious use of them? Does this kind of self-scrutiny provide an economic, and perhaps less unpredictable, way of obtaining the sort of appraisal and advice offered by a management consultant – as it were, a 'distance learning' form of organisational development? Or is it a distraction, and potentially a false comfort?

Hence, in considering how quality models are being used as performance improvement methods, this chapter also explores a broader issue around the use of self-administered diagnostic aids by managers. Before discussing the research questions and method in more detail, the two models need to be located and described.

The two models: origins, approaches, issues

Although both spring from the broad quality movement, the models differ in important respects – in particular, in the contexts for which they were developed, and in their management philosophies, which represent different strands within the quality movement. Though not strictly speaking alternatives, one strand, associated with the idea of Quality Assurance (QA), emphasises organisational structure and procedures, while the other, associated with TQM, gives much more weight to organisational culture and values.

QA and PQASSO. PQASSO is structured in terms of 16 'quality areas'. Some of these (Commitment to Quality, Service Provision, User-centred Service, Monitoring & Evaluation, Complaints & Suggestions) clearly concern the sorts of matters one would expect a quality system to address. Others (for example, The Management Committee, Financial Management, Networking & Partnerships, and Environmental Issues) concern broader issues of management, policy and agency commitments that, however important, are not directly associated with the quality of services provided. Hence PQASSO sets out a broad model for well-run projects and organisations, rather than a template for a focused QA system.

For each of the 16 'quality areas' the 'workpack' sets out a standard, defines the terms used in the standard, sets out three levels of achievement, and suggests the sort of documentary evidence an organisation might provide in order to show that it was consistently operating at that level. It is up to the organisations themselves to decide which areas are important for them, and the levels they need to achieve. The author suggests that level 1 of the standards is perfectly adequate for one-year projects; level 2 is suitable for most on-going projects affiliated to federal organisations, while level 3 is 'very tough' and only appropriate for organisations with a professional management structure.

PQASSO is presented in an attractively designed, loose-leaf pack. It is very clearly written with forms for users to complete, and offers guidance on how it can be used participatively for self-assessment and to build relationships with funders.

TQM and the Excellence Model.   The TQM approach to continuous improvement emphasises the importance of promoting quality and customer service as super-ordinate organisational values and providing scope (and practical problem-solving tools) for staff at all levels to contribute – through quality circles and empowered cross-functional teams. One of the ways in which this approach was promoted was through various quality awards – the best known in the US is the Malcolm Baldrige Award – designed to encourage and recognise the adoption of company-wide quality programmes. Characteristically, such awards involve companies being assessed on a wide range of quality-related practices and achievements. The EM is essentially a sophisticated model of this type which has been developed and promoted primarily as a diagnostic tool, and only secondly as a means of competing for an award.

The EM was introduced in 1991, having been developed and widely tested by senior quality managers and directors from leading European companies (mainly large manufacturers), under the aegis of the European Foundation for Quality Management. The model is structured in terms of nine elements: five 'enablers' (how things are done) and four 'results areas' (actual achievements). The relationship between these and their weights in the scoring system are usually represented diagrammatically, as shown in figure 7.1.[26] The TQM approach is clear in the high weightings given to customer satisfaction and cross-functional processes.

The nine elements are in turn subdivided into 32 sub-criteria, each of which generates a set of scaled questions. The questions – along with user guidance, examples of excellence for the different criteria and graphical display facilities – are presented on disc and can be used in one of three ways: by individuals, by teams (with or without facilitation), and by teams with external validation of the scores. The resulting scores, in total and in terms of the nine elements, can then be compared against those achieved by others, and used to track progress over time. In the UK, the British Quality Foundation has a database of scores from hundreds of companies and public bodies, and though held anonymously they allow comparisons within the same industry or size band.

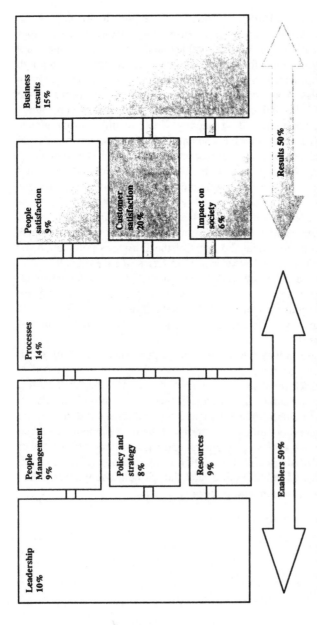

Figure 7.1 The Excellence Model, as of 1997, showing the weighting given to the various 'areas' (after BQF 1997)

Clearly, the two models have much in common. Both *embody a broad and coherent set of assumptions* about what is required for good organisation and management; both provide a set of *generic* standards, and hence a basis for *comparison*, while apparently remaining sufficiently *flexible* to accommodate varied circumstances and different ways of doing things; and both are intended for *developmental* rather than evaluative purposes, under the control of those who choose to use the methods rather than an outside party. They differ in that PQASSO is tailored specifically for smaller social enterprises, and has a narrower focus in terms of the sorts of changes (mainly the introduction of explicit policy and procedure in defined areas) that it is intended to precipitate.

Issues from the literature

As was noted in the last chapter, QA initiatives have attracted criticism for requiring inordinate documentation and formality, making them particularly unsuitable for small organisations (Seddon 1997; North, Blackburn et al. 1998). PQASSO can be seen as an acknowledgement of and response to such criticisms, offering QA in a form more appropriate to small voluntary organisations and projects. Nevertheless, a question remains over when, and to what extent, it is appropriate for a small social enterprise to make its policies and procedures explicit through documentation – rather than relying on informal methods and tacit understandings. As North, Blackburn et al. (1998) put it reporting their detailed data from a mix of small companies:

> An implication of the above is that many small firm owner-managers may not need to implement formal methods to adopt many of the basic tenets of sound quality strategies and that advocates of formal quality standards have no monopoly on effective strategies…. Closely analysed and approached with an open mind, small business owners' use of informal quality strategies very often emerge as a rational way of dealing with customers' needs effectively, relative to the competitive position of the business in the sector and market in which it operates. (p 86)

A second issue for any derivation of the QA approach concerns the questions of the standing and ownership – who is custodian of the procedures to ensure they are maintained and operated? By relying on the trustees or managers of the project (so-called 'first-party' accreditation), PQASSO may reduce the risks of *colonisation* and *de-coupling* that have often been reported when audit is conducted by either a 'second party' (eg funder, contractor) or a 'third party' (eg, independent certification agency). But without any external reinforcement, will an agenda deriving from self-assessment be sustained and carried through?

The literature on quality awards. The high profile of the Baldrige and other quality awards has helped make them controversial, thereby generating some literature. This highlights several issues of relevance to the current study:

- The *scope* of the models has been debated given challenges that it is too broad (by including a range of management processes beyond those associated with quality control), or alternatively too narrow (by not adequately addressing such vital management processes as finance, R&D and marketing) (Garvin 1991; Conti 1997).

- The nature and use of the *scoring systems* have been debated. Critics have been concerned that they stimulate (expensive, even ritual) efforts at looking good or impressing superiors, rather than helping identify weaknesses (Conti 1997). Defenders say the criteria which are 'strongly prescriptive on philosophy but open-minded about practices and procedures' (Garvin 1991) are appropriate, and anyway the vast majority of those who use the models do so with a view to self-assessment and performance improvement, and not in order to enter the award process.

- The *consequences for performance* of conforming to the model have been debated, with critics pointing to the business difficulties experienced by some award winners, advocates claiming that, overall, success in the award is associated with superior business performance, and others saying the evidence is inconclusive (Ghobadian and Woo 1994)

Other research has considered TQM itself, rather than the use of self-assessment models, with a key issue being its *imitability*. It has been argued that TQM involves a combination of 'hard' and 'soft' attributes, with only the former (some discrete practices and techniques) being fairly readily transferable. The latter, including aspects of leadership and empowerment, are tacit, intangible, often culturally at odds with practice elsewhere, and difficult to imitate; indeed it is beyond the capacity of most organisations to restructure their internal and external relationships in the ways required for TQM success. Unless these 'soft' factors in some measure pre-exist the introduction of a TQM programme, its benefits are likely to be limited – which may explain the mixed results that have been observed (Powell 1995).

The focus and choice of the case studies

As usual, the research progressed through key informant interviews and familiarisation with the academic and practitioner literature to the selection of settings for case studies. The cases focused on the ways in which the two models had been (or were being) used over time – always starting with questions about how and why and by whom the models were being used – and what self-assessment actually involved in terms both of process and outcomes. These allowed an exploration both indirectly and directly of several of the issues referred to above. However, through the preliminary 'mapping' phase it became clear that the models were being deployed in two different ways: autonomously, by small and medium-sized organisations; and on a system-wide basis by large organisations comprising many discrete units, or by federations and networks in a particular field or locality. These two modes offered scope for exploring the balance between internal and external purposes (and whether and how use of the model can be sustained in the absence of external accreditation), and the nature of the changes to which use of the models gave rise. The value of the EM's scoring system as a form of measurement was also of interest, as was the appropriateness of what was ostensibly a form of QA, in the context of small organisations.

As well as wanting to encompass autonomous and system-wide uses of both models, the choice of sites was complicated by the desire (and opportunity) to introduce a longitudinal dimension in some cases, and reduce the reliance on retrospective analysis. In the end, the following cases were chosen:[27]

- *The Kids Club Network (KCN).* This is a federation of after-school clubs that began to grow rapidly in the late 1980s especially as the field became a focus for government attention and resources. An important part of KCN's role was to advise many local, very informal part-time projects in their dealings with a range of highly regulated public bodies. What was later to be generalised into PQASSO was developed in this context both as a self-assessment and development tool, and as a 'kite-marking' system, for local clubs (below, it is referred to as proto-PQASSO). It is structurally almost identical, and KCN was chosen as offering not just a wide range of experience but a uniquely long period of use.

- *Hillend* is a drop-in centre for marginalised people – mainly addicts and rough sleepers – in a town on the south coast of England. At the time of the study it had been running for 15 years, and had seven f.t.e paid staff assisted by volunteers. Hillend was chosen as an independent user of PQASSO, and having been one of the pilot sites for its development as a relatively long-term user.

- *The Birmingham Project* refers to a capacity-building scheme that promoted the use of PQASSO in local agencies in England's second city. It was conceived jointly by the Council of Voluntary Service and the (government-funded) Training and Enterprise Council, as a way of meeting the concerns of urban regeneration agencies otherwise reluctant to fund community-based projects. The project provided some funding and initial facilitation, as well as the PQASSO materials, and also supported local networking among PQASSO users. It was oversubscribed, attracting involvement from a diverse range of agencies and projects, four of which were selected for interview as part of the case study.

- *Enterprise and Employment Training Agency (EETA)* was a (different) Training and Enterprise Council providing enterprise support and a range of employment related training in a large town in the Midlands.[28] It employed 80 people and was chosen as a medium-sized organisation which had used the EM, apparently successfully, to help address particular challenges. It was a relatively long-term user of the EM.

- *Ability* is a large national charity working in the field of a particular disability. It provides a wide range of services (residential and community care, schools, employment projects) and operates on about 100 sites nation-wide. It had the attraction of just starting to use the model as the research began. Hence it offered the possibility of a longitudinal, as opposed to a retrospective study. In the event, however, deployment of the model was delayed because financial difficulties pre-empted the management agenda. Hence, though interesting for several reasons, this did not provide an instance of system-wide deployment of the EM, as had been hoped.

Findings: the practice of self-assessment

As before, the principal findings are presented as a series of propositions.

1. *How either model is best applied to a given situation is not self-evident; this usually involves tacit negotiation over how key terms should be construed, whether particular elements are appropriate, and the procedures to be adopted.*

Managers and staff frequently criticised the language of the models for being unclear and unsuitable. The problem was most severe with the EM, despite efforts to make it acceptable to social enterprises.[29] This reflects both specific difficulties over how some of the terms – eg 'customers', 'impact on society' – are to be interpreted, and also the long-standing debate over the appropriateness of business language in nonprofit contexts (the 'genericism' issue). It was seen as one of the major challenges concerning use of the model in the proposal to adopt the EM made to the council of Ability. At EETA one member of staff trained to be an assessor volunteered that she found the language 'quite difficult' and 'manufacturing oriented' which meant they had been 'tempted to re-write all the questions'. In the event she had 'put it in layman's terms for the administrative staff', though it was 'OK for those used to thinking at a strategic level'. These difficulties regularly raise the broader questions about the validity of the model in the context of social enterprises. The idea of 'tailoring' the model to make it more readily and consistently applicable has come up whenever it has been tried out in a particular sector or field (government agencies, local government, charities) as the various reports attest. The trouble, of course, is that this would reduce comparability in relation to other sectors and fields.

Similar concerns were expressed regarding PQASSO in the Birmingham project, despite the efforts that had gone into developing the model specifically for small nonprofits. And this was a major theme in the report on an area trial of PQASSO, with respondents calling for more and better written explanations (McTiernan 1998). However it is very unlikely that this issue could be resolved through clearer expression or more detailed guidance, as participants often suggested. Many of the concepts (like 'quality' itself) are multi-faceted, and the latitude built into both models is there for good reason: in order to accommodate varied circumstances and different ways of doing things, and to ensure those undertaking the self-assessment instil the terms with their own meanings. Hence some debate over how these general terms will be interpreted and applied in a given situation, and how they wish to conduct the self-assessment, are a necessary part of learning to work with the model and to view their situation through the lenses it provides. Thus some uncertainty over how either model will be interpreted and applied in a given situation is inevitable.

A corollary to proposition one is that decisions over whether and how to use the models are the outcome and reflection of micro-political processes within the organisations concerned. A few of the instances encountered in the fieldwork were:

- At KCN it was reported that not infrequently proto-PQASSO was promoted by the staff of Kids Clubs as a way of trying to address difficulties they experienced with the contribution and performance of their management committees.

- In a hospice that was a candidate for a case study, an initial decision to use the EM which had been promoted by the Quality Manager and supported by the Chief Executive, was reversed when the latter left the organisation.

- At EETA, the EM champion took enormous care over the way he introduced the idea first to the Chief Executive (giving him a copy of the questions as 'a sprat to catch a mackerel') and thereafter more widely. Later the Chief Executive was to say '[He] very sensibly did not tell me the full implications of the decision'.

2. Perceived internal benefits from the use of the models were varied and seem to arise from the dialogues to which they give rise, and from the new thinking triggered by the terms of the self-assessment process.

Self-assessment seems to have created occasions on which individuals expressed pre-existing concerns that they had been unwilling or unable to put across in the usual decision-making fora. For example, at EETA the self-assessment provided an opportunity for staff to express dissatisfactions, leading to a shared, 'independent' and later externally verified confirmation of long-suspected weakness – sufficient to convince senior management of the need for action. Likewise, staff at Hillend used PQASSO as a way of prompting their management committee, which had just 'gone on from year to year' with no clear grasp of roles and responsibilities, to review how they worked. By making neglected or excluded topics discussible, self-assessment allowed some new ideas to emerge, or existing ideas to gain wider support. In addition, the conceptual content of the models seems sometime to have stimulated fresh ways of thinking about the organisation and its challenges. This was emphasised at Ability (where the model was described as a 'thinking tool'), but it showed up in very obvious ways among several PQASSO users who noticed 'gaps' in their arrangements.

3. Use of the models is promoted to nonprofits as a means of securing the confidence of external stakeholders; concern for external legitimacy is a major factor in decisions to use the models.

One of the benefits of PQASSO listed in the introduction to the manual is that it:

> provides a common language and frame of reference for grant and contract officers of local authorities, health and probation services and funders representatives.

The EM goes further, providing a series of logos for use on notepaper, publications etc to those organisations with validated scores above particular levels. Although a concern for improvement was also affirmed, external legitimacy was a significant, recurring consideration that surfaced quickly and often spontaneously in fieldwork. At Hillend, for example, the decision to try PQASSO was made when the Centre's funders were beginning to write references to Quality Assurance into contracts. At KCN, it was reported that privately owned clubs (whose motivations might be considered open to question) had shown particular interest in using proto-PQASSO. As regards the EM, a recurring theme in interviews and meeting reports (eg of the Local Authorities Group of the British Quality Foundation, UK guardians of the EM) was the enormous boost use of the EM had received from the introduction of a statutory requirement for Local Authorities to demonstrate 'Best Value', and to use 'Best Value' providers.

4. *Sustained use of both models requires management time and effort, and involves the creation of new sorts of discussions whose relationship to normal decision processes may become problematic.*

Narrowly conceived, using the models involves only the time required for the self-assessment process and ends with agreement on areas requiring improvement. But interviewees generally took a broader view, including the time and effort spent on designing and implementing improvements, as part of 'using the model'. In addition, most saw this as an iterative process of diagnosis and improvement, rather than a once-off review. For these reasons, what seemed initially to be a fairly limited exercise, ended up being a major organisational commitment. At Hillend, despite about six days input from the consultant who was developing the pack, one area (environmental policy) had yet to be addressed and at the time of the fieldwork they no longer expected to complete the process by their target date. Likewise, although they had decided to review two policy areas at a time at the six-weekly management committee meetings (thus covering all areas on an annual cycle) this had yet to start and one respondent was uneasy about the slow progress. On the other hand, it was clear that in order to progress as far as they had, new ways of generating policy and procedure had been introduced – like each member of staff being given two areas to work on, tackling these in pairs, and reporting back to the wider staff group. Staff at KCN reported that making the time for consideration of the PQASSO agenda was the largest single obstacle to its wider use.

At both Ability and EETA introduction of the EM was a major exercise involving the cultivation of internal commitment and the training of assessors who then introduced it to different units or areas. More than a year into the process, those involved at Ability still felt that they had only just started. At EETA, once it was established, the process was driven by a carefully chosen project team, made up on a 'diagonal slice' basis. While this was highly successful in overcoming cynicism, the process experienced a severe loss of momentum when the results were passed to the EETA Board which was then preoccupied, as it was for several months each year, with the latest annual work-planning and reporting requirements coming from Central Government. It took varying degrees of effort over three-and-a-half years to introduce the EM, achieve the first set of verified scores, and obtain Board-level endorsement of the improvement agenda coming out of the Self-Assessment.

Again, these time-scales do not seem to be unusual especially in larger organisations, and a tension between EM-related diagnosis and action planning, and the organisations established decision processes has also been noted by Armistead (1998)

5. *The models can be and are used in quite different ways and for different purposes; within a single organisation the manner of and rationale for use will often change over time.*

KCN, as an umbrella body, was in a good position to observe this diversity of uses, and to promote proto-PQASSO accordingly. For example, it could be used as a planning tool in the set-up phase of a new club, or as a way of handling a major transition (such as expansion or the departure of a founding employee). In Birmingham, an all-volunteer credit union used PQASSO slowly and deliberately over a two-year period to create explicit systems and procedures. The manager and the administrator of an established hostel used it briskly between them as a diagnostic ('A quick tick box enabled us to see what was needed') and then set about developing procedures and practices to fill the gaps. A 10-year-old ethnic minority women's educational project whose founder was the only staff member, seem to have used it to shift from tacit and personalised ways of working to more explicit and shared arrangements. And a social care agency used it for classic QA purposes – as the vehicle to obtain registration with, and hence contracts from, the City social services department. At Hillend, the focus of PQASSO-related activity shifted over time as they worked slowly through the agenda that their self-assessment had generated.

Ability's expectations around how the EM would be used changed even as it was being 'rolled out', with an initial interest in scoring for external comparability being downplayed and put off to an indeterminate future. Then a few months later, anticipating difficulties with his large governing body on which users and carers were heavily represented, the Chief Executive seized on the EM as a means of raising Council members' sights from concerns with particular local services to key issues of strategy and policy. He made some changes to the representation of the model and used it as the basis for a key session at a residential meeting where new members were being inducted and the Council's work for the year was being planned. This was generally agreed to have been very successful (though the staff of Ability who had been trained in the 'proper' use of the EM were shocked at the cavalier way he treated it).

The Chief Executive found it useful regularly to return to this version of the model with the trustees over the next three years. At EETA, a major consideration driving the use of the EM was the need to bind together the staff and activities of the three beleaguered organisations out of which the agency had been formed. Some of the choices over how the EM might be used were recognised quite explicitly: 'We could have gone for 73 small improvements or three large ones – we went for the latter', as the Chief Executive put it.

These different uses are not all positive, and in particular, it remains to be seen how the models will be used over the longer term. In this context it is worth noting that Seddon (1998) reports from extensive experience in the private sector (but drawing also on some exposure to the use of the EM in public organisations) that using the EM can be a matter of 'going through the motions':

> There are larger organisations that have taken to the EM lock, stock and barrel; in some it has become mandatory for managers to conduct a Self-Assessment on an annual basis... In our experience, many become preoccupied with doing things right – meeting the expectations of the hierarchy, conducting a Self-Assessment, reporting a score and having a plan of action against the model – rather than doing the right things... Few find themselves stimulated to question the very assumptions they have been using to run the organisation. (p 32)

6. *The structure and content of both models provide an integrative map or overview of management issues that many users value highly; this seems important in understanding the appeal of the models and why general managers, in particular, remain committed to them.*

The number of spontaneous references to the 'broad picture' which these models provided was striking – both in interviews in the case organisations and in other discussions. A repeated claim was that they showed how other requirements and improvement methods (such as contractual monitoring returns, Investors in People, Quality standards, Customer Care, etc) fitted together. In EETA, for example, 'initiative overload' was a major issue and initially a barrier to the use of the EM. In the event, one of the reasons the EM was accepted was precisely because it set the other initiatives in context: 'a way of pulling all our quality work together under one umbrella'. This was also highlighted in Birmingham, and a trial of PQASSO which a group of local agencies in a rural area reported as one of the 'unexpected benefits': 'They had not expected their new clear thinking, or ability to see the way forward.' (McTiernan 1998) Likewise, in another organisation running homes for people with disabilities, the model was being introduc~d because it promised a way of bringing together financial and professional perspectives that had historically been very separate. This benefit is frequently referred to in other reports on the EM (Darvill 1998; Samuels 1998).

The unprompted frequency of such observations in interviews suggests that this is a significant benefit. A major challenge facing those who used these tools was to structure an agenda for improvement in a coherent and meaningful way, in uncertain and demanding circumstances (eg diffuse cross-functional responsibilities in larger organisations; or the extensive roles with many pressing day-to-day demands of managers in small organisations). These managers seemed to be using the 'maps' provided by the tools to achieve greater clarity and focus regarding an important area of their work, and thereby reducing their own role confusion and uncertainty. Though it goes beyond the data and research design of this study, it would hardly be surprising if they discharged those roles with more confidence and clarity as a result.

Other findings. Some findings were relevant only to one or other of the models. Regarding PQASSO, literature-derived expectations that a broadly QA approach focusing on documentation would be unnecessarily burdensome, perhaps leading to 'colonisation' and 'de-coupling', were not borne out. This was true even though PQASSO was actively promoted to its users by funders, whose confidence it would usually be vital to maintain. There seem to be two reasons for this. First, the funders were very alert to the danger that they might precipitate empty but time-consuming rituals of conformance. Hence they worked with sector bodies to ensure it was adopted wholeheartedly, rather than cynically. Whether this 'development' orientation will be sustained over the longer term remains an open (and important) question.[30]   Secondly, though PQASSO does emphasise documentation, it was being used primarily in contexts where policy and organisational maintenance are frequently neglected, or dealt with erratically, with adverse consequences. Hence it legitimised and facilitated additional attention being given to matters that, by and large, deserved them. Moreover, most organisations signing up for PQASSO sustained a commitment to it, despite the absence of external accreditation. The fact that it was promoted (within KCN and in the Birmingham project) in a way that offered opportunities for peer support and networking may have helped in this respect.

Regarding the EM, doubts about the reliability of unvalidated scoring as a form of measurement appear to be well justified. At EETA the senior management team's initial use of the EM, when they were considering its introduction, produced very high scores – twice what they would produce a year later, completing a more considered Self-Assessment. Consultants with experience of using the model reported that ratings vary widely, and are associated with organisational level. Thus, in one instance the Directors produced ratings of about 750, managers scored around 350, while those on the shop floor were in the region of 180 points (BMI 1998). Validated scoring may be unreliable for other reasons, of course[31] – as well as involving greater expense.

Discussion: making sense of self-assessment

As with the awards considered in the last chapter, 'a striking feature of these cases is the contrast between the way self-assessment is presented and the diverse experiences of its use. The promotional literature implies a well-defined procedure capable of producing an informative, dispassionate and fairly reliable appraisal out of the responses to a series of clear and specific questions. The reality seems to be a process that is necessarily loose and uncertain, which can be used in quite different ways, and which can generate anything from deep scepticism to enthusiastic commitment.

Explaining different patterns of use.   To account for these very different experiences and outcomes one needs to consider how use of the models is absorbed into and impacts on existing patterns of managerial thinking and action in organisations that use them.   Such patterns of thinking and action can be conceptualised in terms of the simple model in figure 7.2.   The managers' cognitive and behavioural world comprises the ideas and constructs in terms of which they think about the issues they deal with; and the behavioural norms that govern the ways in which they interact with each other and with staff, to tackle those issues.   These norms, strategies and assumptions shape the information that is noticed and gathered, as well as evolving in the light of such information. However, an extensive literature attests to the fact that managerial (like other) cultures can be extremely resilient, ignoring or explaining away information that is disturbing (Slatter 1984).

What happens, then, when use of a self-assessment model is proposed and agreed?   At one extreme, within a closed and defensive managerial culture – a Model I theory-in-use, in Argyris and Schon's terms (Argyris and Schon 1978) – managers would either reject the questions presented by the model as not meaningful in their situation; and/or they would construe them within existing assumptions, use only currently available and acceptable information, and discuss the results in the usual decision-making fora.   'Upbeat' and/or highly generalised responses to self-assessment questions would ensure a generally favourable picture emerged, and would prevent threatening discrepancies and disagreements, or just the need for more administrative work, being surfaced by the process.   Such a process might be self-congratulatory, or just safely banal and unproductive ('could do a bit better all round'), or it might quickly become an occasion for familiar skirmishes, as pre-existing agendas were discreetly expressed and pursued through the self-assessment process.

At the other extreme, managers within an 'open' culture (Model II theory-in-use) could be expected to engage with the challenge of thinking in somewhat different and problematic terms about their organisation, and to suspend judgement about its appropriateness.   They would be more interested in new information about their organisation's functioning and performance, and they would be ready to share and discuss this in an appropriate setting outside of the usual meetings cycle.   They would be willing to use the exercise to surface different perspectives and concerns, to explore the information and experience on which these rested, and to accept the implications of such a dialogue.

Figure 7.2 Influence diagram of the effects of introducing a self-assessment model

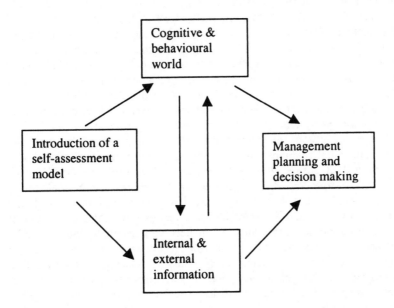

Between these poles are a wide range of possibilities. Even if the culture initially constrains how the model is interpreted and used, it may still introduce some new constructs, throw new light on neglected information, and precipitate discussions between people and on topics that would not otherwise have occurred – from which new understandings and action plans emerge ('sense-making') (Weick 1995). Thereafter the process may atrophy – or one thing can lead to another, with further issues being recognised, or becoming 'discussable'. In short, use of the model may stimulate temporarily or more enduringly some features of a learning organisation, but whether and to what extent this happens is likely to depend on the pre-existing culture and to be path-dependent on the manner of its introduction. For example, one might predict that new thinking and dialogue would be more likely to occur if the model is used, at least initially, in a context (such as an 'away-day', retreat, or planning conference) that is less overshadowed by the current management agenda and its accompanying need to make decisions.

Clearly, this is a reconstruction of what may be going on which needs to be tested in further research. However, it fits with other theory and research, for example, Powell's (1995) proposition that, for cultural reasons, thorough-going TQM is not easily introduced; and Harris's description of her diagnostic procedure as both 'a framework for analysis of existing organisational arrangements...' and a 'technique for organisation development' (Harris 1993b, p 276).

The models as vehicles for the spread of 'quality' practices. These cases also throw some light on how ideas from the quality movement are being adopted and used in social enterprises. While a concern for external legitimacy has been significant in the rapid spread of the models (as institutional theorists would predict – see, for example, DiMaggio and Powell 1983; Lowndes 1996) it is doubtful whether TQM and QA are being spread through the adoption of these forms of self-assessment. The TQM origins of the EM were not widely understood,[32] and indeed, at EETA, the word 'quality' had already been discredited ('In promoting the model to staff, we avoided it like the plague', according to the models internal champion). As for PQASSO, although it uses the terminology of QA, it is unclear whether in this attenuated form it meets the specification for QA systems given by the International Standards Organisation, nor is it often being used for conventional QA purposes (since most users did not have contractual relationships involving detailed service specifications to which they had to ensure close conformance). It is useful in boosting the credibility of the organisation more generally in its dealings with officialdom.

Rather, ideas from QA and TQM are being translated, negotiated and enacted to make sense and be 'workable' in social enterprises. In the process, the meanings and purposes for which the models were originally intended to be vehicles are being reconfigured in line with the evolving preoccupations and purposes of those who use them. Hence, although managers and staff find quality concepts useful, this is *not* because they convey a particular way of managing. Rather, these concepts are loose and uncertain, bringing together and affording legitimacy to the diverse range of an organisation's commitments, without giving priority to any particular one, and allowing recognition of existing good practice and achievements. So although the labels and language of quality are spreading, from the evidence reported here, what these terms signify is evolving and varied. The purposes that were originally embedded in the models are overshadowed by the contextual purposes of those who use them. Hence such institutional isomorphism (DiMaggio and Powell 1983) as is occurring may well be superficial.

Conclusions

Accepting the usual *caveats* about the methodological limitations of the study – in particular, its preference for longer-lasting and relatively successful cases – some implications for practice can still be suggested. If it is thought timely for Board members, managers and staff to stand back and appraise their arrangements, then use of self-assessment tools may be a relatively economical and reliable alternative to engaging a consultant – though some elements of external facilitation will usually make the process more productive.[33] The models provide a stimulus and a loose framework for a particular sort of discussion. It is up to the managers concerned to decide how much time and energy to invest in that discussion, how to conduct it, and how to ensure it serves, and continues to serve, their purposes. Insight and agreement on how to improve performance cannot be guaranteed. Nevertheless, the different ways in which self-assessment models can generate benefits, as well as some of the pitfalls associated with their use, are fairly clear. Self-assessment can be time consuming – indeed, if it is productive in generating new insights and agreement on priorities for improvement efforts, it may generate a considerable change agenda, which is likely, too, to be seen as the result of using the model.

In choosing a model, the key consideration is likely to be whether the assumptions and purposes embedded in the model are more or less appropriate to the internal (and perhaps external) context of the organisation in question – was it developed with such an organisation in mind, or to provide what those considering use are seeking from it? Use of a model developed for a rather different context or to serve a different purpose can still result in a productive dialogue, but the process is likely to be more challenging and time consuming.

At the present time, the language of quality still carries some weight in the institutional environment of many social enterprises. It provides scope for a performance discourse in terms that are specific, categorical and definitive *as well as* enabling a private, intra-organisational negotiation that recognises the shifting, problematic and multifaceted nature of quality in human services. Although often criticised for being ambiguous and contested – for not providing certainties, one might say – if this is recognised and accepted, it seems an advantage rather than a weakness. It may allow managers and professionals to collaborate on important (if often intractable) issues and at the same time to represent their organisation externally as abreast of the times, legitimate, effective.

Sources and resources

Information on PQASSO is available from the website of Charities Evaluation Service (www.ces-vol.org.uk). For the Excellence Model visit the British Quality Foundation (www.quality-foundation.co.uk). Both models have been revised since the studies reported in this chapter were undertaken.

Academic studies on the implementation of quality ideas and approaches over time are sadly lacking. Chapter 6 of Clarke and Newman (1997) contains a gloomy overview of the issues in social policy terms. For a perspective grounded in management and organisational practice, Seddon's reflections on the Excellence Model, based on his experience as a consultant, are thoughtfully informative and entirely credible (Seddon 1998). Finally, Powell (1995), though dated, provides an analytically powerful appraisal of TQM in commercial contexts that relates it to broader themes of strategic management and organisational change.

8 Towards Practice: Choosing a Suite of Measures

From the preceding chapters it is obvious that questions about the performance of social enterprises can be asked from many different perspectives, and a huge number of things can be counted or measured or compared in order to help gauge performance. A problem arises, therefore, in defining a broad enough but manageable set of measures - this is the tension between comprehensiveness and parsimony noted in Chapter 3. Capturing, collating, analysing, presenting and studying information all carry costs. More is not necessarily better, and in any event it is seldom *clearer*. But equally, when things go wrong, one regret will always concern the information that was not available, or that was overlooked. So how *should* the trustees and senior managers of social enterprises decide their reporting priorities? How much performance information is enough - and on what should it focus? This chapter addresses these issues. It offers a tool ('the dashboard') for appraising an organization's measurement and reporting systems, and for clarifying priorities regarding possible changes and improvements. Where is more information needed – and, indeed, where is too much information being amassed and reported?

The discussion starts with an appraisal of the Balanced Scorecard, a framework for designing performance measurement systems that has been widely adopted in the private sector. The difficulties in applying this to social enterprises help clarify what is needed from an alternative. This is then developed, focussing on meeting the reporting needs of Trustees and senior managers. This framework adopts the metaphor of a dashboard – common in France ('tableau de bord') – and hence it is referred to as a dashboard for social enterprises. The use of this tool is then illustrated and the discussion highlights emerging dilemmas of information management. *En route*, a number of topics and cases from earlier in the book are revisited. For although this chapter contains some further researches, it also begins the process of drawing together themes and implications from the studies already reported.

The Balanced Scorecard and taking stock of measurement

The Impact of the 'Balanced Scorecard'. For the private sector, the challenge of defining a well-rounded but focussed suite of measures was famously posed and answered by Kaplan and Norton in their Harvard Business Review articles, and subsequent book, on the Balanced Scorecard (Kaplan and Norton 1996). Their framework was elegantly simple - essentially a set of four boxes representing four key perspectives on a company's performance – see figure 8.1. These were the external financial perspective, the internal business process or operational perspective, the customer perspective, and the learning and growth perspective.

or operational perspective, the customer perspective, and the learning and growth perspective. They argued that a company needed to use a few measures from within each of these perspectives – but which measures should be used was up to the company and depended on their situation. Such a combination of measures would be manageable and by being drawn from all four perspectives it would reduce the risk of managers doing well in relation to what was being measured, at the expense of what was not being measured: 'Even the best objective can be achieved badly', as they put it (Kaplan and Norton 1996, p 73).

Figure 8.1 The Balanced Scorecard (after Kaplan and Norton, 1992)

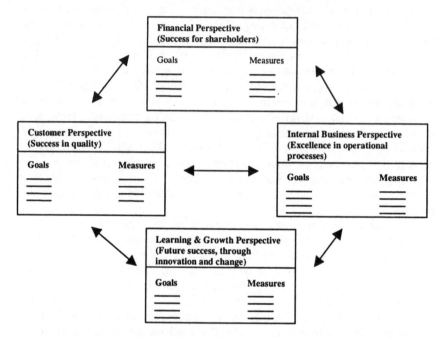

Coming as it did at the end of a decade of experimentation and growth in measurement activity in a wide range of fields (Eccles 1991), the Balanced Scorecard attracted huge interest.[34] It acknowledged the primacy of financial reporting while deftly legitimising a range of non-financial measures and providing a coherent basis for resisting short-term financial results. It has been criticised for considering too narrow a set of stakeholders (employees, suppliers and the community have no seat at the table) (Atkinson 1997). In principle, however, additional, or different, perspectives could be used, if this was agreed to be important (Kaplan 2001). For managers lost among the myriad trees of conflicting priorities and measurement, this was a map of the woods. Even commentators in France acknowledged that the approach addressed familiar weaknesses in the way *tableaux de bord* tended to be implemented (Epstein and Manzoni 1998).

Nonprofit variants. So does such an approach also provide a map for the managers of social enterprises – who likewise need a rounded but focused suite of measures? Some successes have been reported – especially where the balanced scorecard provided blessed relief from narrowly focused financial control systems (Aidemark 2001). But there are several difficulties. Some of these arise from the differences between corporations and social enterprises. The latter pursue a 'double bottom line' of social and financial objectives – so the financial perspective cannot be pre-eminent (as in the Balanced Scorecard). And the customer perspective needs to be duplicated, to accommodate the very different concerns of, for example, donors and beneficiaries. Cutt and Murray (2000) have sketched some quite complex balanced scorecards for different sorts of nonprofits along these lines. However, theirs is more a theoretical exploration than the development of a practical tool, and concerned primarily with constructing a rationalised ('chronologically and casually linked' – p 238) model of performance for accountability purposes (ie institutional-level reporting, rather than the internal management of resources and activities). Further difficulties arise because explanations of the Balanced Scorecard and its use draw on examples from corporate contexts that generally address rather different issues and that assume considerable staff resources are available to gather, analyse and report figures (an exception is given in chapter 8 of Kaplan and Atkinson (1998). Finally, as always, the Balanced Scorecard's simplicity is bought at the price of being very abstract. In consequence, it leaves a great deal for managers to do, in order to apply it in their own organisation.[35]

None of these difficulties is insuperable – and indeed, for large social enterprises operating in a trading environment, it may well be a good enough place to begin. But nor are they trivial. Hence there is scope for a version, or an alternative, tailored to the contexts and concerns of social enterprises. Ideally, this will retain the clarity of the Balanced Scorecard along with its key idea – adopting relatively few measures, but choosing them to represent a range of different perspectives, each highlighting an important aspect of overall performance (a pragmatic blend of focus and comprehensiveness). In addition, it will have two other features. First, it will be conceptually more appropriate, in the sense of accommodating the distinctive features of social enterprise performance. Secondly, it will be presented in ways that relate more directly to the terms and the contexts in which trustees, directors and others think about performance measurement and reporting, and the resources they have available for this.

A 'Dashboard' for social enterprises

Back to basics – distinguishing levels of analysis. The vast majority of the measures that social enterprises use and the enquiries to which they have to respond, are aimed at answering two basic questions. The first concerns efficacy – put simply, 'does it work?' In other words, do the different activities, services, programmes achieve broadly the results intended. The second question is about the social enterprise as an enduring configuration of resources and relationships; in one way or another people want to know 'is it well run?'

These questions are related – part of what we mean by being 'well-run' is delivering effective programmes. But they are not the same and in the short, even medium term, answers can diverge starkly. A valuable and innovative service may be provided by an organisation that is inefficiently administered, or even by one whose funds are being discretely embezzled; and a well administered organisation with excellent morale may be delivering high quality programmes to clients whose needs are slight compared to those of the client group originally envisaged.

Moreover, the distinction between programmes (or projects, in smaller nonprofits) and organisations is often overlooked – not least by funders reluctant to contribute to 'core costs'. In the end, it is the existence of sound organisational practices, cultures and systems that ensures the quality of programmes is sustained over time, that they are renewed as needs change, and that they can be successfully propagated in new contexts (Letts, Ryan et al. 1999). Hence, it does not take long for a narrow or exclusive concern with programmes and their outcomes on the part of funders or trustees, to become self-defeating. Organisations, like individuals, become emaciated and burnt out if they do not take care of themselves as well as those they serve.

The frequency of reporting and review. These broad questions – are the programmes effective and is the organisation well run? – are given focus by the contexts in which they are posed. Essentially, there are two. First, on a day-to-day (or at least, month-to-month) basis, trustees and managers may ask variants of either question about current activities and arrangements. They need to know if they are 'on course', if things are going more or less as expected, or if there are warning signals. Secondly, they may explore these same questions but with a longer term concern for the underlying trends. This is the difference between 'are we doing things right? and 'are we doing the right things?', between single-loop learning and double-loop learning. Every organisation has to operate on the basis of assumptions – about needs, methods, trends – and those assumptions need to be reviewed and revised. But there is a time and a place – no organisation can constantly challenge all its own assumptions and still get work done. So the information required for day-to-day management is different from that required for a more strategic review, with the latter requiring much more environmental information.

Elements of a generic dashboard. Hence the architecture of a dashboard for social enterprises[36] must provide at least four different sets of dials, depending on the question and the context – as indicated in table 8.1.

However, one other area of reporting needs to be introduced. As it stands the matrix provides no space for reporting progress on major changes to the organisation itself, for which trustees or a senior management team may themselves be directly responsible. Lesser change can be carried out by and large within a particular programme or functional area, and reported on that basis; but major changes (eg a new information system, a re-organisation), though still aimed at improving performance albeit indirectly, cannot be – because they are organisation-wide.

Table 8.1 The main reporting requirements

	Short-term/operational context	Longer-term/strategic context
Activity/programme level – what we do (is it working?)	1. Indicators of current goal achievement. Information to answer questions concerned with 'are we doing what we said we would do?'	2. Indicators of underlying performance Information to help answer 'is it worth it, and what else should we be doing as well or instead?'
Organisational level – what we are (is it well run?)	3. Indicators of financial and administrative soundness. Information concerning ways in which the organisation is or might be 'at risk'.	4. Indicators of renewal or decline. Information to help consider 'are we building up our capabilities or at least sustaining them – or are they wasting away?'

Hence, for completeness, provision must be made for reporting on major change projects – those high-level re-development initiatives that the Trustees or senior team supervise directly. This generates a general architecture for Dashboards for social enterprises which contains the five areas shown in figure 8.3. These five areas are discussed and illustrated in turn.

Figure 8.3 The Dashboard as a reporting template for social enterprises

1. CURRENT RESULTS	2. UNDERLYING PERFORMANCE
Monthly checking of progress against key targets eg – Summary achievements – Finance report – Marketing report	Annual reviews of appropriateness and cost-effectiveness of programmes and support functions covering eg – Service outcomes – Business outcomes – External trends and comparisons

5. CHANGE PROJECTS
Regular reporting on initiatives the trustees/senior team are supervising directly.

3. RISKS	4. ASSETS & CAPABILITIES
Monitoring ways the enterprise might be put in jeopardy eg – Liquidity crisis – Legal/procedural non-conformance – Breakdown in key relationships	Annual review of capacity to deliver future performance eg – Physical & financial assets – External reputation and relationships – Expertise and process knowledge

Box 1 – Current Results. The information needed in this area is generally familiar and relatively unproblematic. The requirement, essentially, is for summary control reports from each of the main programme and functional areas, sufficient to enable peer accountability and mutual understanding within a senior management team, and organisational oversight on the part of trustees. Most organisations have a great deal of relevant budgetary and operational information – indeed, contracts often require regular reports on expenditure, activity levels and outputs, against forecasts. Hence the main issues usually concern the selection, the extent of aggregation (a particular problem), the combination, and the presentation of such data – in order to assist the understanding of current performance in each main programme and functional area, on the part of those not so closely involved. On the basis of experience, the questions that arise are:

- Has the presentation of information in reports to trustees and senior managers been reviewed *from the perspective of the information users?*

The pitfalls here are familiar eg a short cover note on top of excessively detailed management accounts or operational reports. Managers who report in this way should not be surprised if trustees are drawn down into operational details and away from policy issues.

- How can summary indicators of social results be routinely reported and presented alongside information on the financial/business performance of programmes? Interestingly, the data on which to base these is almost always available, but it is rarely presented in this way. While of limited value in instrumental or control terms, such headline figures on what is currently being achieved may well have an important symbolic role in reminding everyone what they are really there for.[37]

Box 2 – Underlying Performance. The assumption here is that each main area of activity is subject to a strategic review at some point during an annual (or biennial) cycle. This would be the occasion for more fundamental questions about the effectiveness and continuing value of activities and methods to be addressed. The question therefore is 'what information is required for such reviews?'

As regards programme areas, each needs to be appraised in terms of its *social success* and its *business success*, and for each of these an appraisal needs both *internal* information, particularly trend data, and *external*, comparative information. To illustrate what this can mean in practice, table 8.2 shows the sorts of information needed for programme review at PHS – a good example, because information of all four types was in fact gathered and used.

Ideally, comparable information would be obtained and used in reviewing support functions like fundraising, finance and administration, and HR. The same principles – of clarifying goal achievement taking the views of (internal) customers into account, and obtaining external comparative and contextual information wherever possible – are relevant. In practice, of course, the effort expended on such a review needs to be commensurate with the likely benefits – it is not an end in itself.

Hence many of the measurement practices discussed in chapters 4 and 5 are relevant – administrative or fundraising costs in relation to comparable organisations, outcomes or impact measures (which it will often not be realistic to gather and report more than once a year), and data from occasional benchmarking exercises.

Box 3 – Risk.   All organisations face risks. For social enterprises, nasty surprises may come in the form of a suddenly worsening financial situation, the discovery of legal, contractual or procedural non-conformance, the eruption of board or staff disputes, client complaints or project failures – all of which may then be accentuated by damaging publicity. The question then is, if difficulties were developing in one or more of these areas, would senior managers or trustees be alerted to such a development, or have the information to recognise it?

Table 8.2 PRIM, the Programme Review Information Matrix, illustrated by the case of Pioneer Human Services

	Social performance	Business performance
Internal information	Activity and output levels; Completion rates/client feedback/complaints data/trends in client profiles…	Trends in key indicators of financial and operational performance, eg cost-activity and cost-output trends, margins, etc.
External information	Outcome studies – as per the collaborative project with the University of Washington. Benchmarking data (re-offending rates, or data from comparable projects/organisations). Innovations developed by others. New patterns of social need.	Market share, and competitor analysis (eg how much 'people recovery work' is being funded, by whom? Who else is getting and doing this work, and why?). Market trends (eg regarding public policy).

Hence, this box is about monitoring specific risks to which a social enterprise knows it is exposed. For example, the Groundwork trusts discussed in chapter 4 operate in a particularly uncertain and complex contracting environment and over the years they have devised a set of financial ratios and milestones which help to track progress through the financial year, and to distinguish *serious difficulties* from *normal difficulties*. PHS provides another example: quality assurance is essential for some of its manufacturing and facilities contracts, and hence it tracks the incidence of non-compliance reported. For a national childcare charity the concerns raised by this box centred around child protection procedures and adverse publicity. In general, the issues that arise in this area are essentially those of risk management and they tend to be as much cultural as informational – anticipating possible dangers, cultivating respect for key procedures, not discouraging the reporting of 'bad news', and so on.

Box 4 – Assets and capabilities. Traditional balance sheet items – property, physical assets, investments and reserves – are important for some social enterprises. But usually their key assets are intangible – being recognised and trusted by the public, having a large database of donors and supporters, having positive relationships with particular funders or government agencies, having 'know-how' in a particular field. Using Groundwork and PHS as examples again, both have developed distinctive capabilities in building and maintaining relationships with very diverse commercial and governmental partners, and in holding together the imperatives of business and social concern.   In Groundwork's case this has involved integrating environmental improvement, economic development and community work. For PHS, it has meant becoming practised at working with challenging clients in 'normal' employment situations. These capabilities are diffusely embedded in both organisations in the form of skills, attitudes, working relationships, experience, procedures, policies, training schemes, and so on. They allow both organisations to set up and run new projects and programmes promptly, reliably and with good results, where others new to the field would struggle or fail.

In the language of business, these are matters of brand value and intellectual capital. Over the last decade, protecting and enhancing such intangible assets has been seen as so important for future success that a great deal of effort has been devoted to estimating their value for particular companies (see eg Brooking 1996; Roos, Roos et al. 1997). Whether such efforts have really paid off is doubtful; certainly, anyone who was looking for a simple and reliable metric will long since have been disappointed (Brontis, Gragonetti et al. 1999). On the other hand, the work has produced toolkits for helping recognise where and when key capabilities have been strengthened or undermined.

For social enterprises, these aspects of performance are often only considered intuitively, or within particular functional areas – is the donor list getting old? Do we need to re-write the staff handbook? They are rarely addressed in a more explicit way, on an organisation-wide basis. Nevertheless, managers readily appreciate the significance of these issues, and this area of the dashboard challenges them to consider what the capabilities essential for their organisation's future success really are; what the practices and ways of working that 'carry' these key capabilities are; and (finally) the information that might be drawn together to help judge what is happening to those capabilities.

There are relatively few tools available to help with such reviews, but the self-assessment models considered in the last chapter could well be used for this purpose. Although the Excellence Model is primarily concerned with quality, the 'enablers' are very much concerned with aspects of organisational capability. And PQASSO, which covers a broad array of basic organisational processes and systems, is being used as a capacity-building tool in several local government areas. These tools illustrate the sort of information needed and the process likely to be involved. Much will be 'soft', qualitative and distributed – a matter of experienced staff and managers sharing their impressions and observations. But some information will be formally recorded and more readily accessed. By way of illustration, such information might include: gains and losses in experienced and expert staff over the year, spend on staff development, the adequacy of IT and other facilities for sharing information, ideas and experience ('knowledge management'); the development of cross- and inter-organisational networks and external changes affecting capabilities (eg the departure of key people in *partner* organisations).

Box 5 – Major change projects. Changes like mergers, re-structuring and new IT infrastructures may be challenging for senior managers to plan, negotiate and carry through, but in reporting terms their progress is generally straightforward to monitor. How far the changes, in the end, deliver the benefits intended is a more difficult question, of course. But unless they have become seriously controversial it is not one worth spending scarce time and resources addressing formally.

'Health Rights International' and the limits of measurement

Working with the Dashboard. The core theory implicit in the dashboard is simply that the leaders of a social enterprise need information on performance in the five areas specified. It says nothing about how much there should be or how it should be provided. Through working with it on the reporting issues of a variety of organisations, some additional heuristics – like the programme review information matrix in table 8.2 – have developed. It is a typical consulting or self-assessment tool and a process on the following lines is suggested:

• If necessary, familiarisation with the organisation – its objectives, activities and current reporting practices.

• Developing a model dashboard – that is, a set of suggestions for what in principle is required for each of the five 'dials' in order to meet the organisation's needs, while taking account of its resources and culture.

• Use this in order to stimulate and structure debate among those involved on whether and in what areas some sharpening up of reporting might be warranted.

To the extent that it relies on comparing an analytically derived model with current practice, but does so in a way that those involved can own, the approach is in the spirit of soft systems methodology (Checkland 1981). Hence any idea that some idealised dashboard will be devised, sold and then 'implemented' – as some may hope and others will fear – needs to be emphatically ruled out from the beginning. In practice, thinking hard about a 'dashboard' and performance reporting often raises wider questions, for example, about strategy and the role and functioning of the senior management team. Indeed, in one large national organisation the absence of a tolerably clear and agreed strategy meant it was simply not possible to pursue work with which we had been invited to help. These and other issues are illustrated in the following case.

Health Rights International (HRI). This is a registered charity with an annual budget of c. $5,000,000. Its head office in London has about 12 full-time-equivalent staff, including some volunteers. It employs more than 100 local and expatriate staff in 18 projects in a dozen countries across Asia, Africa and Latin America. When it was established in the early 1980s it concentrated on the introduction of primary health care in extreme situations – marginal communities and those isolated and endangered by warfare. Its mission was summed up as 'working to improve the health of people threatened by conflict', and it saw its role as the development of sustainable systems of primary health care, incorporating traditional and basic western medicine. More recently, it has developed capacities in mass health education, based on the use of popular 'soap opera'-style radio broadcasts in local languages. This means HRI can now claim to reach over 8 million people.

It has e-mail links with most of its projects, and monthly financial reports are made in electronic form using a specially designed spreadsheet. About 85% of its income is from contracts with the Department for International Development or other governmental agencies (including the EU and the UN). These carry detailed reporting requirements which HRI sets out in a comprehensive project managers manual. Most of its remaining income is generated by a small fundraising section supported by some well-known patrons and trustees.

The work with HRI followed an invitation from the Director, and a review of performance reporting systems for the management team was agreed with him. It was a deliberately limited exercise that took the following form:

- a meeting with the management group to talk through the scope and purpose of the exercise;[38]

- a round of interviews with the Director and five other senior staff to establish what sort of information was or might be available;

- the preparation of a report – summarised below – based on these interviews as well as internal documents;

- a day-long workshop with the management team to debate the report and to agree whether and in what ways they would take the work forward.

Current Results (Box 1). The model put forward for the programme areas is summarised in table 8.3. It was argued that all this information was already available, much of it coming back on the monthly spreadsheets from which it could be automatically assembled and presented to show trends. In other cases – eg 'difficulties' and 'slippage' – the model would mean highlighting and making explicit judgements that were being made anyway, and that trustees might need to be aware of, before problems become acute. This also seemed to be the case with the information for the Prospects (marketing) report on progress in identifying fundable and worthwhile project opportunities, and in negotiating support for them. The Director and programme managers had the information, in the sense that they did not find it difficult to offer judgements, but it was not often made explicit.

This model represented a massive *reduction* in the amount of information that would be routinely provided – though it was pointed out that particular project reports could be easily made available, or even appended, if required or requested.

Table 8.3 'Current results' suggestions for HRI

Primary Care	Development Media
Summary achievement indicators	
Number of live projects	Number of live projects
Number of individual health consultations	Number of broadcast hours

Number of person-days local health training	Estimated total combined audience
Control reports	
Variance to budget	Variance to budget
Number of projects affected by significant difficulties	Number of projects affected by significant difficulties
Extent of 'slippage' on projects in a set-up phase	Extent of 'slippage' on projects in a set-up phase
Prospects report	
Number of possible contracts under discussion	Number of possible contracts under discussion
Number of probable contracts being negotiated	Number of probable contracts being negotiated

In addition, the model dashboard suggested the form for simple reports from the fundraising area (eg income raised against forecast and previous year; plus summary narrative on key milestones, difficulties, prospects or events), and from support functions.

Underlying performance (Box 2). As usual, as a way of taking account of the concerns of different stakeholders, the model dashboard offered a way of appraising each programme area in terms of its mission performance and its business performance. Given HRI's modest size and very limited management resource, it was important to consider what additional information for an annual strategic review was particularly important, and how it could be most easily gathered.

Regarding mission performance, the model suggested a range of internally generated indicators – *eg* number and size of projects, results achieved, the nature and frequency of issues affecting projects. Again, most of these were readily available within project reports, but whether they were being accessed and used for such purposes was uncertain. Key categories of external information were also suggested, including longer term outcome/impact information, data on changing patterns of needs, and on any innovative ways of addressing needs being developed elsewhere. It was suggested that some of this information gathering might be funded separately (as research, or through sponsorship of a benchmarking exercise).

Regarding business performance, the model suggested indicators of financial and 'market' performance – such as cost and cost-activity trends, and 'contribution to overheads' achieved; and a five-year graphical summary of forward project commitments and prospects. The sorts of external information proposed included 'market share', and some basic 'competitor' analysis – while acknowledging that this would not be easily obtained. The report suggested drawing together and systematising 'soft' data gathered through discussions with funders in policy fora, and other industry networking that were already undertaken.

The model's suggestions for reviews of Fundraising and PR were straightforward, with internal data providing trends in cost/income performance for different types of fundraising. These would be backed up by brief narratives on major fundraising or PR initiatives agreed at the previous review and which are important but whose results or progress cannot be measured only in financial terms. In addition, the report suggested that it might, from time to time (but not annually), be worth obtaining comparative cost/return data through the 'Fundratios' scheme, or an informal benchmarking club comprising comparable charities. For reviews of the Finance and HR functions the model's suggestions essentially involved making existing practice a bit more explicit. Thus, some possible performance indicators were outlined and the scope for external comparisons, at least on an occasional basis, noted.

Risk. The interviews had identified two areas of perceived risk: staff overload and the potential burnout of key players in a small team, and financial vulnerability. For the former, the problem lay in gauging the severity of overload and stress. Turnover and sickness rates are the standard indicators (and allow external comparability), but in a small organisation they are bound to bounce around somewhat. It was argued that what really matters is the extent and duration of any shortfall between actual staffing level and the requisite staffing level (people can cover for a vacant post for a time, but not indefinitely). In addition, some simple statistics that could be easily generated and tracked over time were suggested – like unused holiday entitlement and the extent of 'late working'.

As regards monitoring financial vulnerability the report discussed liquidity and reserve ratios, but focused more on core funding prospects, where there were no accounting conventions to turn to. It was argued that because projects have to be maintained (for the beneficiaries and to meet contracted commitments), any project shortfalls have to be covered *either* by other project surpluses, *or* from voluntary income *or* by reducing central overheads (the 'core costs'). In principle, drawing on reserves was another possibility, but they were not great and policy was to build them up. Hence, it was essentially a matter of whether, for any forecast period:

Total project contributions + voluntary income > core costs.

Of course, there would be many uncertainties (quite when will a project come on line? What if voluntary income is down on this year? Is a new staff member now unavoidable? etc). Some early warning was already provided by next year's budget forecast, which was updated and examined for this purpose regularly. But this did not match the way managers thought about the core costs issue, or help them focus on it. Hence the model dashboard put forward the idea of trying to capture the significance of the necessary (but programmable) calculations in a simple 'warning light'.[39]

Assets and capabilities. HRI's important assets were all intangible. The report suggested they be considered under three headings:

- 'Brand value' – covering its supporter base, relationships with key players in the main funding agencies, and reputation in relevant networks;

- Partnership capacity – covering field collaborations, and its extensive joint working with complementary agencies;

- Structural and Intellectual capital – covering the expertise and experience of staff, the manuals, pro-formas, standard spreadsheets, and recognised ways of doing things, the electronic and professional/staff networks and routines, to share information and make relevant expertise and experience accessible where and when it is needed.

The report suggested that an annual review or audit, carried out through a simple self-assessment process, perhaps with outside help, be conducted. The process would bring together factual information (various suggestions were made from the data that HRI already possessed) and the views of relevant participants, for discussion and consensus-generation. The output would be a summary statement covering:

i.   what HRI now see as its most important and distinctive capabilities;

ii. what the main changes to those capabilities have been over the last year;

iii. whe capabilities that most need enhancing in the coming year, and how this will be tackled.

Suggestions for reporting on major change projects (Box 5). To keep in step with the relocation of governmental funding decisions to the South, HRI was planning to establish regional offices and reduce the role of the London HQ. That decision needed to be turned into a project plan against which progress could be reported, but in strictly reporting terms this raised no particular issues.

The Workshop and follow through. The report seemed to have t ـn well received and the workshop itself was lively. In the morning it was difficult to maintain focus on the reporting issues[40] and to maintain the discussion within the terms of the Dashboard framework. In the afternoon, after reconsidering the scope and purpose of the exercise, the discussion was more focused and gradually the following issues were chosen as the focus for further work:

- The need to carry out Programme reviews (Box 2). As one person said, 'I'm supposed to be a Programme manager and all I have is a load of project reports'. She undertook to carry out such a review and identified the time in the annual reporting cycle when it would most sensibly be undertaken.

- The need to make their Prospect reporting more systematic and use the information better in preventing unpleasant financial surprises (Box 3). The Director, who had particularly liked the equation in the report, took this on.

- The need to give attention to building the organisations capacities – and hence an interest in exploring the idea of an audit of intangible assets (Box 4). The HR manager committed to pursuing this.

In practice, however, the follow-through on these commitments was very limited – at least in terms of new reporting practices. Over the next six months HRI made major organisational changes, substantially enhancing the roles of the programme managers and adopting a new strategy aimed at growing themselves out of their core funding difficulties. In other words, they addressed the substantive issues (capturing and developing their know-how in programme areas; financial vulnerability) that lay behind the reporting areas about which they were concerned. But they did not significantly change those reporting practices.

Making sense of the exercise. Two interpretations spring to mind: the first is that, for whatever reasons, the managers of HRI missed a trick. How, for example, will they know if they are really improving their 'knowledge management'? And what if their new strategy falters – surely they are still vulnerable to financial surprises?

The second interpretation would be that the HRI team did exactly what they should have done. Measurement and formal reporting are expensive of time and effort; and the design of measurement and reporting systems require scarce managerial time. Hence, although everything can be reported upon and even measured, the opportunity costs of doing so will often be so great that it is simply not worthwhile. Moreover, all organisations, but especially small ones, manage through tacit and informal processes – this is normal, and generally effective *enough*, as well as efficient (see, eg, North, Blackburn et al. 1998). In such situations, organising is fluid, and it is misleading to imagine that 'performance reporting' to the management team (as opposed to the trustees) is a discrete activity set apart from the on-going flow of operational information, discussion and decision making.

While there may be some truth in both interpretations, the second seems much more convincing. But this does not mean that the exercise was unhelpful. Concepts that focus attention on important matters (albeit they are hard to measure) can be useful, even if they are not carried through into new reporting arrangements, let alone measurement.[41]

From performance measurement to information management

The HRI case neatly illustrates what is emerging as a pressing management dilemma for social enterprises. Though by no means a large organisation, it has been steadily increasing its use of ICTs both for record-keeping, for handling operational data, and for communication. No longer is it just a case that accounting information is on the computer – even in quite small organisations, systems are being improvised to handle supporters and donors records, staffing records, standardised field or project reports. Such developments are pervasive – and of course in larger and better-resourced organisations they are being carried out with considerable sophistication. The result is that more and more databases are potentially available for selection, collation, aggregation, integration and analysis. They start to become not just departmental figures but an organisational resource with which to explore performance issues and concerns that were probably never envisaged when the data was first collected.

Two challenges then arise. The first is the need to integrate diverse systems. Managers realise they must bring together accounting information with activity or output or outcome data from professional and operational areas, or from fundraising. They want to understand the choices they are facing and to be able to tell (and show) when, say, spending more on their services is a good thing and when it is a bad thing. But to do this the categories must match – and of course they don't, because they were developed in quite different contexts for different purposes. The second challenge is the need for flexibility, because as we have seen, performance is always a multifaceted and evolving concept, and frequently contested. So, if it is too well integrated an organisation-wide system may be dangerously inflexible – not to mention horridly expensive to develop and maintain.

This is the issue of information management – how far to go in trying to formalise and integrate information systems, and since they are developing anyway, how to make them as efficient as possible, serving a range of users. It is the territory of Executive Information Systems (see, eg, Watson, Houdeshel et al. 1997). Historically, like 'best practice' benchmarking, EIS have been a game for large organisations – and many of them have learned to play it the hard way. But the costs of the technical infrastructure keep falling and the software keeps improving, and so, starting with the larger ones, social enterprises are becoming involved (Graham 1999).

Information politics and information culture. These challenges are severe enough simply in rational, analytic terms. But of course they also have crucial behavioural dimensions. Information is power, and pro-active information management calls in question the structure and culture of many organisations. Moreover, as we have seen, performance is usually a contested concept, and so whose versions of performance become expressed in the measurement system can be a hot political issue. Davenport and colleagues observed different patterns of information politics in large companies, developing in some detail an analogy with different political systems (Davenport 1992). Adapting this schema to social enterprises provides a convenient way of capturing some of the variety of current practice:

(a) *Feudalism* – where the centre is weak and strong barons guard their fiefdoms. Finance, operations/service delivery, fundraising, and Human Resources all have their own separate systems. For example the accounting system does not provide the information fundraising managers' need to analyse and understand the returns on their campaigns. So they gradually develop their own systems for data capture and analysis. Likewise, service professionals develops record systems for different sorts of clients, but then managers cannot match these with cost information because this has been gathered using different categories, is confidential, and anyway key data has not been included. There is hardly a common currency, as different parts of the organisation pursue their own conceptions of what to measure and how, and use different definitions when talking about the same things. There was a time when examples could be found in higher education.

(b) *Colonisation.* This describes settings where the development of accounting and reporting systems has been dominated by the need to meet the requirements of one or more major funders. Hence the systems are devoted to institutional-level reporting, and closely integrated with those of the funder or contracting agency. (Ebrahim, 2002, provides a detailed description and discussion in relation to two Indian NGOs.) The needs of professional and managerial decision making are more or less neglected, but can still be served through informal processes. Health Rights International may be considered a case in point, though not an extreme one. Colonisation is of course more common with smaller organisations or projects, and given a reasonable alignment between the objectives of the funders and the social enterprises this is a perfectly sensible arrangement (a protectorate, one might say).[42]

(c) *Enlightened monarchies* – where a strong centre drives the introduction of a more integrated approach to information systems and performance reporting based on agreed goals and a common set of definitions, but sensitive enough to the needs of different activities to command general support. The drive to develop mission outcomes reporting at PHS has some of these features, as have various other cases encountered or reported (eg Graham 1999).

(d) *Negotiated federalism* – where the centre leads a debate among the departmental barons or the regions and branches over a common framework for performance measurement, and collates the results for all to consider. The Groundwork Federation is a good illustration of this approach.

But these are not much better than speculations. Very little is known about how information management is evolving in social enterprises, and most of the reports are from the perspective of a particular function. Even less is known about the wider effects on management and organisational culture. The research opportunities are wide open.

Conclusions

This chapter has developed the 'Dashboard' as a framework for performance monitoring and review in which managers' (and trustees') needs for information are represented in terms of five discrete domains, in relation to five different sorts of managerial concern. The resulting framework does not avoid the need for hard thinking about what an organisation is really trying to do, what its key resources are, and how desirable outcomes and attributes may be deftly gauged. Its purpose is to stimulate, guide and organise the results of such thinking. Like the Balanced Scorecard, the Dashboard is a general template for the main types of reporting information required. Its use may direct attention to important issues. But the framework itself cannot prescribe answers.

Many of the forms of measurement discussed in earlier chapters were readily located within the framework, as possible ways of meeting particular needs for performance information. However, the approach goes beyond the usual ideas of programme evaluation and external accountability, with their attendant danger, if they are not complemented by other measures, of colonisation. Hence the importance of giving attention to key aspects of organisational performance, for example, regarding intangible assets.

Another important theme has been that performance measurement and reporting do not necessarily mean developing formal systems. Information is expensive, and gathering it can be intrusive. Informal systems may still have much to recommend them. A final implication is that *information management* is and will increasingly be a challenge in social enterprises, and one that requires senior management attention and collaboration. The new ITCs extend the scope for data capture, handling, aggregation and analysis but decisions about when and how best to use these new opportunities are very difficult.

Sources and resources

Kaplan and Norton's book *The Balanced Scorecard* (1996) is clear and straightforward (as are their Harvard Business Review articles). It contains one rather limited example of the use of the approach in a nonprofit context. A much more stimulating instance can be found in chapter 8 of Kaplan and Atkinson's. (1998) *Advanced Management Accounting* where the difficulties with the meaning of the 'customer' perspective are discussed candidly (opinions will differ on how well they are resolved). This case is one of three discussed more briefly in Kaplan (2001) – probably the best general starting point. There are several websites with information about the Balanced Scorecard, including Kaplan and Norton's own site (www.bscol.com).

Work on Dashboards for Social Enterprises continues and the author welcomes examples and experiences of performance-reporting frameworks that have attempted to address the sorts of dilemmas discussed.

As regards information management, Davenport's article is seminal but see also Ebrahim (2002). This important article provides a detailed discussion of two Indian NGOs and the creation and use (or not) of information required by funders.

9 A More Measured Management?

Where we began. The early chapters of this book pointed out that the spread of performance measurement and improvement methods originating in the private sector has been the 'big story' in public and nonprofit management over the last decade. This development has been pervasive - occurring in organizations large and small, in all the fields of activity, and affecting all the functions of management. The central chapters of the book examined instances of this general trend - in the form of particular methods being applied in a varied range of social enterprises. The aim of this last chapter is to stand back and to return to some of the broader questions about this phenomenon. As was pointed out, the methods are often controversial, with very different accounts on offer regarding why they are taken up, and what is actually happening 'on the ground' as they are applied in new contexts. So what light do the various studies reported throw on these broader questions? In particular, are there any general implications for policy-makers, funders, trustees and managers? Of course, the limited number of cases - selected with a deliberate bias towards early adopters, longevity and success - mean all such implications can only be offered tentatively. Nevertheless, they highlight some recurring organizational processes and fit better with some theories than others. Setting out these implications allows them to be scrutinised and tested - either against the reader's own organizational experience, or in future research.

Understanding the spread of performance improvement methods

Generic tools? The genericist position (p nn in chapter 1) claims that the challenges and circumstances for which the performance improvement methods are helpful commonly arise in other sectors, and hence social enterprises will often gain from using them. At first glance, this view seems to be supported. Best Practice Benchmarking (BPB), quality assurance (ISO 9000), Investors in People, the Excellence Model (EM) and Social Audit, have been applied in very different sectoral contexts from those in which they originated. And in various of the instances examined, the claims of success on the part of those who had used them withstood scrutiny.

However, this support for the genericist position needs some important qualifications. First, the practicability of one method, outcome measurement, has appeared questionable. In the two instances examined, both well-resourced, long-standing efforts in favourable organizational settings, outcome measurement remained more an aspiration than an indentifiable practice. The genericist position can be maintained as a broad generalisation by accepting that the circumstances of social enterprises may, not infrequently, make this particular method impracticable. Nevertheless, since outcome measurement is particular method impracticable. Nevertheless, since outcome measurement is the transposition to nonprofit contexts of that most basic business practice of focusing tightly on a single, central purpose, and given that the circumstances of social enterprises are often unfavourable for such measurement, then this is not a trivial concession. Secondly, although social enterprises benefited from using the methods, it was often for the reasons other than those implied by the genericist argument. Quality assurance and BPB, in particular, were adapted and applied in different ways to new challenges and circumstances, and these methods evolved significantly in the process (as is discussed further below). In other words, as the methods spread they took new forms and new uses were discovered for them, and so the class of circumstances for which they were appropriate expanded.

Everything depends, therefore, on quite how the genericist argument is expressed. A strong version might claim, for example, that all of the methods, defined quite specifically, are widely applicable across sectors. By contrast a moderate version would claim only that most of such methods, loosely defined, are applicable in different ways and to different degrees in all sectors. The strong version is clearly mistaken, while the moderate version would seem to be sound, if less remarkable.[43]

Management fads?   The idea that performance improvement methods are fashionable in the management community offered another explanation for their diffusion among social enterprises (see p11). If correct, then those managers of social enterprises who identify with the broader management community would be susceptible to exaggerated claims about their efficacy, but the results of using the methods would be disappointing. It was certainly the case that many managers of social enterprises identified with the wider management community. Large numbers had come across the various methods, and were clearly interested in them. The language and rhetoric associated with the methods was widely adopted. And the results achieved from using the methods were quite often less than had been hoped.

However, as with genericism, this explanation, while superficially attractive, does not stand up well to closer examination. Although many of the managers whose initiatives were studied or whose views were gathered in this study were interested in new management ideas and open to them, they seldom showed much sign of uncritical adoption and inflated expectations. Rather, most appeared sceptical towards anything that might constitute 'hype', and gave the impression of considering what would be appropriate and acceptable in the circumstances of their own organisations. Indeed, given the range of methods on offer, many were weighing up with colleagues whether and which one might be suitable for their situation, rather than being drawn in to a current trend. Likewise, the interest in Social Audit and PQASSO, methods developed especially for social enterprises, does not sit easily with the idea that they were uncritically following a fashion for the adoption of business methods.

This is not to suggest that the managers encountered during the researches were only ever saying and doing things that seemed shrewdly appropriate and well-judged. Some had reasons for thinking particular methods would be appropriate in their situations that seemed idiosyncratic to the researchers;

others seem to have become over-committed to a particular method and were taking it too far. But most were alert to the difficulties and potential pitfalls, and instances were encountered of managers trying a method but then abandoning it because the time and effort involved was excessive in relation to the likely benefits. More specifically, given the difficulty in tracing cases of BPB it is hardly credible that many managers have been uncritically adopting that method, or persisting in its use, regardless of its suitability.

Another major difficulty with fashion as an explanation is that securing the confidence of external stakeholders was often an important consideration in the decision to adopt the methods. Hence resource dependence and the institutional environment, and not just psycho-social processes, need to be included in the account. This was most obvious with PQASSO, where many of the managers of local projects did not identify with the wider management community and did not even know what quality assurance was, but had become convinced that adopting the system would be to their project's advantage.

Perhaps the underlying problem with this explanation is that it is unclear what constitutes 'following a fashion' in the context of management. Curiosity does not equate to belief any more than enjoyment of a consultant's presentation at a conference means uncritically subscribing to the approach in one's own situation. Nor does tactical regard for a 'buzz-word' mean endorsing systematic use of a particular approach. Indeed, the very concept of fashion, strongly associated as it is with non-rational and passive patterns of consumption, may underestimate how most managers actually *use* the new ideas and techniques that are promoted to them. The impression from this research is that most are discerning, not gullible, consumers; occasional and doubting attenders at the church, rather than 'true believers' (Pattison and Paton 1997). For every manager who invests misplaced confidence in a fashionable approach, there are many more who shrewdly observe, select, adapt or simply allude to the new ideas.

Expectations from the institutional environment? Institutional theory offered a third explanation for the spread of the methods, by suggesting it was a special case of a more general phenomenon: that organisations operating within a recognised 'field' tend to become similar (especially if they are more dependent on an institutional, than a trading environment). The argument is, first, that each organisation needs to maintain its credibility in the eyes of powerful external bodies. Second, that the features characterising 'organisational fields' – many equivalent units, power relations involving a dominant body, connectedness and mutual awareness, etc – provide the context within which practices can spread, and participants will want to adopt them (Powell and DiMaggio 1991).

Much of the experience reported fits well with this perspective and its predictions. The great majority of social enterprises operate in institutional environments, marked by the characteristics of 'organisational fields', even if the degree of institutionalisation varies and they are also sometimes heavily engaged in trading activities. The broader political and ideological climate does indeed afford high status to management ideas, especially those originating in the private sector. The government and various public agencies have actively encouraged or required use of the methods,[44] but they have also spread as a result of promotion by and through professional and sectoral networks.[45] And, as we have seen, a concern to build or maintain the confidence of external stakeholders was frequently found to be an important consideration in decisions to adopt particular methods.

There is a twist, however. Although the manner in which the methods have spread illustrates the tenets of institutional theory rather well, it is far less clear that the most celebrated implication of the theory – a trend towards institutional isomorphism – has also been occurring. The cases discussed in chapters 6 and 7 showed diverse applications of methods that were in any case loosely defined. If the organisations were becoming more like each other and more like public agencies and private companies, this was not happening in ways that were either obvious or particularly burdensome. This may yet happen, of course – it has been noted in other contexts that later adopters of organisational reforms do so in different ways and for different reasons than early adopters (Tolbert and Zucker 1983). But it may be that the methods themselves change as they are absorbed into new contexts. They broaden or become diluted, and though the labels remain the same (giving the appearance of practices spreading), they hardly constitute the 'iron cage' feared by Max Weber. These observations reinforce reservations about versions of institutional theory that view organisations as passively internalising the expectations of the institutional environment, and that neglect the agency of organisational actors (see, eg, Mackintosh 1995) Such perspectives fail to account for change and continuing heterogeneity in organisational fields. Indeed, the findings from these cases would seem to fit better with the sorts of elaborations of institutional theory that it has been suggested are needed – eg in terms of 'partial diffusion' and the emergence of hybrids, 'recombination', incomplete institutionalisation, etc (Powell 1991).

Does context matter more than origins? The difficulty for all three theories is that they assume that something constant (a method) has spread. While this can happen – vide, the textbook case of the RSPB, or the use of ISO 9000 at Typetalk – this is not, it seems, the only or the most common thing that happens. More often, the technique or practice changes as it is assimilated; it is adapted, perhaps creatively, to the new rather different contexts. This was very clear in the case of BPB, but can also be seen as an aspect of the application of outcome funding at Groundwork, and in the use of the EM at Ability. However, it was most strikingly evidenced by the remarkable success of PQASSO.

The relationship between small community-based projects – be they in health, welfare, the arts, childcare, young people, economic development, or recreation and sports – and the public bodies to which they turn for financial support is famously problematic. Each needs the other, but they operate in completely different worlds of meaning. The local projects tend to be led rather than managed, based on urgent need or shared enthusiasm, very specific and concrete in their requirements, and relying on informal often tacit processes for planning and organisation. The public body relies on formal procedures, and abstract categories of goals, criteria, logical frameworks, plans, procedures, controls... The local project does not understand the rationale and reassurances that the public agency requires, nor does it know how to provide them. The public agency, even if it appreciates the strengths as well as the weaknesses of the local project's informal arrangements, is not in a position to gradually build up its administrative capacity. The clash of cultures is often debilitating; both parties lose. The case of the Birmingham project, and also other reports, strongly indicate that PQASSO is, for the time being, providing a creative new approach to this issue. It is mediating the relationship in ways that address the concerns of funders while leaving the local projects and agencies in control, equipped with an organisational self-development tool tailored to their situations. This approach is a form of quality assurance – or at least it is presented as such. But who would have predicted that a highly formal system originally developed for ensuring consistency in munitions factories and arms manufacture would be so useful to small social enterprises 50 years later?

It seems, therefore, that the context of use, and how a method is applied, matters much more than its origins. The methods can be applied inappropriately, of course. But on this evidence, the threat that many perceived from the spread of 'alien' business methods was misconceived and exaggerated. As others are now also reporting, the spread of the methods need not and should not take the form of a simple, unmodified transfer (Lindenberg 2001).

Implications for funders and policy-makers

So what are the implications of the research described for governments and other agencies that have thought to promote the performance agenda? The first point is that the studies affirm or clarify the potential of the methods – both positive and negative.

The potential benefits. Clearly, all the measurement and improvement methods can be used to good effect. At the design stage, measurement systems can be used to surface issues around underlying purposes and different meanings of performance, to clarify goals and to communicate priorities. They have the potential to challenge and simplify ossified systems of reporting based on counting activities and outputs. The performance information generated may provide a better basis for demonstrating achievements and for giving recognition. It may be used as a crude filter to direct scarce managerial attention where it is more likely to be needed. It may inform planning and decision making, be used to identify trends, to examine the impacts of new practices, or to provide a challenge requiring that an issue be addressed or an anomaly explained. It can provide a basis for dialogue with stakeholders and for increasing their understanding of the issues. Last but not least, the existence of a functioning system with some interesting (albeit inconclusive) data may in itself reassure funders and purchasers.

The improvement methods can likewise be used to bring about worthwhile changes. They may provide a structure and process for new sorts of discussions, surfacing issues, introducing new ideas, or requiring useful information to be gathered and discussed. Their adoption can reinforce those good intentions that otherwise never reach the top of the priority list, thereby leading to improved policies and practices. They can provide overviews and 'maps of the territory' for managers charged with addressing diffuse cross-functional issues. And like measurement systems, they can provide a reassuring signal to external stakeholders, and in some cases a framework for reviewing and developing relationships with them.

The costs and potential pitfalls. Nevertheless, such benefits are not guaranteed, and the research has also shown that they come at a price. The limitations, difficulties and pitfalls associated with the various forms of performance measurement are very clear, if hardly a great surprise. Thus it is probable that, if taken literally, outcome measurement will be impracticable for many social enterprises. More generally, the features managers hope to find in measurement systems – such as both focus and comprehensiveness, or reliable validity and non-intrusive simplicity – are incompatible and so cannot be realised simultaneously. Moreover, for both internal and external reasons, 'measurement churn' seems increasingly to be a fact of life in social enterprises, as it is elsewhere. So the stability on which much of the logic of measurement depends, is unlikely to be realised.

Then there are the measurement dysfunctions that come with the territory. They may be considered to be limited and contained, and a price worth paying. But they can easily get out of hand – because measurement systems introduce strong temptations for both the measurers and the measured. The former – be they funders, trustees or senior managers – may embrace the figures as convenient certainties that capture what is really going on, precluding the need engage with the ambiguities and inconsistencies of real organisational performance. Indeed, to an extent this is inevitable. People in senior positions have to deal in abstractions just to avoid being overwhelmed. The wiser or more experienced do so knowingly; they remain aware of the difference between the necessary simplicities of the institutional domain and the complicated realities of management and professional practice. Nevertheless, mistaking tidy conceptual maps for the actual terrain, remains an occupational hazard for those in policy work and senior management.

As for those who are subject to the measures, they too may be tempted to choose a single, simplifying solution to the challenge of apparently adverse results. One such solution is to duck responsibility by taking the figures literally and making the measures one's goal – dysfunctions notwithstanding. Another is to act unilaterally, ignoring the figures as irrelevant, and concentrating on making improvements in relation to one's own conception of performance. A third is to focus attention on managing or disputing the figures without taking seriously the possibility of shortcomings in the activities or services themselves.

Likewise, performance improvement methods can be used in ways that gradually become burdensome, an end in themselves, irrelevant to the on-going work. They can become a focus of tension and distrust between managers, and professional or other staff who complain about 'initiative overload', and 'management-speak'. They can be costly, especially in management time (but sometimes also consultants' fees).

Neither necessary nor sufficient. The implication is that the relationship between the use of performance improvement methods and the actual results achieved is indeterminate. Depending on how and why they are adopted and deployed their use may provide scope for important initiatives, or they may be associated with costly and unproductive formalities that aggravate the divisions between those with managerial and service responsibilities. But it is also clear that the use of modern management discourse and methods is not necessary in order to achieve good organisational processes and results. Vide, those who readily 'badge' existing practice with external endorsement or fashionable rhetoric, or the highly committed administrators, of some of the smaller charities whose achievements easily withstood scrutiny and comparison in the ACE ratios studies. These two distinctions – between well run and poorly run organisations, and between those that embrace the new methods and those that do not – generate four possibilities, as shown in figure 9.1.

Table 9.1 Effective and ineffective management cultures

	Use of modern management discourse and methods	
	Little or none	Considerable
Well run and more or less successful	1 Implicit management	3 Explicit management
Questionably run and in difficulty	2 'Time warp' administration	4 Disconnected managerialism

The first possibility – implicit management – might be expected in relatively stable settings where capable and highly committed people have gradually evolved sound working practices through informal processes of organisational learning. Such arrangements might be underpinned by a culture based in professional values and commitments, or by membership of a faith community. The second, labelled 'time warp' administration, may be thought of as the familiar situation where long-serving administrators or managers have been overtaken by developments, slipping into a reactive, fire-fighting mode, and gradually losing the confidence of external stakeholders. The third possibility is 'the way its s'posed to be' – modern management methods being thoughtfully deployed and embedded in ways that staff endorse and external stakeholders appreciate. Finally, disconnected managerialism is suggested as a term for situations where modern discourse and methods are conspicuous (and may even play well externally), but they do not impact the main work, except as noise and a burden. This may happen because they are handed down unilaterally, or because they change too frequently, or because they are overlayed upon unresolved difficulties and divisions.

The danger: promoting disconnected managerialism. A number of points follow from these conceptual distinctions. First, situations approximating all four of these types do arise.[46] Of course, most organisations are neither fish nor fowl; they encompass, to a degree, two (or three, or even all four) types in different areas, at different times. Nevertheless, the distinctions highlight particular possibilities and pitfalls. In particular, that over-zealous attempts to improve performance can have unfortunate consequences – eg moving from cell 2 to cell 4, or even from cell 1 to cell 4. Positive outcomes are most likely when nonprofit managers (and staff) choose the method to suit their situation, and retain some control or influence in the process.

Hence, as earlier chapters have pointed out, managers and funders need to beware the spurious certainties and simplicities of methods that are frequently over-sold, and to avoid pressuring adoption of particular methods and then rushing the implementation process. This is especially the case with measurement systems. Additional performance information will often be warranted, but more realism and less rhetoric regarding its value, and especially regarding the costs, difficulties and pitfalls of obtaining it, are badly needed. Rhetoric has a proper place, of course, in both policy and management; and the fact that we fall short of declared aspirations does not mean we will behave better if we abandon those commitments. The problem is that the rhetoric around performance is sometimes so overblown and so much at variance with the direct experience of staff involved, that advocates of the performance agenda make their own task more difficult, and risk discrediting their entire approach.

How serious is the problem of disconnected managerialism? This warrants a separate study, but Doyle, Claydon et al. (2000) use survey evidence to suggest 'the management disconnect' is widespread, particularly in the UK public sector, in the context of organisational change. And there are signs that such disconnects may themselves be becoming normal and acceptable at quite senior levels. For example,[47] officials in a Regional Health Authority were charged with obtaining performance data from hospitals as part of the Department of Health's latest initiative to drive modernisation. They knew this would be burdensome, and were particularly concerned with one hospital where, through a combination of circumstances, a management team generally viewed as competent was already stretched to breaking point. They resolved the problem by passing on the central directive along with the resources to hire a consultant whom they briefed on how to prepare and present an appropriate set of figures. Nevertheless, even if those involved in implementation have the good sense to do so collusively or in other ways that ensure loose coupling between domains, these initiatives still soak up managerial time and attention and generate costs.

Hence, one message from this research is a familiar one. Put rather simply, policy-makers need to remember that the choice is not just between inviting voluntaristic involvement or imposing central directives. There is a 'middle axiom' (Schumacher 1973) which may achieve more and faster, and with less dysfunction. Thus, several of those involved in the development and evaluation of the UK's 'Best Value' regime for local services have said that its high point was in the early phase when the pilot local authorities had considerable freedom to chose their own methods for pursuing and demonstrating best value. When they realised that they could actually set their own agenda many creative initiatives were set in hand. By the time the scheme was 'rolled out' nation-wide, the 'control freaks' had reasserted their longstanding dominance over the decentralisers, and the procedures were much more prescriptive – in the name of ensuring good practice, of course – producing predictably guarded and formulaic responses from local authorities.

Making judgement calls on performance. An underlying theme of the book has been the difficulty of making judgements about performance in social enterprises. Indeed, figure 9.1 is open to the charge that the conceptual distinction between 'well-run' and 'questionably run' organisations is so facile as to be misleading. Nevertheless, the argument has been that the distinction is problematic, *not* that it is impossible or meaningless. In particular contexts and for particular purposes we can (and must) make thoughtful and informed judgements about performance, even if doing so takes time and effort (which is, of course, why measures with their promise of simplicity and validity are so seductive).

So what comes out of the various studies in this book for funders, or new trustees, or officials in public agencies, or even journalists, who may for one reason or another have to make judgements about a social enterprise and whether it is 'performing'? Given that the clear-cut cases of outstanding success and of multiple, acknowledged failure will be the exceptions, how can we tell the relatively successful from the somewhat questionable? What is the look and feel of a reasonably well-run social enterprise in an era of constantly churning performance management?

One way of answering such questions is in terms of the dashboard, discussed in the last chapter. In other words, whether and how well the social enterprise considers the different aspects of performance defined by that framework. The more aspects of performance that the managers involved are alert to, and the more thoroughly they are able to engage with them, the more rounded and convincing their discussion of performance is likely to be. For example, they are likely to consider underlying performance, not just current results, and to do this in ways that involve external referents, not just comparisons with previous years. They are also likely to be comfortable and informed discussing *organisational* dimensions of performance – various aspects of risk, say, or intangible assets – and not just programmatic outcomes. This does not mean all the information needs to be explicit and routinely assembled, of course. And it *certainly* does not mean that, before one can say a social enterprise is performing well, its facts, figures and reports in all these areas have to be problem-free. Very few organisations indeed, be they for-profit or nonprofit, would pass that test.

Another way of answering this question is in terms of the constructivist perspective that has been an important theme in the book. The starting point is that performance is not an objective attribute independent of those involved and concerned about the organisation and its activities. It is an evolving, often controversial, construct and what different parties see depends on their viewpoints. On this basis it is a promising sign if performance is accepted as multifaceted, contested, contingent, provisional. Of course, this could reflect confusion, so there also needs to be clarity over underlying themes and priorities around which organisational identity has historically developed, as well as recognition that the concerns of the institutional, managerial and professional domains are all legitimate. When this is the case, those involved are unlikely to have much trouble confidently explaining 'performance' for particular purposes, or in particular contexts. Nor are they likely to be seriously discomforted when the goalposts are shifted by their regulatory or contracting overseers – indeed, they may be more likely to see this coming. By contrast, where managers and senior staff take both the meaning and the demonstration of performance as largely self-evident, based on traditional, functionally derived views that are not well integrated, then this could be a cause for concern.

Likewise, if trustees' and managers' attitudes to performance improvement methods is one of sceptical curiosity and interest, this is probably a good sign. If they seem open to new ideas and to being challenged, but have the confidence to select and adapt methods to match their context and current needs – and readily abandon them when they seem to have had their day – then so much the better. By contrast, where such methods are either dismissed out of hand, or seem to be embraced promiscuously, social enterprises may be failing to engage with the performance agenda, or doing so excessively and uncritically. Instead of filtering and tempering the shifting and inconsistent expectations of the environment, senior managers, eager to please external stakeholders or to establish their own credentials, can overdose their organisations with improvement methods and measures.

Implications for managers

Finally, what are the implications for the managers of social enterprises? How do they engage with the performance agenda? As noted in chapter 1, they face a dilemma. In considerable measure they are obliged to support measurement and performance improvement – to object can easily appear self-serving and irrational. Yet, for all the reasons discussed in chapters 3, 4 and 5, they are fully entitled to have misgivings. They seem to face an unwelcome choice:– either they swallow their doubts and commit to the performance agenda, or they join the ranks of the doubters and cynics.

It is clear that significant numbers opt for the first option, building a professional identity out of the language and techniques of the management industry. This is entirely understandable – the roles they undertake are often stressful and unsupported. 'Management' provides an occupational identity and a community of practice – and, of course, management ideas and practices do contain important, usable insights. Yet the dangers are very apparent. The language can easily be heard as jargon, and rightly or wrongly the staff fail to see how the techniques will address the issues they experience. Faced with doubts and negativity, the keen manager can easily become more certain, more positive, less flexible... with all the attendant dangers of generating division and resistance, and making the creative adaptations harder to find.

The alternative – to be negative and distrusting towards performance methods – seems a betrayal of ones management role and responsibility. Indeed, it can easily become so, slipping into a cynical, overly political attitude, in which the gulf between professional stance and private belief grows steadily wider and more uncomfortable. I suspect that many managers, perhaps most, move in a space somewhere between these two positions, but do so rather doubtfully. They do not feel comfortable with either the naïve rationalism of the eager, modernising manager or the debunking and manoeuvring of the cynical manager. And yet their own position may seem confused and indecisive by comparison.

Nevertheless, I suggest that their position is an entirely proper one. They are not so much unsure, as *realistic about the range of possibilities*. It is reasonable to engage constructively with measurement while being very alert to its limitations and misuse, and to approach the performance agenda positively while also being fully aware that every valid and useful method can also become an occasion for goal displacement (by being pursued inappropriately or excessively). One can pursue rationalisation even though the scope for it is limited and any progress will be in constant danger of erosion. In short, they can take performance seriously – but without taking it literally. Drawing on concepts from earlier chapters, table 9.2 further develops this perspective on performance measurement and improvement under the heading of 'the reflective approach' – contrasting it with 'the committed approach' and 'the cynical approach'.

The reflective approach does not mean being detached, or lacking in commitment, as regards the mission of the social enterprise. It is sceptically reflective about the *methods* – perhaps thinking that it is less important which method is chosen than that the organisation adopts one such structured process and works with it inclusively. It is, however, the most demanding of the three approaches. As Forbes puts it in relation to a continuum between acceptance and rejection of effectiveness assessments:

The most successful – and undoubtedly the most difficult – response for nonprofit managers to adopt will be to tread the middle ground of this continuum. Doing so will require managers to look with scepticism on the idea of effectiveness and yet view questions of effectiveness as periodically useful opportunities for reflection, communication and learning ... contemporary managers will also do well to be familiar with the criteria and measures of effectiveness that are relevant to the domains in which they operate so that they can critique, modify and perhaps invent effectiveness measures as it is appropriate in the course of their work. (Forbes 1998, p 198)

Table 9.2 Approaches to methods of performance measurement and performance improvement

Philosophical position	The committed approach Positivist, rationalist	The cynical approach Sceptic	The reflective approach Constructivist
Attitude to measurement	Generally positive	Generally negative	Interested but cautious
Where measures come from	Goals	Someone's agenda	Problems and issues
Expected use of measurement	For learning and accountability	For control	Various – for dialogue, to clarify expectations; for 'challenge, check and conformity'
What matters in performance reporting	The facts	Creative accounting	A grounded narrative and analysis tailored to the concerns of the stakeholder(s) in question
Proper relationship between institutional, managerial and professional levels	Close alignment	Close alignment with own view – failing which, de-coupling	Loose coupling (to accommodate differences, and change, in concepts of performance)
Attitude to new improvement methods	Useful tools	Fads, waste of time	Depends on use and context
Way of applying new methods	Follow the rules, do it properly	Tactically, perhaps collusively, with a view to appearances	Open-minded, willing to improvise, adapt, collude, depending on context
Internal/external orientation	Internal orientation ('integration' or 'emulation')	External orientation ('bearing' or 'badging')	If possible, a dual orientation ('creative integration')
Benefits sought	Improved performance	Maintain confidence of external bodies; preserve autonomy	Develop relationship with external bodies and make some improvements (while accepting one or other may not be achievable)

Managing without managerialism. One final implication from the case studies seems so clear and so important it can also serve as a conclusion. Where the various methods were used most successfully they were 'translated' in the course of their introduction into terms that were concrete and meaningful for those involved. They provided occasions where a range of people in the organisation could discuss the methods, take ownership of them, and then play a part in relating them to the specific circumstances they faced. So the performance agenda, like all the other important aspects of management, has to be pursued with and through people – or else it falters.[48] The measurement and other techniques are at their best when they support and inform dialogue around different concerns and conceptions of performance. They are least helpful when they are seen as an alternative to dialogue (eg with reports being used as the basis for 'management by exception'). And of course, those dialogues are not just internal – they have to include external stakeholders. This is why the managers of social enterprises so often have to be 'multilingual' – capable of moving between and operating successfully within very diverse worlds of meaning. It is also the reason why managerialism – elevating as it does particular roles, perspectives, terminology, and techniques – can so easily become a liability, by making dialogue more difficult.

In short, communication and the people side of management remain fundamental. Familiarity with measurement methods and analytic tools, and the ability to gauge their potential in new settings, are now additional requirements for many managers of social enterprises. But they do not make the basics any less important. Ironically, this is a point that has been established very clearly in studies of private companies (Pffefer 1998) – even if it is one that all of us who manage, in whatever sector, often find hard to remember.

Notes

[1] For the UK Martin Knapp's work is seminal and generally shows voluntary sector providers in a good light. Regarding residential childcare, see Knapp (1986); regarding residential care, see Knapp et al. (1998); regarding community mental health services, see Knapp et al. (1999). Ortmann and Schlesinger (1997) review the studies in a number of areas of health and social services, much of it US-based. Weisbrod (1998) focuses on nursing homes and facilities for those with learning disabilities. Another important study (this time of day care for children in Canada) is provided by Krashinsky (1998).

[2] Apparently, the scheme had tried to introduce continuous improvement in services but without first ensuring a sound structure for those services. It was seen as making marginal improvements to fundamentally unsatisfactory arrangements. The article referred to is Holweger (1995).

[3] As the work progressed and expanded, these aims developed, but never to the point where the enquiries became 'orthodox' (hypothesis-testing) research addressing an issue already formulated in theoretical terms. This does not mean that the study tried to be 'a-theoretical', simply that the choice of an appropriate theoretical frame for the phenomenon was seen as problematic (if it was not to be pre-judged).

[4] For example chapter 3 uses some statistics, chapter 4 makes use of survey findings, and the work for chapter 7 included some action-research.

[5] The information sources and procedures used in the case research are given in more detail in the notes, or references, to the chapters.

[6] The information is available on www.guidestar.org

[7] I am grateful to the staff of the Charity Commission for the interviews which provided this and other information concerning its activities and thinking – see also the following Risk Profiling.

[8] 'The core institutionalist contribution is to see environments and organisational settings as highly interpenetrated' (Jefferson and Meyer 1991 205).

[9] For example the charity Action Aid recently advertised the job of 'Head of Impact Assessment' (*contra* programme evaluation, one presumes).

[10] The third (or voluntary, or nonprofit) sector as a category is usually defined either in economic terms (the non-distribution constraint) or political terms (non-statutory, non-commercial). While suiting the purposes of those disciplines it is problematic for other purposes. For a rather different, *organisational* definition of the territory which also avoids the inappropriately precise connotations of the term 'sector', see Paton (1992).

[11] Namely, Rob Austin of Harvard Business School, Marshall Meyer of the Wharton School and Andy Neely of Cranfield Business School.

[12] The approach can be summed up as using embedded cases studies (Yin 1984) chosen on the basis of theoretical sampling (Strauss and Corbin 1988).

[13] Even though the source data was in the public domain, anonymity was guaranteed in order to encourage participants to speak freely.

[14] Persuading busy finance professionals to attend discussions was not easy, especially in the case of smaller organisations located outside London. Response rates were about 90% to interview requests and 20% to attendance in a group discussion.

[15] The report on the Social Auditing with Voluntary Organisations (SAVO) project is interesting in this respect. In a section entitled 'Resources, resources, resources', the authors state: 'As was to be expected one of the major concerns of [the organisations participating in the SAVO projects] was lack of specific funding to cover social audit activities. Many found it difficult to convince funders of the validity of the activity... The SAVO project was part funded by the National Lotteries Charities Board and the majority of organisations who benefitted from this funding were unsure as to their capacity to continue once the subsidised rate was withdrawn... Some organisations had to scale down to process over time as resources became even scarcer' (Raynard and Murphy, 2000 pp 19–20)].

[16] During the preparation of this book the author met a senior manager from one of the US organisations regularly cited as having made a success of outcome measurement. Still hoping to find a clear example of this, he asked about how she used the information. The result was immediate and unambiguous: not at all. She understood the data had been of some use to local chapters in helping to secure funds, but it was research, and gave her no guidance in planning and decision making.

[17] Anecdotes to this effect are quite common on both sides of the Atlantic.

[18] This conforms to the experience reported elsewhere. Commentators have suggested that some 70% of BPB projects are not carried through. Implementation is the difficult, unglamorous phase, during which the manager may be inclinded to cash in his or her personal learning from the project and move on.

[19] Measurement growth and oscillation – see chapter 3 – are both evident. The 1991 survey involved up to 245 lines of data entry. By 1996 this had grown to 466 – whereupon it was cut back to 388 in the following year in an effort at simplification. But in pursuit of greater consistency the form was thoroughly reviewed for 1998, and the number of lines rose again – to 477. A similar pattern appears on the 'output' side – the 1991 survey produced a 75-page report with 17 main tables and 19 charts. The 1998 survey produced a report of about 100 pages, with two different versions (for large and small charities) of 28 tables, and with more than 20 charts and 'profiles'.

[20] A new Director of Finance established a benchmarking project focused on whole service units and based on the working assumption that all the 130+ centres could break even. The aim was to identify the dynamics and good practices that enabled this in some services and ensure their adoption elsewhere. The project was carried through with assistance from consultants who trained six managers. This team had access to all internal data, developed a detailed questionnaire covering operational arrangements, budget process and

management systems, made day-long visits to 12 selected services, and had access to varying levels of information from three other charities in the field. From this they generated detailed recommendations for good practice and set about running 12 workshops around the country for unit managers, who were, in fact, their peers. Unfortunately it was not possible to review the results of this project.

[21] For example, the use of 'scattergraphs' referred to in the last chapter and discussed further in Stone (1997). In addition, the Groundwork Federation has for 10 years operated a system of triennial Planning and Review (PAR) visits to its constituent local Trusts. These visits are essentially a comprehensive peer review process that takes place over three days and aims to 'exchange and share experience and ideas'.

[22] This is the main way in which benchmarking has been construed and enacted within government policy towards both SMEs and government agencies (DTI 1996; Samuels 1998)

[23] There may also be a collective action problem. The costs of BPB are of two sorts – the managerial and staff time devoted to the exercise; and, for those who join a 'club' or group project, the third-party costs of data definition, gathering, analysis and feedback. The trouble is that in order to spread the third party costs a larger group is required; but this increases the transaction costs, especially for the person(s) initiating the exercise. It is noticeable that in the Trade Associations and Good Practice Unit cases the problem was solved by an entrepreneurial initiative by a third-party obtaining much of the cost of the exercise from a government department – because the scheme would not have attracted sufficient support without the subsidy. Such third-party initiatives (but without external financing) are common among large organisations in the commercial world.

[24] Interestingly, after this research was complete, the GPU was transferred to a large consulting group with experience, expertise and infrastructure to manage the growing service.

[25] Most obviously and simply, popular articles often end with a list of diagnostic questions for the manager to consider, and books comprised entirely of diagnostic checklists have been popular (Rowntree 1996).

[26] This version of the model is the one that was current at the time of the research in 1997–98. It has since been superceded by a modified version. The changes are not trivial, but nor are they so far-reaching as to invalidate the discussion that follows. The same applies to the version of PQASSO discussed in this chapter.

[27] More detailed accounts of these organisations and their experiences with the self-assessment models can be found in Foot and Paton (2002a, b) and Payne and Paton (2002). The hoped-for logitudinal case study of the EM at Ability was never completed, for the reasons given in the text.

[28] The Training and Enterprise Councils were local agencies funded by central government. They have been dissolved and replaced by new arrangements.

[29] A guide to the use of the EM in public and voluntary sectors is available

[30] It would not be surprising if use of PQASSO became obligatory in some areas. Two years after EETA started using it, the EM became obligatory for all Training and Enterprise Councils.

[31] For example, Campbell's law – see chapter 3.

[32] On several occasions it became clear that important precepts of TQM supposedly embedded in the model, had not been recognised or understood by those using it or considering using it. The most notable was the respondent, in an organisation that had considered the EM but decided against it, and who justified the decision on the grounds that it was 'too much focussed on internal processes' and did not give enough attention to service users. Interestingly, Seddon (1998) makes just this complaint about the way the model is frequently used – arguing that such usage misses the whole point of the exercise.

[33] McTiernan considered whether PQASSO worked as a standalone pack or really needed external support, concluding that, although it could be used to good effect without such support, far more tended to be achieved with external facilitation (McTiernan 1998). The BQF takes a similar view regarding use of the EM.

[34] Through the plethora of business seminars, books, consulting activity and specialist software, to which it has given rise, the Balanced Scorecard has probably had more impact on organisational practice than any other management idea since 'In Search of Excellence' (Peters and Waterman 1982).

[35] Apparently some managers prefer to use the Excellence Model in their own organisation for this reason.

[36] In these general terms the framework can be applied to other sorts of organisations, as well. Some of the elaborations in later sections tailor it to social enterprises specifically.

[37] Arguably, the monthly profit and loss accounts of large companies also function in this symbolic way, rather than as a basis for control. Interestingly, the boards of some large companies no longer ask to receive them because they are not a good use of the board members time (Neely 1998).

[38] The research aspect – how useful was the 'Dashboard' as a framework, to whom and in what ways? – was explained and a right to publish (subject to the usual protocols) was agreed.

[39] To develop this and to choose suitable levels for 'amber' and 'red' it would help to understand more about how the equation behaves as things change (sensitivity analysis). At what point does a drop in voluntary income, or a delay in project funding, become serious? What is the relation between the number of projects and the central staffing needed to support them (core costs)? Does growth make the problem worse or better? It was suggested that this might be explored through an MBA student project. I suspect this is still a project waiting to happen.

[40] My notes refer to one senior figure as frequently 'whizzing off into discussion of strategic issues', for example.

[41] This is *not* to claim that this little project itself precipitated the organisational changes. Rather, these discussions probably sprung from and

reinforced a developing awareness and clarity over the need for certain changes.

[42] The difficulties are probably most severe in moderately sized social enterprises where the complexities of detailed fund accounting for a range of funders each demanding reports employing different reporting categories, become a significant burden – what might be called 'multiple colonisation'.

[43] The other problem with a strong version of the genericist argument is that it overlooks size, which has long been recognised as a major determinant of what is appropriate organisational practice. It was clear from the cases, for example, that several of the methods – BPB, the EM and ISO 9000 – bore the marks of their origins in large organisations. Formal techniques requiring a significant on-going commitment of managerial time are generally inappropriate for smaller enterprises – whether social or private.

[44] Two of the BPB cases described were part funded by government departments; the cabinet office promoted the Excellence Model to agencies and public bodies; the 'Best Value' regime in local government required benchmarking in some form and encouraged the adoption of 'kitemarks' and standards-based approaches – and so on.

[45] An informal network of quality consultants and senior nonprofit managers committed to quality approaches promoted a number of the approaches through industry and sector bodies – such as the Association of Directors of Social Service, and the Quality Standards Task Group of NCVO. These bodies were vehicles for spreading awareness of the models through meetings and reports (Astbury and Mayall 1997; CES 1998; Darvill 1998; QSTG 1998). Thereafter, as interest increased, networking meetings at which early adopters shared their experience with those just beginning were arranged through bodies like the British Quality Foundation and the Local Government Association, and proved very popular. CES who held the copyright on PQASSO also produced a newsletter for users.

[46] For a classic, well-documented account of implicit management, see the description of the medical records section of Annersley Hospital (*prior* to the changes it was subjected to), in Berridge (1984). Cases of 'time warp' administration are implied in many reports of renewal and turnaround, as are cases of explicit management. Even if these accounts are often problematic, simplifying and exaggerating the nature of the changes, substantial and lasting improvements in performance can be achieved – as some of the cases in this book illustrate (eg Standish Community High School). 'Disconnected managerialism' as a pattern of organisation is probably under-reported for obvious reasons, though it fits with much organisational folklore, with accounts of measurement dysfunction and with researches on de-coupled processes of audit and inspection.

[47] Recounted to the author 'on good authority'.

[48] The importance of 'translation' and good process was particularly clear to the researchers as regards Groundwork and 'Prove it!', IIP at Standish, ISO 9000 at The House and Home B of the Disability Homes Network, in all the cases involving PQASSO, and in both the cases involving the Excellence Model. Equally, the uneven implementation of the new purchasing system at

the RSPB reflected the severe challenge the project team faced in engaging with enough key people in a large, very disparate and dispersed organisation.

Bibliography

6, P. and J. Forder (1996). "Can Campaigning Be Evaluated." *Nonprofit and Voluntary Sector Quarterly* 25(2): 225-247.

6, P. and J. Kendall, Eds. (1997). *The Contract Culture in Public Services.* Aldershot, Arena.

Abrahamson, E. (1991). "Managerial Fads and Fashions: The Diffusion and Rejection of Innovation." *Academy of Management Review* 16: 586-612.

Abrahamson, E. (1996). "Management Fashion." *Academy of Management Review* 21(1): 254-285.

Ahrens, T. and C. Chapman (1998). *Sustaining Antagonistic Harmony - food margin control in a UK restaurant chain.* Performance measurement - theory and practice; the first international conference on performance measurement, Cambridge, England, Centre for Business Performance, Cambridge University.

Aidemark, L. (2001). "The Meaning of Balanced Scorecards in the Health Care Organisation." *Financial Accountability and Management* Vol 17(1): pp 23-40.

Alberga, T., S. Tyson, et al. (1997). "An Evaluation of the Investors in People Standard." *Human Resource Management Journal* 7(2): 47-60.

Argenti, J. (1993). *Your Organisation: What Is It For?* London, McGraw Hil.

Argyris, C. and D. A. Schon (1978). *Organizational Learning - a theory of action perspective.* Reading MA, Addison-Wesley.

Armistead, C. (1998). *The EFQM and Royal Mail: changing perspectives and attitudes.* Performance Measurement - Theory and Practice, Cambridge, Centre for Business Performance, Judge Institute of Management Studies.

Arnold, J. (1998). personal communication.

Ashby, J. (1990). An Account of the Monitoring of Voluntary Organizations by a Government Agency. Towards the 21st Century: challenges for the voluntary sector - Proceeedings of the 1990 Conference of the Association of Voluntary Action Scholars, Volume 1. London, Centre for Voluntary Organization, The London School of Economics.

Associates, A. (1998). Benchmarking housing performance. London, The Housing Corporation.

Associates, A. D. (1995). Investors in People - the case studies. London, Investors in People UK.

Astbury, R. and H. Mayall (1997). A map of quality standards. London, NCVO Publications.

Austin, R. D. (1996). Measuring and Managing Performance in Organisations. NY, Dorset House.

Austin, R. D., P. D. Larkey, et al. (1998). *Measuring Knowledge Work: pathologies and patterns.* Performance Measurement - *Theory and Practice*; the first international conference on performance measurement, Cambridge, England, Centre for Business Performance, Cambridge University.

Bell, E., S. Taylor, et al. (2001). "Investors in People and the Standardisation of Professional Knowledge in Personnel Management." *Management Learning* 32(2).

Bernstein, D. J. (1999). "Comments on Perrin's "Effective Use and Misuse of Performance Measurement"." *American Journal of Evaluation* 20(1): 85 - 93.

Berridge, J. (1984). Changing Complex Information Systems: Medical Records at Anersley Hospital. London, Harper and Row.

Blau, P. M. (1963). *The Dynamics of Bureaucracy.* Chicago, University of Chicago Press.

BMI (1998). Workshop on the Business Excellence Model, BMI Consulting Group.

Bovaird, T. (1999). Achieving Best Value through competition, benchmarking and performance networks. Warwick and London, University of Warwick and the Department of Environment Transport and the Regions.

Bovaird, T. and A. Halachmi (1998). Citizens, community organizations, the private sector and other stakeholders in performance assessment for best value. Performance Measurement - Theory and Practice; the first international conference on performance measurement ., Cambridge, England, Centre for Business Performance, Cambridge University.

BQF (1997). Voluntary Sector Guide to Self-Assessment. London, British Quality Foundation.

Brontis, N., N. Gragonetti, et al. (1999). "The Knowledge Toolbox: A Review of the Tools Available to Measure and Manage Intangible Resources." *European Management Journal* Vol. 17(No. 4): pp 391-402.

Brooking, A. (1996). *Intellectual Capital.* London, International Thomson Business Pres.

Bruns, W. (1998). *Keynote address: Profit as a performance measure.* Performance Measurement - theory and practice; the first international conference on performance measurement, Cambridge, England.

Brunsson, N. and J. P. Olsen (1993). *The Reforming Organisation.* London, Routledge.

Camp, R. C. (1989). Benchmarking: The Search for Industry Best Practices That Lead to Superior Performance. Wisconsin, ASQC Quality Press.

Camp, R. C. (1995). Business Process Benchmarking: finding and implementing best practices. Wisconsin, ASQC Quality Press.

Carter, N., R. Klein, et al. (1992). *How Organisations Measure Success.* London, Routledge.

CES (1998). Quality in Charities - using the Excellence Model to promote self assessment in charities. London, Charities Evaluation Services.

Checkland, P. B. (1981). *Systems Thinking, Systems Practice.* Chichester, Wiley.

Clark, T. and G. Salaman (1996). "The Management Guru as Organisational Witch Doctor." *Organisation* 3: 85-108.

Clarke, J. and J. Newman (1997). *The Managerial State.* London, SAGE Publications.

Communities, C. o. t. E. (1993). Cycle Management: Integrated Approach and Logical Framework. Brussels, Commission of the European Communities.

Connolly, C. and N. Hyndman (2001). "A Comparative Study on the Impact of Revised SORP 2 on British and Irish Charities." *Financial Accountability and Management* Vol 17(1): 73-97.

Conti, T. (1997). *Organizational Self-Assessment.* London, Chapman and Hall.

Cook, S. (1995). Practical Benchmarking - a manager's guide to creating competitive advantage. London, Kogan Page.

Coopers and Lybrand (1994). *Survey of Benchmarking in the UK.* London, Coopers and Lybrand and CBI National Manufacturing Council.

Cornforth, C. (2002). What do Boards Do? the Governance of Public and Non-profit Organizations. London, Routledge.

Cox, A. and I. Thompson (1998). "On the Appropriateness of Benchmarking." *Journal of General Management* 23(3): 1-19.

Cutt, J. and V. Murray (2000). Accountability and Effectiveness Evaluation in Non-Profit Organizations. London, Routledge.

Cyert, R. and J. G. March (1963). *A Behavioural Theory of the Firm*. Englewood Cliffs, N J, Prentice Hall.

Darvill, G. (1998). Organisations, People and Standards. London, Association of Directors of Social Services and the National Institute of Social Work.

Davenport, T. H., R. G. Eccles, et al. (1992). "Information Politics." *Sloan Management Review* 34(1): 53-65.

Davis, I. C. (1999). "Evaluation and Performance Management in Government." *Evaluation* 5(2): 150-159.

Dawson, S., K. Sutherland, et al. (1998). The relationship between R&D and clinical practice in primary and secondary care: cases of asthma and glue ear in children. Oxford, The Said Business School, University of Oxford.

Dees, G. (1998). "Enterprising Nonprofits." *Harvard Business Review*(January - February): pp 55-67.

DETR (1999). DETR, Circular 10/99 Local Government Act, Part 1, Para 51, Best Value. London, HMSO.

DiMaggio, P. (2002). Measuring the Impact of the Nonprofit Sector on Society is Probably Impossible but Possibly Useful: A Sociological perspective. *Measuring the Impact of the Nonprofit Sector*. A. Hodkinson and P. F. (eds). Washington, Independent Sector and Plenum Press.

DiMaggio, P. and W. W. Powell (1983). "The Iron Cage Revisited: institutional isomorphism and collective rationality in organizational fields." *American Sociological Review* 48: 147-160.

Dow, W. and R. Crowe (1999). What Social Auditing Can Do For Voluntary Organizations. Vancouver, Volunteer Vancouver.

Doyle, M., T. Claydon, et al. (2000). "Mixed Results, Lousy Process: the Management Experience of Organizational Change." *British Journal of Management* Vol. 11(Special Issue): pp S 59-80.

DTI (1996). The United Kingdom Benchmarkiing Index. London, Department of Trade and Industry.

Ebrahim, A. (2002). "Information Struggles: The Role of Information in the Reproduction of NGO-funder Relationships." *Nonprofit and Voluntary Sector Quarterly* Vol. 31(No. 1): pp 84-114.

Eccles, R. G. (1991). "The Performance Measurement Manifesto." *Harvard Business Review*(Jan-Feb): 131-137.

Edwards, M. and D. Hulme (1995). Non-Governmental Organisations - performance and accountability. London, Earthscan.

Elnathan, D. and D. Kim (1995). "Partner Selection and Group Formation in Co-operative Benchmarking." *Journal of Accounting and Economics* 19(2-3): 345-364.

Epstein, M. and J. Manzoni (1998). "Implementing Corporate Strategy: From Tableaux de Bord to Balanced Scorecards." *European Management Journal* Vol. 16(No. 2): pp 190-203.

Farley, T. (1997). Practical Quality Assurance System for Small Organizations. London, Charities EValuation Service.

Ferlie, E., L. Ashburner, et al. (1996). *The New Public Management in Action*. Oxford, Oxford University Press.

Foot, J. (1998). How to do benchmarking: a practitioner's guide. Epsom, Surrey, Inter Agnecies Froup.

Foot, J. and R. Paton (1999a). How social enterprises use IIP: two case studies. Milton Keynes, The Open University Business School.

Foot, J. and R. Paton (1999b). The use of ISO 9000 in social enterprises: three case studies. Milton Keynes, The Open Unversity Business School.

Foot, J. and R. Paton (2002). The Assimilation of Quality Assurance by the Voluntary Sector: Two Case Studies of the Development of PQASSO. Milton Keynes, The Open University Business School.

Foot, J. and R. Paton (2002). Using PQASSO to Build Capacity: the Birmingham Voluntary Sector Quality Development Programme. Milton Keynes, The Open University Business School.

Forbes, D. P. (1998). "Measuring the Unmeasurable." *Nonprofit and Voluntary Sector Quarterly* 27(2).

Frigo, M. (2000). *Current trends in performance measurement systems*. Performance Measurement 2000- *Past, Present and Future*, Univeristy of Cambridge, Centre for Business Performance, Cranfield University.

Gamblin, T. and R. Jones (1996). The financial governance of charities. West Malling, Kent, The Charities Aid Foundation.

Garvin, D. A. (1991). "How the Baldridge Award Really Works." *Harvard Business Review*(November-December): 80-93.

George, C. and S. Casson (1992). "Napier House - a quality assured home." *International Journal of Health Care Quality Assurance* 5(3): 27-33.

Ghobadian, A. and H. S. Woo (1994). "Characteristics, Benefits and Shortcomings of Four Major Quality awards." *International Journal of Quality and Reliability Management* 13(2): 10-44.

Glaser, B. G. and A. L. Strauss (1968). *The Discovery of Grounded Theory*. London, Weidenfeld and Nicholson.

Goffman, E. (1959). *The Presentation of Self in Everyday Life*. New York, Doubleday.

Goldstein, H. and D. J. Spiegelhalter (1996). "League Tables and Their Limitations: statistical issues in comparisons of institutional performance." *Journal of the Royal Statistical Society A* 159(3): 385-443.

Gonella, C., A. Pilling, et al. (1998). Making Values Count: Contemporary Experience in Social and Ethical Accounting, Auditing, and Reporting. London, The Association of Chartered Certified Accountants.

Graham, J. (1999). "Fishing to feed the treasurer." *NGO Finance* n(x): 46-48.

Gray, A. (1997). "Contract Culture and Target Fetishism." *Local Economy*(February): 343-357.

Greene, J. C. (1999). "The Inequality of Performance Measurements." *Evaluation* 5(2): 160-172.

Hadley, R. and M. Goldsmith (1995). "Development or Convergence? Change and stability in a common ownership firm over three decades: 1960-89." *Economic and Industrial Democracy* 16: 167-199.

Hansmann, H. B. (1987). Economic Theories of Nonprofit Organization. *The Nonprofit Sector: A Research Handbook*. W. W. Powell. New Haven, Yale University Press.

Harris, M. (1993 a). Clarifying the Board role: a total activities approach. *Governing, Leading and Managing Nonprofit Organisations*. D. Young, R. Hollister and V. Hodgkinson. San Francisco, Jossey Bass.

Harris, M. (1993 b). "Exploring the Role of Boards Using Total Activities Analysis." *Nonprofit Management and Leadership* 3(3): 269-281.

Hassell, T. (1998). The NGO Finance Charities Internal Audit Checklist, NGO Finance.

Herman, R. D. and D. O. Renz (1997). "Multiple Constituencies and the Social Construction of Nonprofit Effectiveness." *Nonprofit and Voluntary Sector Quarterly* 26(2): 185-207.

Herman, R. D. and D. O. Renz (1999). "Theses on Nonprofit Effectiveness." *Nonprofit and Voluntary Sector Quarterly* 28(2).

Hillage, J. (1998). personal communication.

Hillage, J. and J. Moralee (1996). The Return on Investors. Brighton, The Institute for Employment Studies.

Hoe, S. (1995). *The man who gave his company away.* Wollaston, Northants, Scott Bader Company Limited.

Hoefer, R. (2000). "Accountability in Action? Program Evaluation in Nonprofit Human Service Agencies." *Nonprofit Management and Leadership* 11(2): 167-177.

Hoggett, P. (1996). "New modes of control in the public service." *Public Administration* 74(Spring): 9 - 32.

Holloway, J. A., C. M. Hinton, et al. (1997). Why Benchmark?: Understanding the Process of Best Practice Benchmarking. *Proceedings of the Business Process Track at the British Academy of Management Conference.* London: 271-291.

Holweger, K. (1995). "The RNID's Customer Care Initiative." *Nonprofit and Voluntary Sector Marketing* 1(2): 105-120.

Hood, C. (1998). The Art of the State: Culture, Rhetoric and Public Management. Oxford, Oxford University Press.

Huczysnki, A. (1993). *Management Gurus.* London, Routledge.

Humphrey, N. and M. Hildrew (1992). "Napier House - the Steps to Quality." *International Journal of Health Care Quality Assurance* 5(3): 34-36.

IIP (1996). The Investors in People standard research directory. London, Investors in People UK.

Jackson, A. (1998). *The ambiguity of performance indicators.* First International Conference on Performance Measurement, Cambridge, Centre for Business Performance, Cambridge University.

James, A. (1992). Committed to Quality. London, HMSO.

James, O. (2000). Does the Agency Model Prevent 'Joined-up Government'? the Case of the UK Benefits Agency. British Academy of Management, Edinburgh.

Jefferson, R. L. and J. W. Meyer (1991). Public Order and the Construction of Formal Organization. *The New Institutionalism in Organizational Analysis.* W. W. Powell and P. J. DiMaggio. Chicago, University of Chicago Press.

Kanter, R. M. and D. V. Summers (1987). Doing Well by Doing Good: dilemmas of performance measurement in nonprofit organizations, and the need for a multiple constituency approach. *The Nonprofit Sector: A Research Handbook.* W. W. Powell. New Haven, Yale University Press.

Kaplan, R. (2001). "Strategic performance Measurement and Management in Nonprofit Organizations." *Nonprofit Management and Leadership* **Vol.** 11(No. 3): pp 353-370.

Kaplan, R. and A. Atkinson (1998). *Avanced Management Accounting.* New Jersey, Prentice Hall.

Kaplan, R. S. and D. P. Norton (1996). *The Balanced Scorecard.* Cambridge, Mass., Harvard Business School Press.

Kearns, K. P., R. J. Krasman, et al. (1994). "Why Nonprofit Organizations are Ripe for Total Quality Managment." *Nonprofit Management and Leadership* 4(4): 447-460.

Kendall, J. and M. Knapp (1995). A Loose and Baggy Monstor: Boundaries, definitions and typologies. *Introduction to the Voluntary Sector.* London, Routledge.

Kendall, J. and M. Knapp (2000). "Measuring the Performance of Voluntary Organizations." *Public Management* 2(1): 105-132.

Kennerley, M. and A. Neeley (2000). *Performance measurement frameworks - a review.* Performance Measurement - Past, Present and Future, Cambridge, Centre for Business Performance, Cranfield University.

Kieser, A. (1997). "Rhetoric and Myth in Management Fashion." *Organisation* 4(1): 49-74.

Kingman, A. (1999). "Accreditation - a kitemark for the nonprofit sector." *Alliance* 4(3).

Krashinsky, M. (1986). Transaction Costs and the Theory of the Nonprofit Organization. *The Economics of Nonprofit Institutions.* S. Rose-Ackerman. New York, Oxford University Press.

Krashinsky, M. (1998). *Does Auspice Matter? The Case of Day Care for Children in Canada.* New Haven and London, Yale University Press.

Leland, P. (1998). *The Call to Greater Accountability: Implementing Outcomes-Based Evaluation Systems into Nonprofit Organizations.* 27th Annual Conference of the Association for Research on Nonprofit Organizations and Voluntary Action, Seattle, Washington.

Letts, C., W. P. Ryan, et al. (1999). High Performance Nonprofit Organizations: managing upstream for greater impact. New York, John Wiley.

Light, P. (2000). Making Nonprofits Work. Washington, The Aspen Insitiute.

Lincoln, S. and A. Price (1996). "What Benchmarking Books Dont Tell You." *Quality Progress* 29(3): 33-36.

Lindblom, C. (1959). "The Science of "muddling through"." *Public Administration Review* 19: 79-88.

Lindenberg, M. (2001). "Are We at the Cutting Edge or the Blunt Edge? Improving NGO Organizational Performance with Private and Public Sector Strategic Management Frameworks." *Nonprofit Management and Leadership* Vol. 11(No. 3): pp 247-270.

Llewellyn, S. (2001). "'Two-way Windows': Clinicians as Medical Managers." *Organization Studies* 22(no. 4): pp 593-623.

Lowndes, V. (1996). "Varieties of New Institutionalism: a critical appraisal." *Public Administration* 74(Summer): 181-197.

LRQA (1996). Fitter Finance. London, Lloyds Register Quality Assurance.

LRQA (undated). ISO 9000 - Setting standards for better business. London, Lloyds Register Quality Assurance.

Lynch, R. L. and K. F. Cross (1995). *Measure Up! - how to measure corporate performance.* Cambridge, Mass., Blackwell.

Mannion, R., M. Goddard, et al. (1998). *Assessing the performance of NHS Trusts.* Performance measurement - theory and practice: the first international conference on performance measurement, Cambridge, England, Centre for Business Performance, Cambridge University.

March, J. G. and J. P. Olsen (1989). *Rediscovering Institutions - the organisational basis of politics.* London, Collier MacMillan.

Martin, L. L. (1993). Total Quality Management in Human Service Organizations. London, Sage.

McTiernan, A. (1998). Report on PQASSO pilot carried out for the Community council of Devon for CRISP. Exeter, Community Council of Devon.

Meyer, J. W. and B. Rowan (1991). Institutionalised Organizations: Formal Structure as Myth and Ceremony. *The New Institutionalism in Organizational Analysis.* W. W. Powell and P. J. DiMaggio. Chicago, University of Chicago Press.

Meyer, J. W. and W. R. Scott (1983). *Organizational Environments: Ritual and Rationalilty.* Beverley Hills, CA, Sage Publications.

Meyer, M. (1998). *Keynote address: Finding performance - the new discipline in management.* Performance measurement - theory and practice; the first international conference on performance measurement., Cambridge, England, Centre for Business Performance, Cambridge University.

Meyer, M. W. and L. G. Zucker (1989). *Permanently Failing Organizations.* Newbury Park, California, Sage.

Meyer, W. and V. Gupta (1994). "The Performance Paradox." *Research in Organisational Behaviour* 16: 309-369.

Milward, H. (1994). "Nonprofit Contracting and the Hollow State." *Public Administration Review* 54(No 1).

Morgan, C. and S. Murgatroyd (1994). *Total Quality Management in the Public Sector.* Buckingham, The Open University Press.

Morley, E., E. Vinson, et al. (2001). *A Look at Outcome Measurement in Nonprofit Organizations.* Washington, DC, Independent Sector and the Urban Institute.

Mullins, D. and M. Riseborough (1997). Changing with the Times. Edgbaston, Birmingham, The School of Public Policy, The University of Birmingham.

Neely, A. (1998). *Measuring Business Performance.* London, The Economist/Profile Books.

NEF (1999). Accounting For Ourselves: New Economics Foundation Social Audit 1997-98. London, New Economics Foundation.

North, J., R. A. Blackburn, et al. (1998). *The Quality Business: quality issues and smaller firms.* London, Routledge.

Oakshott, R. (2001). The Inspiration and Reality: The First Fifty Years of the Scott Bader Commonwealth. Norwich, Michael Russell Publishing Ltd.

Osborne, S., Ed. (1996). *Managing in the Voluntary Sector.* London, International Thomson Business Press.

Partnership Sourcing (1997). *Benchmarking the Supply Chain: First cycle of surveys.* London, Partnership Sourcing Ltd.

Paton, R. (1992). The Social Economy: value-based organizations in the wider society. *Issues in voluntary and nonprofit management.* J. Batsleer, C. Cornforth and R. Paton. Wokingham, England, Addison-Wesley.

Paton, R. (1998). Performance Measurement, Benchmarking and Public Confidence. Practice Development Briefing No 1. West Malling, The Charities Aid Foundation.

Paton, R. (1999). "Performance comparisons in fundraising: the case of Fundratios." *Journal of Nonprofit and Voluntary sector Marketing* 5(4).

Paton, R. and C. J. Cornforth (1991). Whats Different About Managing Voluntary and Nonprofit Organisations? *Issues in voluntary and Nonprofit Management.* J. Batsleer, C. J. Cornforth and R. Paton. Wokingham, Addison-Wesley.

Paton, R. and C. Hooker (1990). *Developing Managers in Voluntary Organizations - a handbook.* Sheffield, Dept. of Employment.

Paton, R. and G. Payne (1997). Benchmarking - Passing Fad Or Probable Future? *Dimensions of the Voluntary Sector.* C. Pharaoh. West Malling, The Charities Aid Foundation.

Paton, R. and G. Payne (1999). Benchmarking at the RSPB - a textbook case? Milton Keynes, The Open University Business School.

Paton, R. and G. Payne (1999). Good Practice - What do Users Want? The Experience of a Successful 'Good Practice Unit'. Milton Keynes, The Open University Business School.

Paton, R. and G. Payne (1999). Using Benchmarking to Review an Entire Field. Milton Keynes, The Open University Business School.

Paton, R. and G. Payne (2002). Practising What They Preach: Social Audit at the New Economics Foundation. Milton Keynes, The Open University Business School.

Paton, R., G. Payne, et al. (2002). Performance Measurement in Social Enterprises: Two Case Studies. Milton Keynes, The Open University Business School.

Pattison, S. (1998). *The Faith of the Managers*. London, Cassell.

Pattison, S. and R. Paton (1997). "The Religious Dimensions of Management Belief." *Iconoclastic Papers* 1(1).

Payne, G. and R. Paton (2002). Organizational Self-Assessment in Practice: Using the Business Excellence Model in Government Agency. Milton Keynes, The Open University Business School.

Perrin, B. (1998). "Effective Use and Misuse of Performance Measurement." *American Journal of Evaluaiton* 19(3): 367-379.

Peters, T. and R. H. Waterman (1982). *In Search of Excellence: lessons from Americas best run companies*. London, Harper and Collins.

Pffefer, J. (1998). *The Human Equation: Building Profits by Putting People First*. Boston, Mass: Harvard Business School Press.

Plantz, M. C., M. T. Greenaway, et al. (1997). "Outcome Measurement: showing results in the nonprofit sector." *New Directions for Evaluaiton* No. 75(Fall): pp 15 - 30.

Poppendieck, J. (1998). *Sweet Charity? Emergency food and the end of entitlement*. Harmondsworth, Middlesex, Penguin Books Limited.

Porter, M. E. (1996). "What is Strategy?" *Harvard Business Review*(November-December): 61-78.

Powell, T. C. (1995). "Total Quality Management as Competitive Advantage: a review and empirical study." *Strategic Management Journal* 16(1): 15-37.

Powell, W. W. (1991). Expanding the Scope of Institutional Analysis. *The New Institutionalism in Organizational Analysis*. W. W. Powell and P. J. DiMaggio. Chicago, University of Chicago Press.

Powell, W. W. and P. J. DiMaggio, Eds. (1991). *The New Institutionalism in Organizational Analysis*. Chicago, University of Chicago Press.

Power, M. (1997). *The Audit Society*. Oxford, OUP.

Pugh, D. and D. Hickson (1995). *Writers On Oganizations*. Harmondsworth, Penguin Books.

Putnam, R. (1995). "Bowling alone." *Journal of Democracy* 6(1): 65-78.

QSTG (1998). A 'White Paper' on Quality in the Voluntary Sector. London, Quality Standards Task Group/NCVO.

Raynard, P. and S. Murphy (2000). Charitable Trust? Social Auditing with Voluntrary Organizations. Harrow, London, The Association of Chief Executives of Voluntary Organizations.

Richmond, B. J. (1999). Counting On Each Other: A Social Audit Model To Assess the Impact of Nonprofit Organizations. *Ontario Institute for Studies in Education*. Toronto, University of Toronto.

Rondinelli, D. A. (1994). "Strategic Management in Foreign Aid Agencies: developing a results-based performance system." *International Review of Administrative Sciences* 60: 465-482.

Rooney, P. M. (1997). A better method for analyzing the costs and benefits of fund raising at universities. 26th Annual ARNOVA Conference, Indianapolis.

Roos, J., G. Roos, et al. (1997). . London, Macmillan Business.

Rowntree, D. (1996). *The Manager's Book of Checklists*. London, Pitman.

Salamon, L. and H. K. Anheier (1997). *Defining the Nonprofit Sector*. Manchester, Manchester University Press.

Samuels, M. (1998). Towards Best Practice: an evaluation of the first two years of the Public Sector Benchmarking Project, 1996-98. London, Cabinet Office of Her Majesty's Government.

Sanderson, I. (1998). "Beyond Performance Measurement? Assessing 'Value' in Local Government." *Local Government Studies* Vol. 24(No. 4): pp 1-25.

Sargeant, A. and J. Kaehler (1998). Benchmarking Charity Costs. West Malling, Kent, Charities Aid Foundation.

Sawhill, J. and D. Williamson (2001). "Mission Impossible? Measuring Success in Nonprofit Organizations." *Nonprofit Management and Leadership* Vol. 11(No. 3): pp 371-386.

Schumacher, E. (1973). *Small is Beautiful*. London, Blond and Briggs.

Schuster, J. M. (1997). "The Performance of Performance Indicators in the Arts." *Nonprofit Management and Leadership* 7(3): 253 - 269.

Scotch, R. K. (1998). *Ceremonies of program evaluation; program outcomes and the need for legitimacy*. 27th Anual Meeting of the Association of Researchers on Nonprofit Organization and Voluntary Action, Seattle, WA.

Seddon, J. (1997). *In Pursuit of Quality*. Dublin, Oak Tree Press.

Seddon, J. (1998). The Vanguard Guide to Business Excellence. Buckingham, Vanguard Education Ltd.

Seibel, W. (1990). Organizational Behaviour and Organizational Function. *The nonprofit sector: international and comparative perspectives*. H. Anheier and W. Seibel. Berlin, de Gruyter.

Sheridan, J. H. (1993). "Where Benchmarkers Go Wrong." *Industry Week*(March 15): 28-34.

Slatter, S. (1984). *Corporate Recovery*. Harmondsworth, Penguin.

Smillie, I. (1995). *The Alms Bazaar*. London, Intermediate Technology Publications Limited.

Smith, P. (1993). "Outcome-related Performance Indicators and Organizational Control in the Public Sector." *British Journal of Management* 4: 135 - 151.

Spendolini, M. J. (1992). *The Benchmarking Book*. New York, American Management Association.

Spilsbury, M., J. Atkinson, et al. (1994). Evaluation of Investors in People in England and Wales. Brighton, Institute of Employment Studies.

Spilsbury, M., J. Moralee, et al. (1995). Employers' use of the NVQ system. Brighton, Institute for Employment Studies.

Spilsbury, M., J. Moralee, et al. (1995). Evaluation of Investors in People in England and Wales, 1994-1995. Brighton, Institute of Employment Studies.

Stephens, A. and M. Bowerman (1997). "Benchmarking for Best Value in Local Authorities." *Management Accounting* November: 76-77.

Stevenson, D. R., G. Sales, et al. (1997). *Improving the usefulness of Form 990 service accomplishments data*. Annual conference of the Association of Researchers on Nonprofit Organizations and Voluntary Action, Indianapolis.

Stone, N. (1997). Performance measurement and comparison in charities. *Dimensions of the Voluntary Sector*. C. Pharoah. West Malling, Kent, Charities Aid Foundation.

Strauss, A. L. and J. Corbin (1988). *Basics of Qualitative Research*. Thousand Oaks, CA, Sage.

Tassie, B., V. Murray, et al. (1996). "Rationality and Politics: what really goes on when funders evaluate the performance of fundees?" *Nonprofit and Voluntary Sector Quarterly* 25(3): 347-363.

Taylor, M., J. Langan, et al. (1995). Encouraging Diversity: Voluntary and Private Organizations in Community Care. Aldershot, Arena.

Thom, G. (1999). "Accreditation and Power: fighting the kitemarks." *Alliance* 4(3).

Thompson, J. D. (1967). *Organisations in Action*, McGraw Hill.

Tolbert, P. and L. Zucker (1983). "Institutional Sources of Change in the Formal Structure of Organizations: The Diffusion of Civil Service Reform, 1880-1935." *Administrative Science Quarterly* Vol. 28: pp 22-39.

Unamed (1997). Benchmarking. www.banchmarking.co.uk, The Benchmarking Centre.

Veen, W. J. M. v. and M. M. Veldhuizen (1995). *Self-regulation of fundraising organisations and the public interest.* ARNOVA Annual conference.

Watson, H. J., G. Houdeshel, et al. (1997). *Building Executive Information Systems.* New York, John Wiley.

Weick, K. E. (1995). *Sensemaking in Organisations.* Thousand Oaks, Sage.

Weisbrod, B. (1998). "Institutional Form and Organizational Behaviour." *Private Action and the Public Good.*

Wilkinson, A. and H. Wilmott, Eds. (1995). *Making Quality Critical.* London and New York, Routledge.

Williams, H. S. and A. Y. Webb (1991). *Outcome Funding: a new approach to public sector grantmaking.* Rensselaerville, NY, The Rensselaerville Institute.

Williams, S. and P. Palmer (1998). "The State of Charity Accounting - Developments, Improvements and Continuing Problems." *Financial Accountability and Management* 14(4): 265-279.

Wood, D., J. Jones, et al. (1997). Benchmarking the Finance Function - a practical approach for Small and Medium-sizec Enterprises. London, The Institute of Chartered Accountants.

Yin, R. K. (1984). *Case Study Research: Design and Methods.* Beverly Hills, Sage.

Zairi, M. and P. Leonard (1994). *Practical Benchmarking: The Complete Guide*, Chapman & Hall.

Index